Witness to the Truth

EMILIO F. MIGNONE

Witness to the Truth

The Complicity of Church and Dictatorship in Argentina, 1976–1983

Translated from the Spanish by
Phillip Berryman

ORBIS BOOKS
Maryknoll, New York 10545

First published as *Iglesia y Dictadura* by Ediciones del Pensamiento Nacional, A. Alsina 1280 1 P., (1088)—Buenos Aires, Argentina

© 1986 by Ediciones del Pensamiento Nacional

English translation © 1988 by Orbis Books, Maryknoll, NY 10545

Manuscript Editor and Indexer: William E. Jerman

LIBRARY OF CONGRESS
Library of Congress Cataloging-in-Publication Data

Mignone, Emilio Fermin.
    [Iglesia y dictadura. English]
    Witness to the truth : the complicity of Church and dictatorship in Argentina, 1976–1983 / Emilio F. Mignone : translated from the Spanish by Phillip Berryman.
       p.   cm.
    Translation of : Iglesia y dictadura.
    Bibliography: p.
    Includes index.
    ISBN 0-88344-630-8.   ISBN 0-88344-629-4 (pbk.)
    1. Catholic Church—Argentina—History—20th century. 2. Church and state—Catholic Church. 3. Argentina—Church history—20th century. 4. Argentina—Politics and government—1955–1983.
5. Argentina—Armed Forces—Political activity. I. Title.
BX1462.2.M5313   1988
282'.82—dc19
                            88-1448
                            CIP

Contents

Foreword

From 1976 to 1983, the Argentine people lived through an excruciating martyrdom under a military dictatorship pledged to the "doctrine of national security"—a doctrine that has scourged the whole of Latin America with a reign of terror.

A many-sided reading is necessary to understand what went on in Argentina and the effects it had on the life of the people: the terror tactics; the repression; the arrest and disappearance of thousands, including children; conditions in the prisons; the economic, social, and political devastation, and everything that it meant for a defenseless people who had to go through such torment in order to survive.

In this book Emilio Mignone sketches, with objectivity, the role of the Catholic hierarchy in Argentina during the military dictatorship. It is a story of contradictions, denials, and complicity. He also sketches the role of bishops, priests, and lay persons whose faith welded them to the people. And he analyzes the role of the dictators who called themselves Christians and, in the name of so-called Western Christian civilization, perpetrated atrocious violations of human rights.

The violence of the dictatorship escalated. The bishops and the papal nuncio knew about it and kept silence. Consciously and unconsciously they became accomplices in the injustices, the grave violations of the right to life, the assault on the freedom and dignity of the Argentine people.

This book was written by a man of faith who lives the spirit of the gospel. With determination and regret, he took on the arduous task of researching and compiling documents, statements, and testimony pertaining to the Argentine hierarchy. But he also uncovered another dimension of the church—signs of hope: the martyrology of victims of the dictatorship who lived out their commitment to the poorest and neediest of the people. Among others, he tells the story of Bishop Enrique Angelelli of La Rioja; Carlos and Gabriel, priests assassinated at El Chamical; the French nuns Alice Domon and Léonie Duquet, taken away and never heard from again; the catechists Wenceslao Pedernera and Mignone's own daughter Mónica. In her regard he writes soberly:

> At 5 A.M., on May 14, 1976, a group of heavily armed men took away my 24-year-old daughter from our home in Buenos Aires. . . . We never heard another word about her. Mónica's name was added to the list of the thousands of arrested-and-disappeared.

There probably will be those who will attempt to discredit this book, claiming that it is simply an attack on the church. Nothing could be more erroneous or unwarranted. The text is dispassionate and impartial. It was written by someone who is and who intends to remain a member of that same church, a Christian who felt obliged to contribute, by his analysis, to a major work of exposition and clarification. It is an effort that can help the Argentine church, and all readers, to understand the terrifying reality of Argentina under the dictatorship, in order to correct errors and make up for omissions, and to take steps toward never allowing such a painful drama to be visited again on any people.

It is imperative to direct a summons to the interior of that church, to challenge it to undertake serious reflection on the commitment of Christians to the historical reality of the life of a people. I have often said that a church that does not recognize its martyrs is a church that has turned its back on the Holy Spirit. A church that does not raise its prophetic voice and denounce injustices, a church that does not see in the face of suffering victims the face of the Lord, has forfeited the power and the authority to proclaim the reign of God and its justice. Such a church must recoup its energies in prayer and renewed commitment, so that it can once again use its prophetic and declaratory voice.

Mignone finds in the Argentine experience an example of the teaching of Jesus: "Lord, when did we see you hungry or thirsty or homeless or naked or ill or in prison and not attend you in your needs?" . . . "I assure you, as often as you neglected to do it to one of these least ones, you neglected to do it to me" (Matt. 25:44–45).

The Catholic hierarchy had a serious responsibility. If, during the dictatorship, it had taken a clear and concrete position, as its evangelical duty should have prompted it, it would have saved lives and warded off major evils from the Argentine people. Mignone traces a bilateral convergence: the criminality of the dictatorship and the performance of the church in its church-state dimension. And he clearly delineates the exceptional roles played by bishops and priests who, in fidelity to the gospel, were witnesses of life: Bishop Jaime de Nevares of Neuquén, Bishop Miguel Hesayne of Viedma, Bishop Jorge Novak of Quilmes, Capuchin Father Antonio Puigjané. They constitute signs of hope.

This book, now brought to the English-speaking world, does not portray something distant and foreign. It treats of a way of life and commitment that all Christians and every person of good will should study with humility. It supplies elements for reviewing the attitudes we maintain, as Christians and as human beings, vis-à-vis the needs of our peoples, and it deepens our capacity for solidarity with others.

Mignone says as much when he writes:

In many respects this is a work that simply opens a way to be pursued in further research. I am fully aware of the gospel counsel, "Judge not, lest you be judged" (Matt. 7:1). But, say the translators and commentators of an Argentine Bible, "Jesus is not forbidding us to make an objective judgment about other persons, but rather he forbids us to condemn them without appeal, thus putting ourselves in the place of God, who is the only final judge.''

It is in this spirit that this book should be read: to verify what was said and done, to correct and reestablish our bearings, and to serve as reflection on comportment and commitment, on the attitudes we must adopt as Christians in the historical reality of the life of our peoples. Only so can we contribute effectively to help the church to adopt gospel poverty, to become more prophetic and more paschal, and to be a fountain of life for all humankind.

Buenos Aires, September 1987

Adolfo Pérez Esquivel

Preface

Thus the word of the Lord came to me: Son of man, prophesy against the shepherds of Israel [= the leaders of Israel], in these words prophesy to them: Thus says the Lord God: Woe to the shepherds of Israel who have been pasturing themselves! Should not shepherds, rather, pasture sheep? [Ezechiel 34:1–2].

Readers will discover some passion in these studies related to the hard times Argentina has suffered. Nevertheless, readers should not assume that passion has thwarted the concern for objectivity motivating me as I tried to understand what had happened around me. What I wanted to achieve was a judicious balance between passion and objectivity. And I hoped that such balance would not lessen any interest possibly aroused by what has been going on in Argentina [José Luis Romero, *La experiencia argentina y otros ensayos,* Buenos Aires, 1980, p. 2].

Argentina has begun a healthy debate over what happened from the 1970s until the restoration of constitutional government in 1983. The role played by the Catholic Church, and especially by its hierarchy, should be part of this discussion. This is absolutely necessary both for our country and for the church, which must increasingly develop its own internal public opinion, in which diverse assessments have every right to be expressed, reasonably and respectfully.

With this book I intend to make a contribution to that need, within the limits of my capabilities. I do so in response to an imperative of conscience. As a Christian and Catholic, I would have no peace unless I had written it. In these pages, I have gathered together data, documentation, testimony, and personal experiences. For these purposes, I found the archives of the Center for Legal and Social Research (CELS) quite valuable and it has complemented the publications and notes I have been keeping for a number of years.

In many respects this is a work that simply opens a way to be pursued in further research. I do not claim to pronounce definitive judgments. I am fully aware of the gospel counsel, "Judge not, lest you be judged" (Matt. 7:1). But, say the translators and commentators of an Argentine Bible, "Jesus is not forbidding us to make an objective judgment about other persons, but rather he forbids us to condemn them without appeal, thus putting ourselves in the place of God, who is the only final judge." *

El Libro del Pueblo de Dios—La Biblia, translation, notes, and commentaries by Ar-

My striving for objectivity does not prevent me from having a legitimate passion, for I was an active and suffering witness of this lamentable period in Argentine life. I have sought to combine passion with objectivity, and document honest opinions with proper respect for persons and institutions. It is up to readers to judge whether indeed I have really done so.

I am convinced that I am providing a service and satisfying a demand: I have received numerous requests to do this both from fellow citizens and from beyond the borders of Argentina.

In writing these pages I have been thinking of my wife and my children, especially Mónica, whose name is frequently mentioned here. I have written them in order to clarify things, and without any pretension. I hope that neither spite nor contempt will be found in these pages. With regard to all my fellow creatures, I believe I am a debtor, not a creditor. If I narrate experiences from my own life, it is not to seek glory for myself, but rather to collaborate with the society and church to which I belong.

In short, I hope to be of service both for consolidating Argentine democracy and for renewing the church.

---

mando J. Levoratti and Alfredo B. Trusso, Madrid/Buenos Aires, Paulinas, 1980, p. 1987.

Acronyms

APDH	*Asamblea Permanente por los Derechos Humanos,* Permanent Assembly for Human Rights
CAC	*Corporación de Abogados Católicos,* Corporation of Catholic Lawyers
CAR	*Conferencia Argentina de Religiosos,* Argentine Conference of Religious
CAUSA	*Confederación de Asociaciones para la Unificación de las Sociedades Americanas,* Confederation of Associations for the Unification of American Societies (a Moonyite organization)
CELAM	*Consejo Episcopal Latinoamericano,* Latin American Episcopal Council
CELPA	*Centro Experimentación Lanzamiento Proyectiles Autopropulsados,* Experimentation Center for Independent Projects
CELS	*Centro de Estudios Legales y Sociales,* Center for Legal and Social Studies
CIAS	*Centro de Investigación Social y Acción Social,* Center for Social Research and Social Action
CIDH	*Comisión Interamericana de Derechos Humanos* (in English, ICHR)
CLAR	*Conferencia Latinoamericana de Religiosos,* Latin American Conference of Religious
CODETRAL	*Cooperativa de Trabajo de La Rioja,* La Rioja Labor Cooperative
CONADEP	*Comisión Nacional sobre Desaparición de Personas,* National Commission on Disappeared Persons
CONICET	*Comisión Nacional de Investigaciones Científicas y Técnicas,* National Commission on Scientific and Technological Research
CONSUDEC	*Consejo Superior de Educación Católica,* Higher Council of Catholic Education
FAMUS	*Familiares y Amigos de los Muertos por la Subversión,* Relatives and Friends of those Killed by Subversion (relatives and friends of military personnel)
FEDEFAM	*Federación de Familiares de Detenidos-Desaparecidos de América Latina,* Federation of Families of the Arrested-and-Disappeared of Latin America

xv

ICHR   Inter-American Commission on Human Rights (in Span-
            ish, CIDH)
JEC   *Juventud Estudiantil Católica*, Young Catholic Students
JIC   *Juventud Independiente Cristiana*, Independent Christian
            Youth
JOC   *Juventud Obrera Católica*, Young Catholic Workers
JUC   *Juventud Universitaria Católica*, University Catholic Ac-
            tion
LCS   *Lucha contra la Subversión*, Struggle against Subversion
            (an Argentine government program)
MEDH   *Movimiento Ecuménico por los Derechos Humanos*, Ecu-
            menical Movement for Human Rights
OAS   Organization of American States
PRN   *Proceso de Reorganización Nacional*, Process of National
            Reorganization (the official title of the military dictator-
            ship in Argentina, 1976–1983)
SERPAJ   *Servicio Paz y Justicia*, Peace and Justice Service

Witness to the Truth

Mónica Maria Candelaria Mignone

CHAPTER ONE

The Military Vicariate

MÓNICA

At 5 A.M. on May 14, 1976, a group of heavily armed men took away my 24-year-old daughter from our home in Buenos Aires (*avenida* Santa Fe 2949, 3° A). We never heard another word about her. Mónica's name was added to the list of the thousands of arrested-and-disappeared.

Right from the beginning, my wife and I were convinced that this was a standard procedure carried out by members of the military. I have explained why we believed so in statements to the Inter-American Commission on Human Rights of the OAS (Organization of American States), to the National Commission on Disappeared Persons (CONADEP), and in the suit brought against members of the first three military juntas, introduced in the Federal Appeals Court for Criminal Matters in the capital.[1]

Ever since that ominous May morning we desperately appealed to all kinds of authorities in order to find out something about Mónica. The same was true of the families of six of her friends who lost their freedom that same day.

Throughout these efforts, we never accepted the explanations offered at that time, to the effect that the military government had nothing to do with the disappearances. From the start, both privately and publicly, we held the armed forces responsible, and we soon understood that the method of making political dissenters disappear "in the fog and in the night" was part of a repressive method conceived and carried out in cold blood.

Most Argentinians were confused and uneasy, but those who belonged to the well-informed sectors of society—military officers, high officials, diplomats, and political, social, financial, business, and labor leaders, as well as journalists and bishops—were quite well aware of what was going on, and many of them justified it, welcomed it, and even cooperated in it.

I have a vivid memory of one incident during this period. In early April 1976, I was invited to a reception organized by representatives of the Inter-American Development Bank to welcome a delegation that had come to discuss financing. Most of those present were officials in the new administration whom

1

I did not know, the majority of them in military uniforms. When I spotted a friend, an economist named Carlos Brignone (who has since died), I went over to him. He introduced me to the man he was talking to, Walter Klein, the father of the number two man in the Ministry of the Economy, who bore his father's name. We were near the door. Suddenly we saw General Alcides López Aufranc stride in elatedly. He had just been appointed president of the Acíndar steel company, replacing José Alfredo Martínez de Hoz [minister of finance in the military junta]. López Aufranc came over to our group and said hello. Klein congratulated him on his appointment: "They needed someone energetic like you in that spot." López Aufranc smiled with pleasure. Then the conversation turned to rumors about a possible strike by steel workers, and Klein said he had heard that twenty-three union representatives had been arrested. Assuming that I was one of those who held power, the general sought to calm him: "Don't worry, Walter," he said, "they're all six feet underground."

ARCHBISHOP TORTOLO

One of the first persons my wife and I tried to contact was Archbishop Adolfo Servando Tortolo. There were many reasons for doing so. At that time, Tortolo was archbishop of Paraná, vicar for the armed forces, and president of the Episcopal Conference of Argentina. Previously vicar general of the diocese of Mercedes, in the province of Buenos Aires, he knew many of the younger generation there, including Jorge Rafael Videla and Orlando R. Agosti, both of whom were members of the first military junta. Tortolo was their friend and advisor. His influence, when he decided to use it, was crucial.

Tortolo was very closely connected to the events leading up to the coup on March 24, 1976, and could not have been unaware of the repressive methods the armed forces had decided to use. The night before the declaration of the coup, two of its leaders—General Videla and Admiral Emilio Massera—met with leaders of the episcopacy in their office (Paraguay 1867, Buenos Aires). On March 24 itself, the three chief members of the military junta had a long meeting with the military vicariate, according to a report in *La Nación* the next day.

As he came out of the meeting, Tortolo stated that although "the church has its own specific mission . . . there are circumstances in which it cannot refrain from participating even when it is a matter of problems related to the specific order of the state." He urged Argentinians to "cooperate in a positive way" with the new government. Political option replaced gospel mission.

Some bishops, including Tortolo, had anticipated the coup. On September 23, 1975, in a homily given in the presence of General Roberto Viola, the army chief of staff, the vicar for that branch of the service, Bishop Victorio Bonamín, wondered aloud, "May not Christ some day want the armed forces to go beyond their normal function?" And on December 29, that same year, during a lunch in the Argentine Chamber of Advertisers at the Plaza Hotel,

Archbishop Adolfo Tortolo prophesied that "a process of purification" was drawing near.[2]

My wife and I had known Archbishop Tortolo since the 1940s, when we were both active in Catholic Youth Action in the city of Luján, in the diocese of Mercedes. However, various circumstances gradually drew us apart from him. In 1949 the pastor, Father Armando Serafini, expelled us from Catholic Youth Action, because we questioned the use of the resources of the Basilica of Our Lady of Luján for commercial activities. Bishop Anunciado Serafini (no relationship) of Mercedes encouraged these activities. I repeatedly spoke about these matters with Tortolo, who was then his vicar general, but got no response. We had another disagreement around the National Marian Congress, held in Luján, for which there arrived from Rome an anachronistic and ridiculous entourage of Pope Pius XII, including a papal knight with cape and sword, but which made no contribution to authentic religion.

In 1960 my wife, children, and I moved to Buenos Aires and then in 1962 we went to the United States. Meanwhile, Tortolo became bishop of Catamarca and was later promoted to the archdiocese of Paraná. After our return from the United States, on a trip to Entre Ríos in 1968, my family and I paid him a visit. He left a very bad impression on us. As we were leaving, my daughter said, "He strikes me as a hypocrite." I tried to defend him. I now realize she was right. Mónica had a martyr's intuition.

"I AM NOT AWARE THAT HUMAN RIGHTS ARE BEING VIOLATED"

When Tortolo administered the diocese of Mercedes, his style of cultured spirituality earned him a good image, although his affected and sweet mannerisms and speech did him no good. In this small city, which had an infantry regiment and other military installations, he lost no time in establishing links to the military, paving the way for his being named military vicar to replace Cardinal Antonio Caggiano. When I saw him again in 1968 in Paraná, I realized that he was openly opposed to Vatican II. Again the next year he expressed this position to me when we happened to be traveling together in the same airplane. From that point on, the seminary of the archdiocese of Paraná and its periodical review *Mikael* became exponents of a preconciliar point of view.

I met Tortolo in the cathedral of Buenos Aires several days after the arrest and disappearance of my daughter. He told me that he had received many similar reports from others, but there was nothing he could do.

Several weeks later I saw him again. I was with a group of parents of persons who had disappeared. Tortolo did not intend to deal with us, but we caught him by surprise as he was going into a building. He became very nervous and avoided any kind of commitment. When I said he was in a position to win their freedom and to prevent the use of clandestine procedures, he closed off the possibility of any further meetings. Later on, he wrote to me stating that he had no proof with regard to what was being said about torture.

On October 14, 1976, when hundreds of disappearances were taking place and the murderous orgy unleashed by the military was at its height, Tortolo stated to the press, "I have no knowledge, I have no reliable proof, of human rights being violated in our country. I hear about it, I listen, one hears rumors, but I have no proof." He was lying. In 1977, when no one was unaware of the procedures being used, he reaffirmed his support for the military regime:

> The church thinks that the circumstances at this time demand that the armed forces run the government. . . . Hence the conviction that in accepting this very serious responsibility at this time, the armed forces are carrying out their duty.[3]

From other bishops I later found out that in meetings of bishops he had justified torture, using arguments from medieval theologians and popes, contradicting the explicit teaching of recent popes, and especially Paul VI. I have the impression that his disgraceful behavior included sympathy with Bishop Lefebvre.

What Tortolo did is important for he was the president of the Argentine Bishops' Conference and of the military vicariate from 1976 to 1978. By reason of the latter post, he should have demanded that the military under his pastoral care behave in accordance with the Ten Commandments and the values of the gospel. Obviously, he did not do so. On the contrary he helped elaborate a pseudo theology that tried to justify genocide and torture.

For several years, until his death on April 1, 1986, Tortolo, due to a serious case of arteriosclerosis, which made him hallucinate, was a patient in sanatoriums in the capital. Students from the seminary of Paraná took turns caring for him. One night, a student heard him in his delirium: he was crying out in anguish that his mother was among the "disappeareds."

BISHOP BONAMÍN

After Mónica was arrested, besides contacting Tortolo, I tried to meet with the provicar for the army, Bishop Victorio Bonamín. I was well aware of his ideology, but in my naivety, I thought that when faced with flagrant violations against a human being, a bishop of the Catholic Church would feel obligated to take a stand.

I made connections through someone who had been a student of his at the Salesian high school in Rosario, José Luis Cantini. Then I went to the bishop's office, located behind the Stella Maris chapel, next to the naval headquarters. His secretary, a petty officer, received me. When I explained the purpose of my visit, he replied that his instructions were to tell me that the vicar did not deal with questions of disappearances, arrests, and layoffs, "because he did not want to interfere in the army's course of action."

That answer was very clear. When faced with a choice between his duties as a priest in the church of Christ and his status as a military officer, Bonamín opted for the latter.

From his position as vicar for the army for many years, Bonamín contributed a great deal to the elaboration of a pseudo-religious doctrine aimed at backing the armed forces' exercise of political power and their use of any means to attain their ends.

Bonamín stands over six feet tall, weighs over two hundred twenty pounds, and has a powerfully loud voice. In Rosario, where he was principal of a Salesian school for decades, he developed a bombastic and vacuous speaking style based on a notion of Catholicism as national ideology. His insistence on that theme opened up for him the doors to the military vicariate.

Blood and death were his favorite themes. He was a prophet of genocide. On September 23, 1975, the very month in which the military high command decided to rebel and approved the system of clandestine repression, Bonamín proclaimed it. In the homily cited above, given in the presence of General Viola, army chief of staff, he greeted the military as "purified in the Jordan of blood so that they could place themselves at the head of the whole country." He added, "The army is expiating the impurity of our country. May not Christ some day want the armed forces to go beyond their function?"

Such expressions led Luis León, a Radical Party leader, to protest, for he saw them as encouraging the overthrow of the government, but for the most part they went unnoticed.

On January 5, 1976, in the Stella Maris church, the vicar returned to one of his favorite topics, exalting and glorifying the armed forces and their leaders:

> In Tucumán our nation recovered its greatness, which had been sullied in many circles, and betrayed by many officeholders. It was the Argentine army that saved this greatness in Tucumán. It was written, it was in God's plans that Argentina must not lose its greatness and it was saved by its natural guardian, the army.

[In the 1970s guerrillas retreated to the northern city of Tucumán where the army dealt them a crushing defeat.]

After the military coup, Bonamín's oratory became more explicit. In Tucumán, on October 10, 1976, in the presence of General Bussi, he said, "Providence entrusted the army with the duty to govern, from the presidency all the way to intervening in a union." A week later he asserted that when a military man is carrying out his repressive duty, "Christ has entered with truth and goodness."

The exaltation of the military by this successor of the apostles knows no limits, going beyond the bounds of doctrinal orthodoxy and defying common sense. Any occasion will serve. In Santa Fe on December 3, 1977, he taught that "the best defense is to attack rather than show patience and tolerance." On November 20, that same year, he said, "If I could speak with the government, I would tell it that we must remain firm in the positions we're taking:

foreign accusations about disappearances should be ignored."

Flattery of political/military potentates was another of the strings Bonamín liked to pluck, and he struck notes higher than any others in Argentine history, which has seen a good deal of this kind of adulation. "The members of the military junta will be glorified by generations to come," he said on November 3, 1981, from the Cristo Rey chapel that Videla had installed in the Casa Rosada ["Pink House," Argentine presidential residence]. That wild statement came undone only four years later when former commanders received penal sentences.

Bonamín expressed his basic position in many speeches, and especially in a conference given at the Universidad Nacional del Litoral, as reported in the Santa Fe newspaper *El Litoral* on December 6, 1977. At that time he said that the world is divided along ideological lines by two incompatible philosophies, "atheistic materialism and Christian humanism." The armed forces, which in his eyes represented Western Christian civilization, must use any means to combat their enemy:

> The antiguerrilla struggle is a struggle for the Argentine Republic, for its integrity, but for its altars as well. . . . This struggle is a struggle to defend morality, human dignity, and ultimately a struggle to defend God. . . . Therefore, I pray for divine protection over this "dirty war" in which we are engaged [*La Nación,* May 6, 1976, and October 11, 1976].

Finally, it is worth noting that, despite the fact that as a bishop he was a member of the Bishops' Conference of Argentina, Bonamín, the military vicar, never attended its meetings during the military dictatorship, thus sidestepping the problem of having to sign its mild statements or listen to any criticism.

THE MILITARY VICARIATE

From their beginnings the Argentine army and navy had the services of priests to provide officers and troops with spiritual aid, especially during moments of danger on military campaigns. However, it was only with laws 4,031 and 4,707, passed in 1905, which gave the armed forces their present form (their exclusive system for officer training, their system of promotions and retirement, and the imposition of obligatory military service) that the presence of chaplains was organized as a permanent body within the institution and subject to its discipline.

This reflected the Prussian idea of an army as an organization with total control over the individual. Under such a system, priests who belong to the armed forces are subject to military regulations and to the authority of the military command. In rank they are officers and receive the corresponding salary, and have a right to promotion, retirement, and other privileges. From a religious standpoint, prior to the establishment of the military vicariate, chaplains were under the bishop in whose diocese they were incardinated, but in practice that canonical tie was a pure formality.

The result of this situation was that priests who became military chaplains tended to be those who were attracted to an easy life with a good income and few obligations. Such priests had often had problems of a moral nature in their own dioceses. In order to improve this situation, the church moved to organize the military vicariate for the armed forces, and it was set up by agreement between the Aramburu government and the Holy See on June 28, 1957. The vicar was to be a bishop appointed by the pope with the consent of the president of the nation. The rules governing it were approved in decrees 5924/58 and 22,113/73. The military vicariate was set up as a diocese, in which chaplains acted as pastors and the military and their families were parishioners. Although this step sought to solve a real problem, it led to two pernicious effects. First, it widened the gap between the military and the rest of society. Secondly, it set the conditions for the elaboration of a religious doctrine to suit the aims and mind-set of the armed forces.

The first military vicar was Archbishop Fermín Lafitte of Buenos Aires, who was followed by Cardinal Antonio Caggiano. Neither had much impact, for both were absorbed in their functions within the archdiocese of Buenos Aires, although they were conspicuously present at military ceremonies. Alain Rouquié points out, for example, that on October 2, 1961, at the Senior War College, Cardinal Caggiano was present along with President Frondizi at the inauguration of a course on counterrevolutionary warfare in which there were French instructors, veterans from Indochina and Algeria.[4] Most obligations fell on the shoulders of the former chief chaplains of the three branches of the armed forces, who were now called provicars.

The picture changed when Archbishop Adolfo Tortolo of Paraná became vicar, after Cardinal Caggiano retired in 1968. The preferences of the top officers had a decisive influence on this election, which took place during the Onganía military regime. In contrast to his predecessors, Archbishop Tortolo threw himself into his task, visiting all the garrisons in the country and keeping in close contact with commanders and officers. Thus, there gradually took shape a religious notion of the armed forces that was to play a decisive role in the events of the 1970s.

BISHOP MEDINA

In 1981 Archbishop Tortolo resigned from the military vicariate, due to illness. One year later, Pope John Paul II accepted his resignation and on March 29, 1982, after a long negotiation process with the military government, appointed the bishop of Jujuy, José Miguel Medina, to replace him. The army wanted Archbishop Bonamín to take the position, but the Holy See believed his age was an impediment.

Bonamín, in fact, retired on December 22 of that same year. At that time, the army commander-in-chief, General Cristino Nicolaides, presided over a testimonial dinner at which he presented the bishop with the army's highest medal. In making a speech marking the farewell, he was unsparing in his praise and gratitude, making it plain that the bishop was identified with the ideological notions behind the "dirty war." "Both troops and command," said Nicolaides, "used to welcome him, avid to hear his preaching, the irreplaceable spiritual sustenance for keeping up the struggle and overcoming the lack of understanding. . . . His advice clearly pointed the military sword in the right direction." Blending the military and the religious, he called him a "true soldier of Christ and of the nation."

In contrast to his predecessors, Medina was replaced in the diocese of Jujuy so he could work full-time with the armed forces. The new vicar had followed an administrative career in the see of Buenos Aires until being made bishop of Jujuy.

Medina's behavior left no room for doubt about his position. As *Clarín* explained in the news about his appointment (March 30, 1982), when in that northern province he had persistently denounced "Marxist elements." On various occasions, he criticized the human rights organizations of the mothers and relatives of the arrested-and-disappeared—with whom he never met—and Amnesty International. Even more serious is the testimony given by the victims of repression to the National Commission on Disappeared Persons (CONADEP) and in the trial of the former commanders, which shows that the new vicar believed the procedures used during the period of repression were acceptable.

In *Nunca Más* ["Never again"], a report issued by CONADEP, there is a transcription of part of a statement by Ernesto Reynaldo Samán (file 4841), which reads: "When I was in the prison in Villa Gorriti, Jujuy, Bishop Medina said Mass, and in the sermon he said that he knew what we were going through, but that all this was for the good of the country, and the military were working for good and we ought to tell everything we knew. For that purpose, he offered to hear confessions."

That report also includes the statement by Eulogia Cordero de Garnica (file 4859) in which she recounts:

> While I was in jail in Villa Gorriti, and was alone in a cell, cut off from all communication, Bishop Medina came to see me. He told me I had to tell all I knew. I replied that I had no idea what I had to tell him, and that the only thing I wanted was to know where my children were. Medina answered that they must have been involved in something if I didn't know where they were. He insisted that I had to talk and tell everything, and then I would find out where my children were.

Mrs. Garnica and her son Miguel had been arrested on July 20, 1976, in their home in Calilegua, Jujuy. Miguel's brother, Domingo, had been abducted from a nearby sugar mill where he worked. Miguel and Domingo have never been heard from. Señora Garnica was freed on March 5, 1977.

For his part, Mario Heriberto Rubén López (file 4866) says that he met Pedro

Eduardo Torres (a "disappeared") "in early June 1976 in the Villa Gorriti jail, and I was able to speak with him. He told me they had said they were going to kill him. Bishop Medina, who often visited the jail, told me he had been 'transferred.' "[5]

In the trial of former commanding officers, Carlos Alberto Melián said that, in the presence of the lawyer Collado, Alberto Saracho, Hugo Condori, Mario Ricci, and Julio César Bravo, Bishop Medina had stated that seven disappeared persons (including Mario Giribaldi, Alicia Ranzoni, Dominga Alvarez de Scurta and a lawyer named Turk) "were transferred from the Villa Gorriti prison to Tucumán, sentenced, and shot to death."

Despite the wide circulation of the commission's report, Bishop Medina has not spoken out, nor has he denied what these persons have said.

EPISCOPAL ABSURDITIES

Bishop Medina was enthusiastic about being made military vicar. He thought this position would enable him to lecture to the whole country. On September 29, 1982—"feast of St. Michael the Archangel, prince of the angelic armies"—he published an *Introduction to Pastoral Work with the Military*[6] and set out to give sermons, sending copies to the newspapers, and giving press interviews. His preaching prompted me to write an article for the newspaper *La Voz* (October 21, 1982), under the heading "Bishop Medina's Absurdities." It had quite an impact in ecclesiastical circles, particularly because at that moment the Bishops' Conference was meeting in San Miguel. After that, the bishops were more discreet. I quote some paragraphs from that article:

> Scripture says that the Holy Spirit distributes his gifts "as he wills" (1 Cor. 12:11). If that is the case, it is obvious that the third person of the Blessed Trinity decided some time ago not to give "wisdom for speaking" or "knowledge for teaching" (ibid., 12:8) to military vicars. Now is not the time—although such a time will come—to recall the ambiguities of Archbishop Tortolo or the startling statements of Bishop Bonamín, both of whom are now retired. However, the absurdities of the present military vicar, José Miguel Medina, are now taking their place and are a matter of concern to the bishops meeting in San Miguel.
>
> The new vicar's viewpoints are well known. Some of us recall that when he was bishop of Jujuy, he publicly defended the legitimacy of torture. Now he is clearly moving into the political realm: he is devoting himself to defending "the legitimacy of the military profession, the indispensability of the armed forces, union with them, and unity among them."
>
> In addition to such subjects, his language is also noteworthy, both naive and out of date, with its ridiculous ornateness. He is clearly out of contact with the real situation and with contemporary theology. Argentinians have been astonished at how inappropriately he has spoken of a

supposed "esteem the military enjoy among the people." He has said that "without the armed forces we would be in an anticonstitutional situation" (he said this when the government was not elected but imposed).

Aware of how ready he is to speak, reporters question him on each journey, for he is visiting the various army bases. On one occasion, showing where his bellicose thoughts lead, Medina said that justice is prior to peace and that in our republic there is no justice. Alarmed, *La Nación* wrote an editorial criticizing him. The paper feared that such words encourage popular movements to settle injustices. In response, the vicar felt forced to state that he was not questioning the rectitude of the judicial branch of the government, but was only referring to individuals.

As if this were not enough, in Mendoza Bishop Medina stated that there should be an investigation of the Malvinas/Falklands war and of the "disappeared," but that he did not believe the results should be made public. He said it would be "antipedagogical," like a father who does not tell his 5-year-old child everything. In this case the teachers are "the bishops and the authorities," and thus one can deduce that he believes it is dangerous for other adults to find out the truth. In Medina's eyes, we citizens of the republic, except for the military and the bishops, have the mental capacity of a child. It is clear why his brother bishops at the San Miguel meeting have advised the military vicar that it would be better if he kept his mouth shut.

As a corollary to these doctrinal aberrations, in April 1982 Bishop Medina stated, "Sometimes physical repression is necessary; it is obligatory, and thus licit." In other words, torture is justifiable.

THE ROLE OF MILITARY CHAPLAINS

Within the framework of the military vicariate, chaplains to the military, the police, and the prisons—who were operationally under the control of the armed forces—cooperated with tortures. Much of the testimony presented to the courts and CONADEP makes this clear. It stands in sharp contrast to the contemporary teaching and doctrine of the Catholic magisterium, as expressed by recent popes and by the Argentine episcopacy.

Father Astigueta, air force chaplain in Córdoba, heard the confessions of prisoners before they were secretly shot to death. He never made a public denunciation, as he should have by law. Later he had to be institutionalized for psychiatric treatment. Father Gallardo, chaplain to the III Army Corps, also at Córdoba, used to visit the secret detention center in La Perla. He once told former congressional representative Musa, when he was being held there, that it was a sin to torture only if it lasted more than forty-eight hours. Father Julio Mackinon, who also frequently visited the same base and the prison in Córdoba, spoke to several prisoners, including Vaca Narvaja, before they were executed. Father Regueiro, chaplain of the General Paz Military School in Córdoba, who also worked in the San Fermín parish, stated during a diocesan deanery meeting in 1976 that Father Nicolau "would have to be killed." Father Nicolau was abducted, tortured, and killed in San Nicolás, during the period when Regueiro was working as a priest in that city.

Father Ala, a Salesian who was close to the intelligence services, used to give talks to the military on communist infiltration. He said that the Medellín documents proved that communism had made its way into the church. He also said that Bishop Angelelli was the spearhead for subversion in the sphere of religion. He denounced Father Italo Gestaldi, a member of his own congregation, who was thus forced to leave the country. Testimony presented in CON-ADEP (file 4952) accuses Father Felipe Perlanda López, chaplain of the prison system, of having justified torture. "Son," he told one of those arrested who was screaming because of the torture to which he was being subjected, "what do you expect if you are not willing to cooperate with the authorities who are interrogating you?" Señora Iris de Avellaneda states that the chaplain, Father Francisco Priorello, took part in her torture in Campo de Mayo. Father Guadagnoli, a member of the II Army Corps, was present at torture sessions. Other accusations made to CONADEP implicate the chaplains Father Astolfi (file 2680); Father Biagoli, a member of the air force (file 6048); Father Armando Monzón, (file 3382) of the I Army Corps—with whom I once had a distressing interview; Father Félix Ignacio Olmedo, of the federal police, who visited illegal prisons; Father Pedro Fernández, of the Army Mechanical School (files 187 and 776); and Father Ortiz y Dusso.

Above and beyond these facts, the main role of the chaplains—who took their orders from the military vicariate—was to distort and soothe the conscience of repressors, by legitimating violations committed against the dignity of the human person. "When we had doubts," Admiral Zaratiegui has said, "we went to our spiritual advisors, who could only be members of the vicariate, and they put our minds at ease." They went so far as to compose sacrilegious prayers. One of them goes "Impart skill to my hand, so the shot will hit the mark."

THE CASE OF MONSIGNOR GRASSELLI

One of the unresolved enigmas surrounding the relationship between the armed forces and the church is the role played by Monsignor Emilio Teodoro Grasselli in the military vicariate.

Grasselli was Cardinal Antonio Caggiano's *familiar* and moved with him from Rosario to Buenos Aires in 1959 when Caggiano was transferred. According to the dictionary of the Spanish Royal Academy, a *familiar* is "the ecclesiastic or page, dependent and table companion of a bishop." The expression has disappeared from the Code of Canon Law, and today bishops have private secretaries like everyone else, but not a *familiar*. However, the function still existed when Caggiano was archbishop of Buenos Aires.

As military vicar, Caggiano had Grasselli become military chaplain and private secretary, and he remained in that capacity under Tortolo and Medina. In May 1985 Grasselli told the federal court, when the former commanders were on trial, "I was [between 1976 and 1982], and continue to be, the private secretary of the military vicar." Because he was called *Monseñor,* Argentinians mistakenly regarded him as a bishop. He was only a priest who had the title of monsignor bestowed by the Holy See, no doubt at the behest of Cardinal Caggiano, whose protegé he was. [The Spanish title *monseñor* is used for both bishops and monsignors.]

Grasselli's office was located in the Stella Maris church, headquarters of the military vicariate at the corner of Comodoro Py and Corbeta Uruguay, in the Retiro district. At this site, which belonged to the armed forces and was heavily guarded, Grasselli received thousands of family members of the arrested-and-disappeared from March 24, 1976 [date of the military coup] onward. Word that he was receiving inquirers spread rapidly and victims' family members came forward, hoping to obtain some information. My wife and I also went to confer with him, and we saw the hallways full of persons waiting. On our second visit, he told us he had not been able to obtain any information. We did not go back, but others did so repeatedly.

For each case, Monsignor Grasselli filled out a card, and filed it alphabetically. In his statement to the federal court he said that he had never counted them, but he calculated that there must be some twenty-five hundred cards. I have the impression there were more. These cards recorded information inquirers supplied. Grasselli said he was taking down this information with Archbishop Tortolo's approval, and he then sought further information from the Ministry of the Interior, from the police, and from military commands. He said he presented these lists to the military vicar who sometimes showed personal interest in obtaining information, but there was never any success. Grasselli said that he located a disappeared person only once—a girl who was in the third police district station in Lanús. Her mother was able to visit her. She was held for nine months.

On the other hand, many of those who visited Grasselli say that he often had indications that turned out to be true, and that he made statements, encouraged their hopes, or indicated that the worst had already happened. At first the families felt they were being received by a priest who was only an observer and who wanted to help them, and wanted to offer advice. But as time went on, family members felt they had been deceived or had been the object of a sinister maneuver, and there came to be a general reaction against Grasselli. Today his name is mud.

I can cite some documented cases. In CONADEP records, Jorge Alfredo Barry (file 270) said that Grasselli gave a physical description of his son Enrique "commenting that his nickname was 'Penguin' and producing other information that proved that he knew where the victims were; he added by saying that Enrique had been killed by firing squad." Adelina Burgos Di Spalatro (file 1526) told the commission:

Forty days after the disappearance we went to see Monsignor Grasselli, who told us to come back a week later. When the time had passed, we went to see him and Grasselli showed us a list with a lot of names, and told us to check to find our son's name. A cross beside the name meant that the person was dead; if there was no cross, alive. By that indication, our son was alive.

Carlos Oscar Lorenzo (file 1560) testifies that Father Amador sent him to see Monsignor Grasselli:

> He told us that the young persons in question were taking part in an operation aimed at rehabilitating them, which has been carried out in houses set up for that purpose. . . . He said that Videla had been the charitable soul who had contrived the plan so that these young persons would not lose their minds. . . . He said that they were working with psychologists and sociologists, and that perhaps in the case of those who could not be recovered, some "pious person" might give them an injection so they could sleep forever.[7]

In addition, something should be said about travel arrangements. On several occasions, Grasselli worked to get passports and tickets for those who had been freed, especially from the Navy Mechanical Training School, and their families. The destination was usually Venezuela. This matter is being pursued in several lawsuits and it prompted Grasselli's long speech in the federal court at the trial of the former commanders. At first he tried to deny the implications, but when faced with testimony by witnesses, letters, and other documents, he ended up accepting it, explaining that it was the best thing that could be done. That is what he did in the cases of the Quiroga, Roldán, Milesi, Abregú, Iglesias, Castillo, Pisariello, Dalo, Actis, Cubas, and Forti families.

The Cubas and Forti cases are especially illustrative. They are set forth in a detailed way by Grasselli, transcript #5, in *El Diario del Juicio*. Circumstances led him to admit that he knew of the existence of the secret detention center in the mechanical school. Grasselli was legally and morally responsible, because he could have denounced the existence of detained-and-disappeared victims and of secret jail cells, even though he was a government employee. He was guilty of complicity and subterfuge.

The most important question is that of the role of Grasselli and his superior, Tortolo, within the machinery of repression. A benign interpretation is that both of them as priests saw Grasselli's mediation as a way to provide a service to victims' families and help them find their loved ones. But Grasselli's utter ineffectiveness as an instrument—aside from getting passports and air tickets for a few persons who had already been freed—makes that interpretation insupportable. It is clear that the military commanders allowed—or perhaps even encouraged—this activity on the part of Grasselli because it aided their own plans, created confusion, encouraged family members to keep up their hopes, and tempered their fighting spirit. When a similar process for registering complaints was started in the Ministry of the Interior, the effect was the same. Given the knowledge of the facts that Grasselli came to have, thanks to his daily contact with hundreds of witnesses, one can only assume that under the direction of the vicar, his function was that of an accomplice within the sinister machinery of genocidal repression.

PRIESTS AND TORTURE

The following testimony of Eusebio Héctor Tejada is found in a CONADEP report (file 6482): "In the Caseros prison, around March 1980, I was subjected to torture sessions by the officer in charge of interrogation, along with the officer in charge of the prison, in the presence of Father Cacabello, because I refused to cooperate with them."[8] The priest in question is probably Alejandro A. Cacabello, who in the 1977 ecclesiastical directory of the archdiocese of Buenos Aires is listed as auxiliary chaplain to the army's medical unit. He had come from another diocese.

There was also a military chaplain named Manuel Jorge Cabello, who joined the armed forces in 1959, and served as secretary-chancellor of the military vicariate. I recall meeting him more than thirty years ago when he came to ask a favor of me when I was working as general supervisor of schools in the province of Buenos Aires during the Mercante governorship. I later heard that he had joined the army.

Fathers Jorge Vernazza and Rodolfo Ricciardelli have told me that in 1976, when Fathers Orlando Iorio and Francisco Jálics were among the disappeared, they went to the military vicariate to seek information. They were able to see Cabello, whom they knew. Of course he said he knew nothing about the matter. In the course of the conversation the two visitors were alarmed to note that Cabello regarded the use of torture as absolutely justified.

MILITARY CHAPLAINS AND THEIR TEACHING

The role of military chaplains does not stop with their attending spiritually to their flock and shedding light on their problems of conscience. Many of them teach classes or give conferences to both officers and troops. This indoctrinating activity has contributed to shaping the mind-set of our armed forces and to paving the way for genocide.

I am not going to analyze the content of such courses in general terms, so as not to duplicate what is found elsewhere in this book. I will limit myself to some specific points.

A fitting guide is a book by a military chaplain, Marcial Castro Castillo, which I have before me. It is entitled *Fuerzas armadas—Etica y represión* ("Armed forces—ethics and repression") and is published by Nuevo Orden (new order) press. The very name of this publishing house, which refers to the kind of political order that fascism and nazism tried to impose on Europe, amounts to taking a position.

> In the Introduction, the author writes: This book is intended for the offi-cer in combat. It was not written for theologians, philosophers, or legal experts, but to respond to the needs of action, by illuminating it with the clearest and most practical traditional teaching in Christian thought and law. . . . the need for spiritual direction among the military and my close friendship with many combatants were the kinds of concerns that moved me to examine the moral problems involved in modern warfare.[9]

Castro Castillo tries to find the basis for his teaching in Thomas Aquinas and Francisco de Vitoria, without paying any attention to the fact that these think-ers, who in their own time were forward-looking, were responding to a politi-cal, cultural, social, economic, and technological context utterly different from our own.

The basic idea of the book is to be found in its justification of war, when its purpose is to defend, impose, or reestablish a supposed "natural order," which amounts to a state in which the authoritarian principles defended by the author are in effect. He says that repression demands not only that the combatants of the other side be punished but, most importantly, that those responsible for disorder—ideologists and politicians—be punished. What this amounts to is the exoneration of murder and torture when carried out by the armed forces. The great enemy is democracy, whether liberal or socialist, and it is the cause of every evil. Thus, democracy must be destroyed, along with the principles of equality and freedom on which it is based.

After an enthusiastic defense of the death penalty, Castro Castillo takes up the difficult question of torture. In principle, he says, citing quotes from Pius XII, it is wrong. He then raises the possibility of exceptions "for very special cases." In such cases, he says:

> We believe that the man who is exercising competent and responsible authority, must judge according to his conscience and act accordingly. He is probably acting well if in each particular case he manages to give a satisfactory answer to these three questions: Is the threat to the common good so grave? Am I unable to protect the common good in some other way that is licit? Is it really indispensable that I do this?[10]

Such a position obviously paves the way for the indiscriminate application of torture, for officers will consider it indispensable. This is the argument mil-itary officers use in their private conversations and what they have presented to bishops. However, the church's official teaching since Pius XII and especially under Paul VI, holds that torture is never legitimate or permissible, no matter what the consequences might be. Paragraph 531 of the Puebla document, which was approved by John Paul II, states:

Condemnation is always the proper judgment on physical and psychological torture. . . . If these crimes are committed by the authorities entrusted with the task of safeguarding the common good, then they defile those who practice them, notwithstanding any reasons offered.

With Castro Castillo's casuistry, an absolute principle of Christian morality becomes relative. His crusader ethic evaporates when confronted with the official teachings of the church.

Curiously Castro Castillo's book bears no ecclesiastical approval, an oversight that runs against his traditionalistic notion of ecclesiastical authority. No one in the chancery office was willing to be compromised by legitimizing such a doctrine. This fact demonstrates that the supposedly Catholic teaching received by military officers is not in agreement with the present magisterium of the church. Nevertheless, the military vicar, who should have pointed it out, did not step in, thus signaling his own complicity in the matter, and the fact that military chaplains were cut off from ecclesial communion. Other chaplains with similar ideas, such as Rodobaldo Ruisánchez and Egidio Esparza, teach courses in war colleges and the national intelligence institute. All three are Spaniards whose stone-age education bears the imprint of Franco.

Defense lawyers for the former commanders, especially Alfredo Battaglia, Galtieri's lawyer, have used ideas and quotes from Castro Castillo in arguing their case before the federal court.

In a text for a course on counterrevolutionary war given in 1977 in the Superior War College, one reads this statement: "Democracy based on universal suffrage or popular sovereignty is an effective means for encouraging legal subversion." At that same institution, Father Daniel Armando Zaffaroni, made this statement:

Democracy is government by the people. Therefore, if a people is not mature enough to govern, democracy makes it responsible for its own downfall. Let us not forget that here and in other countries subversion arose under democratic governments.

THE MILITARY DIOCESE

On April 21, 1986, Pope John Paul II raised the twenty-nine military vicariates around the world to the status of dioceses, with military jurisdiction, and governed by a prelate who is accorded the same rights and privileges as a bishop. There are twelve such vicariates in the Americas, including Argentina, nine in Europe, three in Africa, three in Asia, and two in Oceania. The decision is found in the apostolic constitution *Spiritualis Militum Curae*. It was published on May 5, 1986, and went into effect July 21, 1986. I think this measure was a grave mistake on the part of the Holy See, and means that a dangerous direction has been taken.

The military diocese has under its jurisdiction those faithful who are in the military, civilian employees working for the armed forces, and members of their families—spouses and children living in the same house. This will lead to innumerable conflicts with diocesan prelates. Military bishops are authorized to build seminaries, confer the sacrament of holy orders on students trained there, and have their own clergy. For that purpose they will be able to incardinate priests from other dioceses who agree to carry out their pastoral work with such bishops.

This measure is based on article 569 of the 1983 Code of Canon Law, which states that "military chaplains are under special laws." This is the only precept in that whole extensive body of law referring to this idea.

NEED TO SUPPRESS THE MILITARY DIOCESE

The harmful effects that flow from the existence of a military clergy are obvious from what has been said. "No one can serve two masters," we read in the Gospel according to Luke (16:13). These words are applicable to the bishops and chaplains who are subject to a double hierarchy, military and ecclesiastical. Ordained to serve God, they end up obeying Mars. That will inevitably happen when priests are subordinated to military regulations that bestow on them rank, salary, promotions, and privileges, and impose on them corresponding obligations. In Argentina they betrayed the gospel by justifying and supporting state terrorism.

The perspective becomes even more alarming with the possibility of seminaries in the new military dioceses. There the moral, spiritual, and intellectual deformation of candidates would be complete. There is a danger that we will see seminaries take their place alongside schools for junior officers in the Campo de Mayo. And what might we expect of a young man who would decide to enter a seminary for military chaplains?

Military dioceses are unacceptable from both an ecclesial and a political point of view. It is not a good idea for the church to create sectors with their own hierarchy within the jurisdiction of dioceses and parishes. What is needed at present is a strengthening of equality and community between Christians, not separating them. For our country, it would mean consolidating the military ghetto and caste, when everything demands that the armed forces be incorporated into society.

The disproportionate number of priests incardinated into the military diocese of Argentina is alarming. Moreover, everyone knows that their pastoral work leaves a lot to be desired, and takes up little of their time. There are some 270 chaplains in military ranks, who serve around 500,000 faithful. Meanwhile the diocese of Morón, with a million Catholics, has 130 priests, Quilmes has 61 priests to serve 800,000, San Justo with 900,000 Catholics has 92 priests, and Santa Fe with 600,000 Catholics has 133 priests.[11]

In 1972 during the imposed government of General Lanusse, a serious conflict gave evidence of how disadvantageous the existence of a military vicariate is for the church. When the strike took place in El Chocón, Bishop Jaime de

Nevares ordered that no priest of his diocese celebrate Mass there when national authorities came to visit. Lanusse then went to Bonamín, the vicar general of the army, who sent a military chaplain to celebrate the liturgy, under the pretext that he was doing it for members of the armed forces.

I think the time has come for the Argentine government and the Holy See to agree to suppress the military diocese and change the status of chaplains incorporated into the military structure. This is the only way to eliminate an ideological focal point that represents a danger for the effort to consolidate democracy. Such a change is an indispensable measure within the reform of the military, and would be part of the process of reintegrating the armed forces back into Argentine society. I think many bishops and perhaps even the bishops' conference would support it, for they are aware of the problems I have pointed out.

Such a decision would not affect the right of citizens in uniform to spiritual attention. On the contrary, such attention would be more genuine. The solution is simple. Married officers and junior officers, and many single ones as well, live off base, and hence they would be able to go to their own parish or the church they prefer, as other Christians do. With regard to officers and junior officers who live in military units and especially those who are on maneuvers, their commanding officers could simply make arrangements for spiritual care with the bishops of the local diocese or directly with pastors. For remote bases, such as in the Antarctic, or on long sea voyages, it would be possible to make special arrangements to have suitable priests. The same is true for recruits of other religious beliefs, who have been ignored until now.

Diocesan priests or members of the various religious orders and congregations would bring the gospel message more effectively to the armed forces, and would be free to judge the moral conflicts that arise in the military.

This would be the case in peacetime, which is the normal situation. In case of war, there will always be priests who will volunteer to go along with combatants. They should avoid the ludicrously triumphalistic and antievangelical harangues of Father José Fernández, broadcast during the Falkland Islands conflict.

Finally, the solution I have proposed would meet the demands of the principle of freedom of conscience. Presently, soldiers, junior officers, and officers of other beliefs, as well as atheists and agnostics, are forced to take part in Catholic religious ceremonies. This overlapping of the military and religious spheres violates the norms set down in article 14 of the constitution and the idea of religious liberty developed by Vatican II.

CHAPTER TWO

The Bishops

THE BISHOPS AND THE MILITARY DICTATORSHIP

Prominent Catholic bishops were fully informed of the plans to overthrow constitutional rule and set up a long-term military dictatorship that would lead to a new political and social order. As I pointed out in the previous chapter, the night before the change was announced, two of the coup leaders, General Jorge Videla and Admiral Emilio Massera, met with members of the hierarchy at the headquarters of the bishops' conference. The very day of the coup, March 24, 1976, members of the military junta met for a long time with Archbishop Adolfo Tortolo of Paraná, who was the military vicar and president of the Bishops' Conference of Argentina.

In these extensive meetings at the critical moment when basic decisions were being made, there must have been a thorough examination of the situation and the consequences that would ensue. Repressive methods to be used must have been taken up in that analysis. Thus it was foreseeable that the relatives of victims, in their desperation, would ask the bishops to intercede, as indeed was the case.

The subsequent course of events revealed what kind of agreement they had made. The regime would get a green light for its repression and would enjoy the support of the episcopacy, in exchange for taking on the defense of "Western Christian civilization" and bolstering the privileges of the church.

The Argentine episcopacy is made up of more than eighty active prelates, including heads of dioceses, auxiliary bishops, and military bishops. Only four of them took a stand of open denunciation of the human rights violations committed by the terrorist regime: Enrique Angelelli of La Rioja, who was murdered by the armed forces in what was made to look like a traffic accident on August 4, 1976; Jaime de Nevares of Neuquén; Miguel Hesayne of Viedma, who joined the Permanent Assembly for Human Rights; and Jorge Novak of Quilmes, who was made a bishop on September 19, 1976, and who joined the Ecumenical Movement for Human Rights (MEDH).

Bishop Tortolo and Cardinals Aramburu and Primatesta, who in 1976 made

19

up the Executive Commission of the bishops' conference, closed their doors to the victims' families; only in rare cases did they meet with them. With the exception of the instance already described, when we caught the archbishop of Paraná by surprise, I never managed to meet with them. They took the same attitude toward human rights organizations, which they labeled "communist" and subversive.

Without taking a public stance, other bishops met with those affected by the repression and made private inquiries, which were never successful. These same bishops raised questions in the bishops' meetings but they were never a majority. Among them I recall bishops Zaspe, Ponce de León, Kemerer, Marengo, Devoto, Laguna, Marozzi, and Maresma—and I do not want to be unjust to anyone I am not aware of. More numerous, however, were those who expressed themselves aggressively and in a manner contrary to the gospel, going so far as to malign the arrested-and-disappeared, their relatives, and the institutions that helped them come together.

THE BISHOPS' FIRST STATEMENT

Immediately after the military coup the bishops were assailed by the families of the "disappeared," those imprisoned, exiled, missing. They had not expected this and they felt they had to say something.

The first pastoral letter of the bishops' conference, signed in San Miguel on May 15, 1976, is symptomatic. The bishops state in general terms that kidnaping and murder are illegitimate—as if we did not know it from the time the commandments were proclaimed on Mount Sinai—but they maintain a steadfast ambiguity about who is responsible and they strain to find attenuating factors and justifications for the military government imposed on the nation:

> There are deeds that are more than an error: they are a sin, and we condemn them unqualifiedly, whoever might be responsible. . . . It is murder—whether preceded by abduction or not, and no matter what side the person murdered is on. . . . But we must keep in mind that it would be easy to err with good intentions against the common good, if one were to insist . . . that the security forces must act with the chemical purity of peacetime, while blood is being shed every day; that the kinds of disorders, whose depth we all know quite well, were to be straightened out without the drastic kinds of measures that the situation demands; or that we should be unwilling to accept for the sake of the common good the sacrifice of the measure of freedom that this moment requires; or that with justification allegedly based on the gospel, there should be an attempt to impose Marxist solutions.

The document then goes on to point out in the same generic style:

> One could err if out of a concern to attain such security, which we intensely desire, there should occur indiscriminate arrests, incomprehensi-

bly long detentions, lack of knowledge of the whereabouts of those arrested, persons held incommunicado for unusual periods of time, a denial of religious services . . . if for the same reason some constitutional guarantees were to be suspended, or the right to legal defense were to be limited or postponed . . . or if, in the quest for the security we need, the generous efforts carried out to defend justice, which are often Christian in their roots, and to defend the very poor or the voiceless were to be confused with political subversion, Marxism, or guerrilla activity.

All these generalities, written in the conditional mood and weighted down with balancing qualifications that make it sound like the bishops are apologizing, were published in the midst of the terror unleashed by the regime, when agents of the military and the security forces were carrying out hundreds of murders, abductions, and tortures every day. The bishops who signed this letter were not unaware of that fact. When matters had reached this point, they were quite aware that private and personal efforts led nowhere. If at this moment the bishops' conference had reacted vigorously, directly pointing an accusatory finger at those responsible, tens of thousands of lives would have been saved. The powerful image of Cardinal Aramburu using the pulpit of the metropolitan cathedral to denounce this criminal activity—like Saint Ambrose in Milan before Theodosius—could have stopped the genocide. Such was the very grave responsibility of the Catholic bishops of Argentina.

After the bishops' meeting the executive commission of the episcopacy met with Videla, the imposed president. After the meeting, Cardinal Primatesta said that the document "had not led to a difficult situation and was accepted for its *real value.*" He added that he could not reveal what Videla had said (*Clarín*, May 19, 1976). When there is understanding, words are superfluous.

I admit that it is possible that the kind of stance I have urged would not have succeeded in changing the course of events. But that is not the issue. The mission of the pastors of the Christian flock, in accordance with the example of their Master, is not a matter of guaranteeing results but of giving witness to the truth, even if it costs their life. Let us recall Jesus' charge to his disciples: "You are the light of the world. . . . Men do not light a lamp and then put it under a bushel basket. They set it on a stand where it gives light to all in the house. In the same way, your light must shine before men" (Matt. 5:14–15). We should also recall how the prophet Isaiah condemns perfunctory leaders: "They are all dumb dogs, they cannot bark" (Isa. 56:10).

One could object that it is not fair to blame the bishops for what happened when other equally important sectors of society—political and Jewish leaders—were also silent. I do not intend to defend them, and others can carry out that kind of analysis. But it is important to point out with utter clarity that in the circumstances surrounding the March 24, 1976, coup, the Catholic hierarchy was in a position to have a decisive influence. The military regime had claimed that it based itself on the defense of Christian values. It could not have withstood open criticism by the bishops.

"BUT THAT WOULD MEAN BREAKING OFF . . ."

In this connection, I recall an illustrative example. In 1979, if I remember correctly, I was visited by a family whose son was in the Sierra Chica prison in Olavarría and was subjected to all kinds of tortures. I advised them to go see Bishop Manuel Marengo, then in charge of the diocese of Azul, where the prison was located. I knew he was concerned about the problem.

Marengo explained to them that he was aware of the problem and that it affected all political prisoners, and he had made many efforts on their behalf, without any improvement in the situation. "I've met with the warden, with the local military commander, with the director of the prison service, with the minister of the interior, and with President Videla, and torture still goes on," he said. "I've exhausted all levels of government and I can't do anything more."

They came back and told me about the conversation. I urged them to go back to Azul and to tell Bishop Marengo, who knew me, "It isn't true that you've exhausted all means. You have a cathedral where you celebrate Mass on Sunday, with army officers and their families in the congregation, for there are many regiments in the area. On such occasions, you preach the homily. Next week, I beg you to go up to the pulpit and make a very solemn denunciation of what is going on in the Sierra Chica prison, and that you point out how serious it is, and accuse the military government of these violations of human dignity. The rest of us citizens do not have the same opportunity."

Marengo listened to them, they later told me, and lowering his arms and looking down, he answered, "But that would mean breaking off. . . ." His answer is important: it indicates a mind-set. There is no question that this bishop is virtuous, and that his heart is in the right place. He met with the victims of repression and really tried to do something for them. But these were only private efforts. He never made a public statement, or provided any ongoing family-prisoner service, or supported a human rights organization. Anything like that would have meant breaking with the military government, and no matter how serious the violations of human dignity might be, breaking with the military dictatorship does not seem to find a place in the mental horizon of an Argentine bishop, even one with the good qualities of Bishop Marengo. What, then, could be expected from an Aramburu, a Primatesta, a Tortolo, a Bonamín, or a Plaza, to name simply the most notorious?

The answer Marengo gave bespeaks historical conditionings, a compromise with temporal power, even a certain theological position. It means that witnessing to the truth takes second place to subjection or loyalty to a despotic political regime that savages human rights and dignity, as long as that regime claims to be the defender of the church. It bespeaks a temporal political option at the cost of fidelity to the gospel message.

THE EXAMPLE OF SAINT AMBROSE

There is a difference between this attitude and the example given by great bishops of the Catholic Church over the centuries.

On March 26, 1983, in a commentary in *La Voz* on a regrettable statement by Bishop Antonio Quarracino of Avellaneda, who was then the president of CELAM (Latin American Episcopal Council), I recalled an episode from the life of Saint Ambrose, bishop of Milan. I quoted the historian Henri Marrou:

In the year 390, Saint Ambrose could not prevent the savage repression ordered by Emperor Theodosius in Thessalonica, in which seven thousand persons were rounded up in a circus and mercilessly exterminated, but he demanded and obtained public penance from the one responsible.[1]

By contrast, Quarracino, I said in that article, was proposing a "law to let bygones be bygones" *(ley de olvido),* aimed at making blameless and unpunishable those military figures who were responsible for the cold-blooded murder of twenty or thirty thousand prisoners, without demanding any contrition. [Contrary to the general public sentiment in favor of bringing the military to justice, the bishops urged "reconciliation" understood as a universal amnesty for the military.]

FAINT ACKNOWLEDGMENT

As was to be expected, the restoration of democratic rule has led to a public debate about the way the bishops acted under the military dictatorship. To defend themselves against anticipated criticism, the bishops' conference in June 1984 published a pamphlet entitled "The Church and Human Rights—Extracts from Some Documents and Minutes of Some Interventions Made by the Bishops' Conference of Argentina regarding Violence and Various Human Rights, 1970–1982."[2]

This pamphlet is intellectually dishonest: it does not include texts favoring or excusing the military government, texts that more than outweigh general statements of Christian ethics, which never accuse anyone directly. Bishop Carlos Galán, the bishops' secretary general, well known for his contemptuous attitude toward the victims of state terrorism, is hardly sincere when in the Foreword he says that "the purpose of this publication is simply to offer a small amount of material for easy reference for anyone interested. Nothing else." He adds a quote taken from the document "Democracy, Responsibility, and Hope," which the bishops' conference published when constitutional rule was established. This statement attempts an apology, but it does not excuse the bishops for their grave omission, for which they were blameworthy. The statement reads:

The Argentine bishops may not have been right in everything they said and did. We bishops are limited human beings; but we can state that we always tried to act and speak in accord with the dictates of our conscience as pastors.[3]

Some bishops, by their own statements, have confirmed the accuracy of my assessment, which is what any well-informed person who speaks frankly will say. In January 1980, when Pope John Paul II asked that the situation of the disappeared be clarified, Bishop Miguel Hesayne of Viedma tried unsuccessfully to have the permanent commission of the bishops take a clear stand. He went on to say that "particular statements by a number of bishops are equivocal or soften the demands of the pope's gospel-inspired statements" (January 22, 1980).

In May 1983 Hesayne wrote to the former (unelected) President Videla, reacting to his statement that one should read the final statement made by the armed forces in the context of the statement by the Argentine bishops. Hesayne said to Videla:

> The basis of my concern is the need to make the faithful entrusted to me aware that what you have said has no legitimacy. The fact that you present yourself as a Christian is confusing to the flock the church has entrusted to me. . . . In 1979, in reply to a letter from me, you said, "We have not done anything that requires repentance." Nevertheless, I now publicly want to make a new call for you to be converted in Jesus Christ.[4]

Finally, in 1984, the bishop of Viedma said that he was "personally in anguish":

> If I had been aware of everything I'm now coming to realize, I would have acted in another manner. I never would have stood on the platform with a government imposed by force, and I am making myself a promise never to do so again.[5]

"The Argentine church must examine its conscience with regard to the stance it took during the military dictatorship," said Bishop Jaime de Nevares on April 9, 1984.

Speaking about the problem of the disappeared over Vatican Radio on June 3, 1984, Bishop Justo Laguna of Morón said:

> The church cannot be accused of having remained silent. It spoke and continued to do so after 1977. However, for myself, I certainly cannot say that I am at ease. Although it is true that we spoke clearly, our denunciation was not always accompanied by deeds, by concrete actions.

In issue number 16 of *El Diario del Juicio* [special newspaper to cover the trial of the military commanders], Bishop Jorge Novak of Quilmes was asked: "What was the role of the Catholic Church in Argentina during the coup of 1976? Can one speak of some kind of complicity?" The core of his response was:

I am not in a position to say to what extent the church, in the person of its pastors, may have advised in favor of a coup or not, because I was not a member of the bishops' conference at that time. But what I can observe is that the kind of spiritual care given in military chaplaincies should be purified of everything that is not in accordance with the church's social teaching, the teachings of Vatican II, and the documents of Medellín and Puebla. One wonders about officials in the recent military government who suspended the constitution and at the same time participated in Masses, listened to the word of God, received communion, and professed their faith. They must have posed the moral issues involved, so someone must have been counseling them. One can draw the logical inferences.

I think these statements are clear enough and they corroborate what I have said about the connection between the hierarchy, especially the military vicariate, and the military dictatorship and its behavior.

DOCUMENTS OF THE BISHOPS

In late 1982, when anyone could see that military rule was tottering and a certain opening enabled human rights organizations and the press to bring to light the crimes committed by the government of the armed forces, the bishops' conference published a book entitled *Documents of the Argentine Bishops 1965–1981: Complete Collection of the Postconciliar Teaching of the Bishops' Conference of Argentina.*[6] In this book are found messages, letters, and statements related to human rights issues. For that reason there was a good deal of interest, and the first printing of two thousand copies was soon sold out. The second printing added something new, a text entitled "Memorandum: Document Handed to the Honorable Military Junta by the Executive Commission of the Bishops' Conference of Argentina," dated November 26, 1977. This message had been kept secret until that moment. The reason for publishing it was undoubtedly to defend the behavior of the bishops, which was coming under scrutiny with the reinstatement of a democratic system.

It would be interesting to make a complete analysis of this material from a religious as well as a social and political viewpoint, but I am simply going to comment on the postcoup documents insofar as they are related to the human rights violations committed by the military dictatorship.

I have already said that right after the announcement of the coup by the military, the bishops and the apostolic nuncio, Pio Laghi, were flooded with anguished appeals for help from relatives and friends of persons who had mysteriously disappeared after being arrested by agents of the state. The church officials felt a great deal of pressure. Whatever the religious affiliation of the victims, all their friends and relatives went to the bishops, conscious that at that moment they were the only force that might successfully intercede. The repeated professions of Christian faith coming from the lips of the military holding power resounded in the ears of the population.

Some of the bishops, especially those in the provinces, felt disconcerted and distressed when they were thus besieged and their efforts proved in vain. Having previously shared in political and social power, they had never encountered a similar situation. Previously, a telephone call or a letter to the police commissioner, the local base commander, or the government usually managed to solve such problems or lead to an explanation. Now, rebuff was the normal response, sometimes followed by the suggestion that it was not a good idea to become involved in such an issue.

The reaction of most bishops was to accept in a formal manner the government's explanations and not press the matter. Many bishops, especially the more prominent, refused to meet with the families of the disappeared, or delegated such meetings to lesser chancery office staff. Others showed open hostility to such visitors and especially toward the organizations that began to make it possible for these persons to come together. Bishops were also heard to use the well-worn expression, "There must be something there. . . ." The few who really fulfilled their pastoral duty to aid the persecuted and tortured scarcely had time for anything else, such was the distress of the relatives and friends of thousands of persons who had disappeared.

Public pressure demanding that the bishops intervene can be clearly seen in the various episcopal documents published after March 24, 1976. The circumlocutions they use make it clear that the bishops' conference would never have spoken unless it had been pressured.

In this connection, the reply made by the bishops' conference on August 12, 1976, to a letter sent by the Conference of Religious, is significant. I have not seen the text of the letter from the religious, which was signed by Father Leonardo Cappelluti, S.C.J., but from the answer it received from the bishops it is clear that the letter was urging the bishops to step in to defend persons who were coming under attack by the armed forces:

> We are not unaware of the various events or conditionings referred to in your letter. . . . But it is our duty to make a pastoral judgment about what is good for our people and to try to weigh different positions, keeping in mind the sole objective of the glory of God and the common good.
> . . . Convinced that there is a *tempus loquendi* and a *tempus tacendi,* we regulate our comportment to effectively seek the greatest good for the body of the faithful.

From what has been said, it is obvious that it was a time to keep silent, apparently so as not to hinder the genocidal activity of the military, a silence hard to reconcile with the greater glory of God and the good of the people.

Not much before that, on July 7, 1976, the Executive Commission of the bishops' conference, then made up of Cardinals Primatesta and Aramburu and Bishop Zaspe, wrote to the military junta "about the unspeakable extermination of a religious community in the parish of San Patricio in Buenos Aires." But the very next line relieves those responsible of any guilt:

> Because of what the minister of the interior said, and because the Minister of foreign affairs and worship, and high-ranking military officers were present at the funeral, we know that the military government shares in our sorrow, and, we dare to say, that they are as stunned as we.

In fact those who signed the document, like any well-informed person, were quite aware that it was agents of the state who carried out the mass murder and that the authorities were in a position to know who they were. Evidence of such involvement was immediately gathered and I understand that it was sent to Rome through the nunciature. In any case, the military junta did nothing to punish those responsible. General Roberto Viola, army chief of staff is no doubt referring to this incident in the secret directive that is part of annex 5 of ordinance 504/77, published by CELS in *La Voz* on November 6, 1984. The text reads:

> The particular characteristics that the LCS [*Lucha contra la Subversión*, Struggle against Subversion] had to use led to results in the form of various denunciations. The adversary skillfully took matters to the church, so as to commit it to carry out its pastoral mission to defend all those principles that are the essence of Christian teaching, challenging the government and the armed forces. This situation became more serious due to certain chance occurrences affecting members of the clergy, particularly as a result of the carrying out of certain operations, which were not always correct but were certainly justified.

Obviously, everything was justified, even the crime at San Patricio. Those in command were committed to covering up the crimes, even the most excessive, committed by mid-level officers. The bishops took the same stand.

1977–1978

The year 1977 was critical for the bishops. There were increasing accusations of disappearances, murders, torture, and long detentions. The victims' families had begun to get organized, and when all the bishops or the permanent commission met they were confronted by hundreds of persons striving to meet with the leaders of both groups and to hear a word of hope—a word that never came. The large gatherings in front of the Maria Auxiliadora retreat house in San Miguel were especially distressing. Under the surveillance of the police of the province of Buenos Aires—whom the bishops allowed in—fathers, mothers, children, brothers and sisters, spouses, and friends of the arrested-and-disappeared spent long days, hoping for nothing but contact with some bishop who was sensitive to the problem, such as Zaspe, de Nevares, Novak, Hesayne, or a quick, bland meeting with Bishop Galán, secretary of the bishops' conference, or the press secretary, Father Berg. My wife and I were personally involved in many of these long and fruitless hours of waiting and we shared in the frustration created by such a heartless attitude.

I have at hand a news clipping chosen at random, dated April 25, 1978, which is similar to many others and bears the headline: "Waiting for the Bishops." It reads:

> Yesterday more than fifty men and women, most of them middle aged, spent a long and fruitless time waiting on the grounds of the María Auxiliadora retreat house. They were unable to achieve their main goal, which was to meet with the president of the Bishops' Conference of Argentina, Cardinal Raúl Primatesta. Instead they passed the bishops a letter.

On one of these occasions I had the chance opportunity to talk with the second vice-president of the bishops' conference, Archbishop Vicente Zaspe of Santa Fe, who has since died. Discouraged, he told me, "I have no doubt that some years from now the church is going to be pilloried for this." Zaspe understood the human and pastoral problem connected with the bishops' position. Within the bishops' inner circle he certainly must have struggled for a stance more in accord with the gospel. But he was not firm and decisive enough to break free of the web of mediocrity, cowardice, and complicity all around him, or to overcome his own intellectual conditionings.

In this climate the bishops produced three documents—one of them secret—in which it gave the military junta its view of things, without making the junta responsible for what was happening, as it should have.

THE MARCH 17 LETTER

The first is a letter sent by the permanent commission dated March 17, 1977. As always, it begins with flattery and an apology:

> Your Excellencies, with whom the presidency of the bishops' conference has had the opportunity of speaking on several occasions, are aware of, and appreciate our position, from your own vantage point as rulers and devoted Christians. Thus it is without any fear or the danger of being misunderstood that we today want to communicate to you, by means of this letter, the concerns that have been coming to our attention from all sides for some time now. . . . These concerns have to do with the situation of a considerable number of our fellow citizens whose relatives or friends claim that they have been abducted or have disappeared at the

hands of groups of persons who claim to belong to the armed forces or police and act in their name, although in the vast majority of cases it has not been possible for those grieving or the church authorities who have so often interceded for them to obtain any information about their cases. In addition, there is the situation of many prisoners detained by the National Executive Power—whose authority to arrest suspects within the existing legal framework we acknowledge—and of other persons who have been apprehended and whose cases are in process. According to the accounts of their relatives, they have been subjected to illegal kinds of pressures, whose nature and characteristics we would always have regarded as incompatible with the Argentine character and certainly unacceptable to a Christian conscience. The truth is, your Excellencies, that there is a growing outcry about this in our country, which we can in no way ignore. One further point: prisoners are seeing their cases drag on for years, and no sentence has been passed on them one way or the other. With regard to prisoners, we should also point out that they find it difficult to get spiritual attention, if they desire it. As one final point to round out this picture, which does not intend to be exhaustively descriptive, we must note cases presented to us of abuses against property in repressive operations: all kinds of objects that have nothing to do with a proper police investigation disappear.

The rest of this long letter seeks to balance the bad impression that this listing of claims might project. And the bishops simply transmit statements, without taking any stand on whether or not they are true. Their letter continues:

Indeed, we recognize that our country is going through an exceptional situation. We know what a threat to our national life subversion has represented and represents. We understand that those who are responsible for the welfare of our country have felt forced to take extraordinary measures. . . . We likewise recognize that for a whole series of reasons, in which all kinds of interests play a role, an international campaign seems to have been unleashed against Argentina, one that pains us as citizens who love our country. In no sense would we wish to have anything to do with accusations, of whose origins we are ignorant. . . . We are well aware that for some time now the forces of evil have been at work and their activity has translated into all kinds of attacks on the life and good name of individuals—military figures themselves often being the victims—as well as attacks on property. We have condemned all this, both individually and as a body, on more than one occasion.

They go on like this for several pages, finally concluding with the docility of a lapdog:

Thus it is, your Excellencies, that with all due respect, and indeed certain that we will be heard, we request that you take specific measures to restore the confidence of so many of our citizens, who find themselves under attack and do not know who should be blamed, and who understand that those responsible should be punished, but within established procedures.

THE MAY 7 TEXT

Meeting in their Easter assembly, the bishops issued on May 7, 1977, the most widely circulated of their documents on the issue. Its title, "Christian Reflection for the Citizens of Our Homeland," indicates they are not speaking to those who hold the reins of power and are responsible for the atrocities recounted. Instead, they chose to direct their meditations to the whole society, as a way of lessening the blame and spreading it to everyone.

The text is divided into three parts. The first lays out doctrinal principles on the dignity of the human person deriving from the gospel message and the church's magisterium, on the respect for personal rights, which no "theory about collective security may destroy," the fact that it is wrong to murder one's enemy, to practice moral or physical torture, to deprive someone of freedom illegitimately, or to eliminate all those who conspire against collective security, as well as the need to proceed within the framework of law. This section concludes with the ethical principle that the end does not justify the means, "which finds vigorous expression in Saint Paul" (Rom. 3:8).

The second part is called "Events Observed" and repeats the bishops' concern about situations, "denounced or presented by relatives and friends," that contradict the principles just laid out. Once again there are references to abductions and disappearances, persons tortured, imprisoned, their houses ransacked, always based on statements made by third parties, thus neither affirming nor denying their truth and exempting the government from responsibility. One finds the usual flattery and apology, which in the light of what our country now knows, sounds like hypocrisy or cowardice. "We are aware of and we appreciate," the bishops say, "the effort made by our rulers and officials, their disinterested commitment to serve our country, which in many instances has meant sacrificing their own lives . . . as well as renouncing personal gain. . . . We have often heard that the military government wishes to stamp its own activity with a Christian character."

Finally, they issue a call to hope, urging conversion on "those who initiated, sowed, and continue to sow subversion with violence and hatred," and they express their appreciation "toward those priests and religious who, in union with their bishops" console the afflicted and preach to those who stray.

Despite its extremely moderate tone and its elaborately roundabout expressions, intended to balance its content and avoid making any accusations, the document led to some irritation in military circles. There were some nervous meetings, but the choice was to opt for cynicism, of which Videla was a master. *La Razón* on May 13, 1977, reported:

Referring to a statement by the bishops, Videla pointed out that the government of Argentina accepts this reflection on the part of the church, which in fact is about something real. He gave five possible reasons for disappearances: that the persons in question went underground; that for whatever breach of loyalty they might have been eliminated by their own organizations; that they may have gone into hiding to withdraw; that out of despair they may have committed suicide; that they might be the result of possible excesses of repression by the armed forces.

THE NOVEMBER 26 MEMORANDUM

I have previously pointed out how the bishops' conference, in order to justify itself before public opinion, included in the second edition of its collected statements a text that had been kept secret until that point: "Memorandum: A Document Handed to the Honorable Military Junta by the Executive Commission of the Bishops' Conference of Argentina," dated November 26, 1977. It takes up more than four pages but ellipsis points (. . .) indicate that some paragraphs have been omitted. It would be helpful to be able to see the whole document, as well as the private letter sent to the military junta in July 1976, which is mentioned in the text but has never been made public. Only when there is access to all the existing documentation, without any subterfuge, will we be able to come to a correct assessment of events and the roles of the various participants.

The content of this memorandum reflects the difficult situation in which the bishops found—and still find—themselves due to their compromises with the military dictatorship, and the social pressure demanding that they live up to what the gospel demands:

> It would have been just for us to expect that the quality of Christians found in the armed forces would have led to a clearly Christian response to the expositions made previously [by the bishop's conference]. To our sorrow, we have found that such is not the case. The result is that the church is discredited. Other sectors of society more and more openly and extensively accuse it of going along with what is happening, or they accuse the hierarchy of being timid for not speaking more often and for not publicly using harsher terms to describe situations that are clearly not Christian.

The memorandum complains about the way the military government has acted toward the church, despite the bishops' efforts to be cooperative. "Another equally important point is the attitude toward the church in general or toward its prelates and priests on the part of some government officials or members of the armed forces, as reflected in testimonies we receive." Episodes occurring in schools are recounted, as well as the frequent accusations that the church has been infiltrated by subversion. The tone is more confidential than that found in public communications:

> Even in July 1976, in a private letter to the honorable military junta, we had expressed a sensation of fear spreading through the country; regrettably we must state that it is still true today. . . . We had not the slightest suspicion of the picture that has subsequently become all too sadly familiar: thousands of accusations that persons have disappeared, most of whom have never been heard from since. This situation, which is so regrettable, and which we felt we had to point out in our exhortation of May 1977, is today as much a reality as it was then. Not only has there not been a valid explanation for what happened previously, not only has the mantle of silence over what has happened to so many persons not even been partly lifted, but abductions and disappearances, although at a somewhat slower rate, have continued to sow concern, perplexity, and a deep feeling of anguished desperation—which tends to lead persons to all kinds of irrational misgivings—in many Argentine families. . . . The families of the disappeared, or the institutions that have shown concern for them, and the church·itself, when they go to the authorities with a perfect right to do so, often either receive no answer, or they are told that there is no information about such a person. Naturally, such an answer, which might be comprehensible in a few cases, when it is repeated thousands of times, leads such persons very understandably to mistrust the veracity of the information given, and indicates, in the best interpretation, an unacceptable failure on the part of the agencies that the state must have in order to defend the rights of its citizens. . . . In broad sectors of the population there is an underlying conviction that power is exercised arbitrarily, that people had no adequate means of defense, and that the citizen is helpless in the face of a police-style, all-powerful, authority.

Thereupon follow, as in previous statements, expressions of understanding for the actions of the armed forces:

> We bishops know that this aspect of the situation has its origins in the wide network of subversion that came to the point where it threatened the very life of our nation. . . . We are quite well aware that the exceptional circumstances through which our country has passed demanded firm authority and rigorous implementation. . . . We know that the decision to turn to violence in order to impose changes was not taken without deepened premeditation.

This previously unpublished document makes it clear that the military government and the bishops share the same ideology and language (their expressions are similar). The bishops decide to speak only because they feel pressured by society all around them, labeling them weak. They do not back up the reported facts with their own assessment, but, as they repeatedly state, those facts come to them through the witness of third parties. Nevertheless, they are aware, even though they do not say so, that the responsibility for the picture they describe lies unqualifiedly with the military dictatorship. They try to justify themselves before the eyes of other human beings by formally fulfilling their duty, but they are not justified before God, who reads the depths of the heart.

A mendacious reply from Videla, between one lunch and another, was enough to make the bishops forget the issue, which does not reappear in episcopal documents except when they call for reconciliation—that is, forgiveness for the military. The formalities have been observed, as though there had been a prearrangement: each side would carry out its proper role, since in fact their objectives and ideologies are similar.

The November 16, 1977, memorandum was given to the imposed president, Videla, on November 30, at a lunch at which those who made up the executive commission of the bishops' conference (Primatesta, Zaspe, and Aramburu) were present. It took Videla five months to compose his three-page reply. The text was analyzed at a similar meal at government headquarters on April 10, 1978. According to Primatesta, the meal took place "in a cordial atmosphere." The unelected president objected to applying the term "political prisoners" to those arrested, and stated that the priests in jail were not there as priests. With regard to the disappeared, Videla held that "the government cannot be held responsible for events that subversives bring about in order to discredit the process of national reorganization. Nevertheless, each case will be investigated." They talked about the Puebla meeting, for the government was worried that it might lead to a condemnation by the Latin American bishops.

On April 24, 1978, the bishops began their Easter assembly. Behind tightly closed doors, they were told about the lunch at government headquarters and Videla's reply. There is no indication that any decision was made. However, the communiqué published at the end of the meeting, on April 29, is noteworthy. It weakly states that the bishops "are continuing their efforts to bring peace to the Argentine family, which has been shaken by many situations of pain and sorrow." There is not a word about the disappeared or about the denunciations expressed in previous documents, including a letter from Primatesta to the president on March 14, 1978, in which he again emphasized "the need, for the sake of the tranquility of the population, to clear up as soon as possible the situation of so many persons about whom there is no news." At a press conference, Primatesta said, "I believe in the good will of many. . . . I think we have to be frank and acknowledge that violence exists. The situation has reached such a point that it cannot be straightened out overnight" (*La Prensa,* April 24, 1978). As I pointed out previously, the president of the Bishops' Conference of Argentina would not meet with the relatives who went to San Miguel. The bishops focused their concern entirely on the Puebla meeting.

AFTER 1978

In my view, the April 1978 bishops' meeting sought to close the book on the problem of human rights violations and of the arrested-and-disappeared, which had spilled out in May 1976. From that moment onward the bishops' documents are devoted to other problems and they allude to this issue only to connect it with the need for peace, reconciliation, forgiveness, forgetting. . . . A statement on May 8, 1978, exalts the world soccer championship. Other statements deal with peace, the Marian congress, the church's rights in the realm of education, the Puebla meeting, dialogue, youth, labor unions, reconciliation. In a document by the permanent commission of the Bishops' Conference of Argentina on this latter topic dated December 14, 1979, there is a regrettable statement, untruthful from any angle. It reads:

> The disappeared. Although it is true that the government has cleared up and made known the situation of many of them, and that law 22,068 deals with absence and presumed death, thus attempting to resolve some questions about legal and patrimonial rights, nevertheless the problem of disappeared persons still remains, whether as a result of subversion, or of repression, or of free choice.

This statement is false and the bishops who signed it knew it was false. The military government never gave information about even one person who had disappeared. The bishops themselves said so in their previous statements. Bishop Justo Laguna, a member of the three-prelate commission that held weekly meetings with representatives of the armed forces to pass on to them the accusations that had come in, told me on one occasion that they had never received a single reply. Law 22,068 was passed in order to declare dead the arrested-and-disappeared, and not to facilitate a solution for legal and patrimonial problems, for which there already were adequate legal means. Moreover, there is no basis for saying that some of the cases denounced as disappearances by families were due to acts committed by subversive groups, or that individuals had gone underground—in Videla's terminology. It is not only a lie, but a public disgrace.

OUR QUARREL WITH ARCHBISHOP QUARRACINO

So that readers may be aware of how baseless was this statement by the bishops, I am going to refer to the communication my wife and I sent to Archbishop Antonio Quarracino, which prompted him to retract a statement he had made, so as not to be found guilty of calumny and complicity.

The nineteenth assembly of CELAM was held in Port-au-Prince, Haiti, in March 1983. At this session, Bishop Antonio Quarracino finished his term as secretary general and was appointed president of CELAM. He was then bishop of Avellaneda, but subsequently was made archbishop of La Plata, when his Colombian predecessor as president of CELAM, Alfonso López Trujillo, was named a cardinal. (Unfortunately, CELAM, which aroused so much hope when it was created in 1955 and led to the Medellín conference of 1968, is now controlled by a reactionary clique led by Quarracino and López Trujillo who handpick the staff and direct its policy. But that is another story.)

It happened that as he was leaving Port-au-Prince, Quarracino very casually said that he knew some Argentinians who had disappeared and who were living outside Argentina. The news item was picked up by the media. In reaction to such a statement, on March 22, 1983, my wife and I sent him the following cable:

Having become aware of your statements in Port-au-Prince, Haiti, published in Argentine newspapers in the middle of the present month of March, we are requesting that you make public the names of arrested-and-disappeared persons who appear on the list of the Permanent Assembly for Human Rights (APDH), who, according to your statement, are outside the country. If you do not respond to this request within ten days, we will begin legal action against you for false testimony, complicity, calumny, and damages.

Quarracino heard about it as he was reading a Colombian newspaper on his way back from Haiti to Argentina. Bishop Rubén Di Monte, then the auxiliary and now in charge of the diocese—a great friend of Súarez Mason, Nicolaides, and other military figures—was preparing a triumphant reception for him. When Quarracino got back to his see he found our letter. In that letter we had specified that we were talking about those arrested-and-disappeared who were on the APDH list to prevent him from going off on a tangent and giving the names of persons who had never been declared disappeared. The archbishop, who often makes off-the-cuff remarks, became alarmed and he replied to us within a telegram:

In response to your letter sent to this chancery office and published internationally, I state that at no time nor under any circumstance have I declared or stated that among the names of the arrested-and-disappeared listed by the so-called Permanent Assembly for Human Rights, as you call it, are included persons who are now outside the country. Moreover, I have not mentioned the organization you indicated nor any similar organization. The same is true about any list.

Thus it is clear, through the word of a distinguished member of the Bishops' Conference of Argentina, that contrary to their reckless statement, the bishops were and are unable to identify a single truly arrested-and-disappeared person living outside the country.

STATEMENTS BY CARDINAL ARAMBURU

On November 19, 1982, the Buenos Aires magazine *Radiolandia 2000* printed an interview done by its correspondent in Rome, Fernando Elenberg, with Cardinal Juan Carlos Aramburu, archbishop of Buenos Aires, along with a photograph of both of them. It was at the time when mass graves were discovered at the cemetery in Grand Bourg, in the province of Buenos Aires. This discovery prompted a search that led to some four thousand bodies buried in similar conditions in different graveyards in our country.

Cardinal Aramburu ratified some statements that had already been published in *Il Messaggero* (Rome):

> In Argentina there are no common graves; each body has its own casket. Everything was registered in the proper books. The common graves are of persons whom the authorities were unable to identify after they died. Disappeared? Things should not be mixed up. Do you know that there are some "disappeared" persons who today are living quite contentedly in Europe?

Such incomprehensible statements about facts that were publicly known and indeed notorious can be understood only by taking into account a preceding sentence: "I don't understand how this question of guerrillas and terrorism has come up again; it's been over for a long time." For Cardinal Aramburu, and to some extent for the bishops' conference, with well-known exceptions, the issue of the violation of human rights is over and done with. It is obvious that after the formal protests in the 1977 documents and with the meetings with Videla at the end of 1977 and in April 1978, they decided the matter was finished. From 1979 onward, as we will see in the next chapter, most bishops became increasingly irritated every time the issue was raised. They came to the point of proposing a "law of letting bygones be bygones" and seeking an amnesty for the military who were responsible for these crimes.

The rest of Aramburu's responses reflect the same tone. About the disappeared, he said:

> The church responded to all the requests it received . . . but I don't recall whether there were any results. . . . I don't have any mission (in Rome) related to the disappeared. . . . The church has published a book that documents all its statements. . . . The problem should be dealt with in realistic and reasonable terms.

OPTING FOR THOSE IN POWER

I have already said that the bishops could have saved thousands of lives and changed the direction of events had they reacted vigorously to the clandestine repressive procedures utilized by those responsible for the March 24, 1976, military coup. That did not happen. Nevertheless, due to external pressure from society and internal pressure from those bishops who were aware of the situation and from some religious and priests, during 1977 the bishops' conference produced both the public and the private documents I have described above. In these statements they transmitted the accusations they were receiving and reiterated Christian principles about the issue.

The bishops' conference never reported on the answers given by President Videla during their long lunches, a method he used (and which the bishops accepted) to prove that relationships between the two kinds of authority were cordial. On October 14, 1977, in a public dialogue with the minister of the interior, Albano Harguindeguy, Bishop de Nevares said that the government's answer was not positive. That is all we know. After these meetings there is no other episcopal document denouncing the atrocities. As I have noted, they talk only of peace, reconciliation, and forgiveness.

What happened? Here is my hypothesis. The military government never provided any explanation, and it justified the way it acted with the familiar arguments about the dangers of guerrillas and Marxism, the defense of Christian civilization, the possibility of World War III, and the fact that the military dictatorship and the bishops were united in their objectives. In effect, they repeated the expression of General Vaquero, commander of the V Army Corps, when he was unable to refute the facts Bishop de Nevares was presenting: "We had to do it." (De Nevares cited that expression in the presence of a APDH delegation, of which I was a member, to the executive secretary of the CIDH [Inter-American Commission on Human Rights] of the OAS, Edmundo Vargas Carreño, when that body visited Argentina.)

Given this reaction, the bishops' conference decided not to go any further. Between the gospel and those who held political power, they chose to maintain their friendship with the latter even at the cost of the Lord's command. Unlike Peter and John, the bishops did not say, "We cannot help speaking of what we have heard and seen," nor did they say to the authorities "Judge for yourselves whether it is right in God's sight for us to obey you rather than God" (Acts 4:19). They did not dare accuse those who were responsible even though they knew who they were, or to indicate with deeds and actions the seriousness of the crimes committed. They feared the consequences of a break or a conflict with the government. They abandoned the poorest and most humiliated among their flock: the disappeared.

The disappeared are utterly abandoned. The armed forces abduct them with impunity, isolate them and keep them from knowing their whereabouts, they cover their heads with hoods, torture them to the limits of endurance, abuse them, insult them, humiliate them, and then—days, months, years later—they murder them cravenly and in cold blood, not letting them die near their parents, their sisters and brothers, their friends. Finally, they dispose of the bodies, preventing any observance and public mourning. I am thinking about my daughter Mónica and of her friends who underwent this Calvary—and about Jesus who was also abandoned, in the words of Psalm 22, found in Mark and Matthew, *"Eloi, Eloi, lama sabachthani,"* "My God, my God, why have you forsaken me?" (Mark 15:33; Matt. 27:46). As a contemporary theologian observes:

> Here is the peculiarity of his death. . . . Jesus found himself left alone, not only by his people, but by the one to whom he had constantly appealed as no one did before him. . . . The mockery at the foot of the cross, reported in a variety of ways, underlines vividly this wordless, helpless, miracle-less and even God-less death.[7]

THE FINAL DOCUMENT

Confirmation of what I have being saying can be found in connection with the so-called final document. As is well known, this statement, made by the fourth military junta (Nicolaides, Franco, and Hughes), sought to close the book on the human rights violations committed by the military government. It was announced that all the arrested-and-disappeared in Argentina were dead. Except for the ever cynical Videla, who called it an "act of love," this document met with utter rejection. Political parties, foreign governments, international organizations, and all kinds of institutions reacted angrily to this outrageous ploy.

On Wednesday May 4, 1983, in a public audience in St. Peter's square, Pope John Paul II unmistakably referred to the sinister report:

> These days world public opinion is focused with new and understandable sensitivity on the painful drama of the disappeared in Argentina, showing solidarity with the families of the victims of that anguishing situation. The pressing problem of the disappeared has always been with me and it continues to be even more so now. To the families, whose hearts are pierced with the sharp thorn of the fate of their loved ones, I wish to convey once more that I share in their feelings at this moment when it appears that any hope they may have still nourished has been broken. With all my heart I pray to the Most Holy Virgin Mary, the Mother of Sorrows, that she may obtain consolation for the families that have had to undergo so much suffering and that she may aid them in this hour of bitter grief. I invite everyone to join me in this heartfelt and fervent prayer.

A news report from Rome, headlined "Vatican Condemns Junta's Report on Disappeared," stated:

> The document, with which the military junta on April 28 acknowledged that all the disappeared in Argentina are dead, is neither comprehensible nor acceptable to the Holy See's newspaper *L'Osservatore Romano.* Observers believe the condemnation issues directly from Pope John Paul II.

. . . "The [Argentine] government states there is no reason for further efforts to determine the truth," says the Holy See's daily paper. . . . "The anguished search by so many families, wives, and mothers—and so many innocent children—has been left without any voice and has been acknowledged to be hopeless." In the opinion of observers in Rome, the fact that the Vatican newspaper publishes its harsh observation on the communiqué of the Buenos Aires junta on the disappeared in Argentina in a box on the front page indicates that the condemnation comes directly from Pope John Paul II [*Clarín*, May 4, 1983].

The only group that attempted to defend the communiqué was the executive commission of the Bishops' Conference of Argentina, made up of Cardinal Aramburu (now the conference president), Cardinal Primatesta, and Archbishop Jorge Manuel López of Rosario, a replacement for Zaspe, who had been shunted aside because he had pressed for a firmer stance toward the military government.

In this connection, the political commentary in *Clarín* on May 5, 1983, is significant:

For the military, this has certainly been the worst week so far this year. The unfortunate report on the disappeared reinforced Argentina's international isolation and an avalanche of criticism—even from the pope— came crashing down on the junta. What shook up the men in uniform was the attitude of Italian President Sandro Pertini, who used frank and cutting language about the government's explanation of the consequences of the antisubversive struggle. . . . The bishops' statement on the official document that declares the disappeared dead provided relief to the government. Internationally chastised and meeting vigorous rejection within the country, some voices in official circles had begun to express disagreement with the decision to publish the report. The Italian reaction was the high point of the international response, and the vigorous protest by the undeniably antifascist president, Sandro Pertini, provoked an emotional reaction in the highest echelons. . . . Pope John Paul II tightened the screw one more turn, albeit in a much more diluted context. . . . Given this situation, had the bishops launched the final broadside attack, they would have broken the back of the official position, which was utterly isolated. . . . But the patient suddenly revived with a gust of fresh air: the bishops opted to provide a moderate vision, making the objective of reconciliation outweigh other considerations. The bishops regarded the document as having "positive aspects, which may constitute a step toward reconciliation."

After the publication of the statement by the executive commission (of which he was no longer a member), the archbishop of Santa Fe, Vicente Zaspe, gave a sermon, broadcast by radio, sharply criticizing the military's report, in contrast to the bishops' document. Never before had he spoken with such vigor and clarity. It was obvious that he disagreed with the stance taken by the executive commission. In his view, the "final document" contains "the unspeakably immoral principle of reaching a desirable end by intrinsically perverse means." He condemns "the astonishing fact that torture, abduction, clandestine murder, arrest without trial, handing children over to strangers, and the shameless sacking of homes are called acts of service. . . . In recent months, many hidden aspects of the Process [the 1976–1983 military dictatorship called itself the "Process of National Reorganization"] have come to light and have not been refuted. They make any justifications of that Process very vulnerable." He concluded:

> Can we still speak of excesses when the whole antisubversive process was a result of premeditated planning? Can we still say we need more information, when the intelligence services exercise a rigorous surveillance on individuals, groups, institutions, and telephones? [*Clarín,* June 6, 1983].

A few months after this homily, no doubt anguished by the weakness of the bishops' conference, on whose executive commission he had served, Zaspe suddenly died. His heart could not hold out any longer.

The document by the executive commission of the bishops' conference prompted other commentaries. "As Christians we are being cheated by this document," said Néstor Vicente, then a member of the Christian Democratic Party. "I regard it as insufficient," was the careful comment of Antonio Cafiero, leader of the Peronist party. And with a similar courtesy, Ernesto Sábato, well-known writer and chairman of CONADEP under the constitutional government, said that "the least thing that could be said of the bishop's position is that it was weak." Bishop Laguna, who had not participated in writing the statement, as he had on other occasions, tried, unsuccessfully, to explain it. However, he added, "I recall that in 1977 the church published documents that were clearer and stronger than the present ones" (*Clarín,* May 10, 1983).

To bring this chapter to a close, I will quote my article in *La Voz* of May 8, 1983, which points to some backhanded procedures that will receive further commentary in the following chapters:

> Inexplicable is the mildest term that can be applied to the declaration published by the executive commission of the Bishops' Conference of Argentina on May 5 with regard to the document of the military junta on the antisubversive struggle. I say "inexplicable" because only the existence of sordid and secret political agreements with the top levels of the military can serve to explain this regrettable text, which flies in the face of truth, common sense, the firm conviction of the public, the teaching of the gospel, and even what the Holy See and several Argentine bishops have said about the issue.

It is true that the executive commission of the Bishops' Conference of Argentina, presently composed of Cardinals Aramburu and Primatesta and Archbishop López, is authorized to act on its own in emergency situations when it is not feasible to have a meeting of the full assembly of the bishops' conference. However, to treat as unimportant an issue of such magnitude, in which the credibility and honest intentions of the hierarchy of our Catholic Church have been irreparably compromised, is highly irregular. Those who signed the document were aware of what was in the military government's report during the plenary meeting of the bishops April 18–25, but they kept silent and did not check to see what their colleagues thought. Even if they did not do so on that occasion, they were under obligation to check once more when they encountered the well-founded opinions of several bishops, which brought out the radical opposition between the ideology found in the military document and Christian teaching, and showed that military statements and assessments were objectively false. Even the Justice and Peace Commission, which is under the bishops, broke its usual silence with a courageous, clear, and independent statement.

But it was all in vain. Contrary to the prevailing opinion, the executive commission believes that the document of the military is, on balance, positive, and its only and timid criticism is that it is "insufficient." It even goes so far off the mark as to take seriously the military document's assertion about the "ethical dimension of the state" and the need to protect that dimension from being accused of holding "totalitarian theories about security, which it does not really hold." That means, add the bishops who signed the document, "a rejection of the theory of state security condemned by the Puebla conference." As if the military junta's report did not take anti-Christian notions to their greatest extreme when it justifies crimes against humanity—abduction, torture, and clandestine murder carried out by agents of the state—thus placing the military estate above revealed and natural morality, the nation, the constitution, and the law! It would seem that seven years of unlimited exercise of power, with many thousands of such incidents, about which the bishops on the executive commission have exhaustive information, were not enough for them to prove that our armed forces subscribe to that doctrine. That doctrine is very plain in statements by the military where they show no signs of regret and are ready to apply it again "whenever necessary," in accordance with "the sole and supreme judgment of the military leaders."

CHAPTER THREE

The Nuncio and the Vatican

PIO LAGHI

One of the most controversial church figures during the period of the military dictatorship was Archbishop Pio Laghi, the papal nuncio to Argentina, who was to become apostolic delegate to the U.S.A.

I should like to use the information I have at my disposal to help clarify questions about him, and to communicate my own viewpoint.

Laghi's name, which had not previously been mentioned in connection with disappearances, suddenly came into the spotlight when it appeared in a list of 1,351 persons connected with the repression published in the magazine *El Periodista de Buenos Aires* in November 1984. The appearance of his name in that list prompted a long series of denials and protests, both in Argentina and elsewhere.

El Periodista explained that the list had been drawn up by the National Commission on Disappeared Persons (CONADEP) based on documentation, but that it had not been included in the earlier CONADEP report, *Nunca Más*.

President Alfonsín and some CONADEP officials denied that there was such a list. I am assured, however, that in fact it was drawn up by members of the commission, but that they decided not to publish it after a discussion with President Alfonsín, who received a confidential copy of the list. It was inevitable that the list would become known. The magazine obtained a copy from someone who worked for CONADEP.

The list was compiled by placing in alphabetical order the names of persons mentioned in one or other of the hundreds of testimonies the commission received. On the list are fifteen Catholic priests, including Archbishop Antonio José Plaza of La Plata, Bishop Blas Conrero of Tucumán, and Bishop José Miguel Medina of Jujuy, Monsignor Emilio Grasselli, about whom I have already written at some length, Father Christian von Wernich, and several military chaplains, mentioned in chapter 1, above. Although the testimonies that refer to the other ecclesiastical figures appear on pages 259–63 of *Nunca Más*, the name of the nuncio did not appear in that report. The same is true of Plaza and Conrero.

It is worth noting that anger broke out only over the mention of Laghi. No one, including the Bishops' Conference of Argentina, bothered to defend the others, as though their presence on such a list were taken for granted. Bishop Conrero was dead by that time. Plaza did not protest, not because his colleagues would not have supported him, but simply because he had never denied his close link with the forces of repression.

At the time, I explained what had happened in an article in *La Razón* (November 8, 1984):

This reference to Laghi was nothing new for the human rights organizations dedicated to documenting what happened during the military dictatorship. On December 10, 1981, the Argentine citizen Juan Martín, released in Madrid a detailed testimony about his illegal imprisonment by the army in Tucumán, and he sent it to the Human Rights Division of the United Nations. That statement was ratified by CONADEP and has been in the files of CELS for some time. Thus, his statement is not anonymous or anything of the sort, as Laghi seems to believe, when he demands that "this person who has accused me show his face."

On page 45 of his report Juan Martín says he met the nuncio in the heliport at the Nueva Baviera sugar plantation, which was the command center for operations in the area. He had been transferred from a nearby clandestine detention camp.

Later on, Juan Martín was in Buenos Aires and I explained to him that in the documentation department of CELS there is information only about one visit of Laghi to Tucumán, which was extensively reported in *La Nación* on June 27, 1976. However, Martín was arrested in October of that year, and he estimates that the meeting took place in November or December. There is no proof of another trip during those months and Laghi emphatically denies it. Thus, the dates do not agree.

I questioned Juan Martín for a long time, inquiring about all kinds of details in connection with the incident. He repeated that he was brought in from the detention camp to the helicopter pad and put in a line the moment several bishops were landing and getting out. One of them came up to him. He believed it was Laghi because that was the name he was later given. In a low voice, he was able to pass on a brief request that the bishop look up his family and inform them. The description of the visitor's height and dress, including the round kind of hat used in Rome, agrees with a description of Laghi. But he did not say who he was, nor could Martín check to see whether he had an Italian accent.

I have no doubt about the truthfulness of what Juan Martín says, but because up to now it has not been possible to prove any other trip by Laghi to Tucumán, I feel impelled to conclude that it was another bishop.

Even if it were Laghi, it would not mean that he had visited a clandestine detention center, as was said in some articles. He would have been introduced to some prisoners—who might or might not be legally imprisoned—at the helicopter pad of the sugar plantation.

REACTIONS TO THE ACCUSATION OF COMPLICITY

In response to this incident, many others, besides the bishops' conference, came to the defense of the nuncio in Buenos Aires. President Alfonsín and Interior Minister Antonio Tróccoli expressed their displeasure over the publication of his name and were unsparing in their praise of the one accused. Two members of CONADEP, the president, Ernesto Sábato [well-known novelist] and Professor Gregorio Klimovsky, stated that Laghi had showed intense concern for the situation of the disappeared and had helped save many individuals. Similar statements came from Cardinal Raúl Primatesta, Bishop Jaime de Nevares, and the former bishop Jerónimo Podestá, who is usually critical of Catholic Church authorities. Father Miguel Ramondetti, of the diocese of Goya, Corrientes, and one of the founders of the Movement of Third World Priests, said that the nuncio had helped him leave the country. I have proof that he similarly helped others, including the Jesuits Francisco Jálics and Orlando Iorio, who were arrested-and-disappeared sometime between May 23 and October 23, 1976. Monsignor Emilio Grasselli says the same about several others who were released.

When it published my article, *La Razón* added an editorial note, stating, among other things:

> *La Razón* does not engage in polemics with its columnists or writers. Nevertheless, it does feel obligated to provide its readers with some items of information that of necessity should complement the article by Dr. Emilio Mignone. . . . The assistant editor of *La Razón,* Jacobo Timerman, has confirmed that Pio Laghi was very attentive to his family when he was abducted and held by the military dictatorship. . . . At this moment Laghi is certainly in the thick of controversy but it is just as true that he will occupy a brilliant page when the history of those terrible years is written.

Laghi has emphatically denied that he visited the Nueva Baviera sugar plantation and the Holy See has vigorously supported him.

LAGHI'S COMPORTMENT

The foregoing should suffice to clarify with the information at my disposal the alleged meeting between the nuncio, Pio Laghi, and the prisoner, Juan Martín, as well as the reaction that followed its publication.

That, however, is a minor issue, which has no bearing on the underlying problem I want to deal with—Pio Laghi's comportment during the military dictatorship, which is of course set within a wider context.

To enable readers to form their own opinion, I am going to lay down certain significant facts side by side.

Early on the morning of July 4, 1976, three priests and two seminarians in the community of the Pallottine Fathers in the parish of San Patricio in Buenos Aires were murdered. In connection with this crime, Robert Cox, former editor of the *Buenos Aires Herald,* said the following in the federal court in the capital during the trial of the former commanders:

> I would like to insert something I consider important, in connection with Pio Laghi, who was then the papal nuncio in Argentina. I lived very close to the nunciature at that time (1976). I frequently went to visit Pio Laghi, a wonderful man who from the beginning was one of the few who tried to call the military to task about the disappeared and who again and again tried to change what was going on. I was friendly with Pio Laghi's secretary and we were in frequent contact. I asked him to set up a meeting with Pio Laghi to speak about the murder of the Pallotine Fathers.
>
> We met in a room in the nunciature, the two of us alone. Laghi had the same impression as I—that is, that it had been done by security forces and that it was not an isolated event; it was one of the pieces of this puzzle that were falling into place. Naturally, he knew a lot more than I did, and he was truly horrified. I recall very clearly the look on his face. I recall what he said in great detail. He said to me, "I had to give communion to General Suárez Mason during the Mass I celebrated at the church of San Patricio. You can imagine what I felt as a priest." He made a gesture and added, "I felt like hitting him in the face with my fist."[1]

Before the crime in San Patricio and after the arrest and disappearance of my daughter Mónica—that is, between May 14 and July 4, 1976—I met with Laghi three times. I must confess that I found it disturbing. During the first meeting he agreed with everything I said, and he expressed concern about what was happening. He added that he would report the incident to the government as he was doing with hundreds of similar accusations, but he let me know in advance that he was powerless. During the second meeting, he scarcely listened to me, changed the subject, and tried to find excuses for the authorities. At the third meeting he told me we were being governed by criminals, an opinion that I quoted to Admiral Massera two years later. He looked surprised and answered, "I find it odd that Laghi would say that: we get together to play tennis every two weeks."

During one of these conversations Laghi told me he was afraid. I replied that as a nuncio he was not in danger. It was we Argentinians who were in danger, I said. I pointed out that as a bishop he ought to be ready to give his life for his neighbor, following the example of Jesus ("the good shepherd lays down his life for the sheep," John 10:11).

The fact is that this wonderful man, in Cox's words, who will occupy a brilliant page when the history is written, in Timerman's inflated phrase, and who had no doubt about the magnitude of what the military was doing, at this very period, on June 27, 1976, was willing to visit the zone of operations in Tucumán, at the invitation of one of these leaders whom he called "criminals," the commander of the Fifth Infantry Brigade and the governor of Tucumán, General Antonio Domingo Bussi. *La Nación* reported:

> Before starting back to Buenos Aires, Archbishop Pio Laghi spoke with the commanders and officers in the army post at Tucumán, and gave them a papal blessing. . . . He said to the officers, "You know well how to define Homeland." He then mentioned the activity of troops in the sphere of antisubversive operations, and said that they were being asked to offer "a good deal of sacrifice; be both submissive and courageous in following your orders, and keep your interior serenity."

In response to a speech by Bussi, Laghi said that "the mission of the troops was self-defense." Before returning to Buenos Aires, commenting on that expression, he told reporters, "In certain situations, self-defense demands that one take particular stances, which means that in this case the law should be respected *as far as possible"* [italics added].[2]

On the same occasion Laghi explained that the church formed part of the "process of national reorganization" and was cooperating with the armed forces "not only with words, but with actions." This shows his solidarity with the ideology of the military dictatorship despite his knowledge of its crimes.

THE UNDERLYING PROBLEM

From what has been said, there is evidence that from the very beginning Laghi knew the nature of the repressive system set up by the military regime, and he was in anguish over what was happening. In the nunciature he met with and listened to the victims' families and kept a list that was regularly transmitted to the military government.

Many found Laghi understanding and helpful, particularly in cases where persons were legally arrested, such as the Timerman family and the family of María Consuelo Castaño Blanco, who wrote a very moving letter from jail when she heard about the accusations against him. (María Consuelo, with whose case I was involved, was arrested, illegally, and concealed by the army during a visit of the Inter-American Human Rights Commission. Thanks to the vigorous efforts made by this organization, she was legally arrested and sentenced to eighteen years in jail by a military court. The military government pardoned her before the change of government. However, her husband, who was arrested with her, never reappeared. That is, he was murdered.)

Looking closely, one observes that Laghi's efforts to help persons leave the country were successful in cases where they had been legally arrested or were released. Apparently he could do nothing to prevent or mitigate disappearances or secret executions, much more common.

Sometimes Laghi was ill-humored in meeting the families that went to see him. He strikes me as moody, alternating between extroversion and depression, and that explains his fear. When he was leaving Buenos Aires in December 1980, he said that the most difficult problem he had had to deal with during his time there was that of human rights. He was glad to be leaving. He said, "The nunciature was a place which many people resorted to in order to ask for help. We tried to listen and help." [3]

In statements made in the United States, he repeated that he had feared for his own life, noting that he had received a death sentence from an Argentine National Socialist unit and that he took the threat very seriously. [4] I wonder if this made him more reserved, and I refer to the thoughts I expressed above.

Nevertheless, the underlying problem is something else. Given the seriousness of the situation, why did Laghi not take a stance of public denunciation? Or did he actually believe that by playing tennis with Massera he could change his plans? What was the nature of the private pressures that he is supposed to have brought to bear? As nuncio, did he not have means at his disposal that he failed to employ to restrain the murderous fury of a regime that proclaimed its Catholicism to the four winds? I do not think it would have been necessary to punch Suárez Mason, but would it not have been proper and would it not have been more effective to deny him communion, for Laghi was convinced of his guilt, when the man cynically and sacrilegiously went up to receive communion at the Mass celebrated for the Pallotines? How can one justify his elaborate praise for the armed forces, when he was convinced that what they were doing was criminal? Is there not something two-faced in such a procedure?

Through what I have read and heard, I am familiar with the attempts to answer these questions. Nuncios, it is said, are representatives of the Apostolic See to sovereign states and must be careful not to interfere in their internal affairs. An imprudent attitude could lead to a breaking of relations and could worsen the situation. Moreover, in the case of Argentina, after January 8, 1979, the pope was acting as a mediator in the conflict with Chile and hence Laghi's position was even more delicate. Finally nuncios are supposed to respect the judgment of the local Catholic hierarchy, and it is not their role to take their place.

I am leaving aside reference to mediation of the conflict over the Beagle Channel, for that began when most of the events being examined here had already taken place [ownership of islands in the Beagle Channel has repeatedly caused dissension between Argentina and Chile].

With regard to other arguments, I must beg the reader's indulgence and make a historical and theological detour into the issue of nunciatures. Such an inquiry will be useful for getting at the root of the problem.

NUNCIATURES

Legates or nuncios of the bishop of Rome first appeared in the fourth century, but their major expansion took place during the twelfth and thirteenth centuries, when papal power was on the rise. Institutionally, nunciatures took on a clearly diplomatic character in the sixteenth century. Their present form is a product of the nineteenth-century pontificate of Pius IX, who initiated a period of intense centralization of the church.

This strengthening of the role of nunciatures became fixed in a note of Leo XIII's secretary of state, on April 13, 1885, after the nuncio in Madrid had censured a Spanish bishop.[5] This course of action, "which obviously expressed the pope's will and was intended to serve papal diplomats as a precedent they were expected to keep in mind, made it clear that nuncios were not only representatives to governments, but the natural instruments of the Holy See vis-à-vis the faithful, the bishops, and their delegates, to the extent that the pope, whom Vatican Council I has solemnly declared to be the universal pastor throughout the church, deems it opportune to confer on them his authority."[6]

As is well known, despite the tenacious opposition of the Roman curia, Vatican II made progress in collegiality and in reaction to centralism. The document on the church, *Gaudium et Spes,* as well as a specific decree on the subject, *Christus Dominus,* clearly state that both the mission and the collegiality of the bishops are of divine origin—that is, they are included in the revelation contained in scripture—and they derive from the sacramental character of episcopal consecration as such, and not from jurisdiction conferred by the Holy See. Nunciatures, on the other hand, are merely administrative creations of the papacy.

As a logical corollary of this doctrine, Bishop Joachim Ammann of Münsterschwarzach, Germany, made a proposal on the council floor that nunciatures be abolished. His initiative was not successful, but I believe that the Catholic Church should consider it in the near future as one way to deemphasize its temporal and diplomatic aspects, and thus accentuate its evangelical and pastoral mission. The day should come when the pope, as the universal pastor, visits the particular churches scattered throughout the world as a simple pilgrim, with none of the pomp of his present journeys and the pernicious effects of his political involvement due to his inappropriate status as a head of state.

However, in this aspect, as in so many others, there has been a retreat from Vatican II. The synods of bishops have become a mere formality. The Code of Canon Law promulgated by John Paul II on January 25, 1983, lays out the function of nuncios with a centralizing bent that I believe is opposed to the episcopal collegiality accepted at Vatican II.

Article 364 grants to papal legates a role in supervising local churches, and a decisive influence in the appointment of bishops.

I am convinced that the Catholic Church would benefit from the elimination of these expensive functions of diplomatic representation, generally exercised by short-sighted clerics who have no pastoral experience and who live in permanent conflict with the particular churches that constitute the people of God. As bureaucrats who are used to the refinement of diplomatic salons, they meddle in a way that is irreconcilable with the idea of a prophetic church that has taken a preferential option for the poor, founded on the word of God and guided by the Holy Spirit.

My personal experience only confirms these assessments. I have known several nuncios in Buenos Aires: José Fietta, Humberto Mozzoni, Lino Zanini, Pio Laghi, and the present nuncio, Ubaldo Calabresi—and who knows which one has been worst?

I met with Calabresi twice. The first time, shortly after he arrived, I tried to explain to him the situation created by state terrorism. It was useless. He is ignorant of the most basic aspects of Argentine history and life, and he has not become a part of the church in our country. He acts like an informant, and is influenced by inappropriate advisors, those who cultivate their contacts with the palace of the nunciature on avenida Alvear (another absurdity). He is notorious for his intellectual limits and his gaffes. He maintained that "Showing the film *Je vous salue Marie* [controversial Godard film depicting the Virgin Mary in contemporary forms that some found highly offensive] is prohibited by the national constitution for it states that the Catholic, apostolic, and Roman religion *is the official religion.*"[7] His statement is not exact; the Argentine constitution does not adopt Catholicism as the religion of the state. It does not seem to have occurred to him to read the basic law of the country in which he is a papal representative.

When it was announced that John Paul II would be visiting Argentina, I went to see Calabresi to ask that the human rights organizations have an audience with the pope. A few days later he sent me a letter, explaining that the brevity of the visit would make it impossible. I realized that there was bad will on his part. On June 4, 1982, when I saw in the papers the proposed schedule for the visit, I became alarmed about certain aspects and wrote a letter that I took to the nunciature right away. Because I did not trust Calabresi, I sent a copy of the letter to foreign news agencies, which sent it out, so that it appeared the next day in several European papers that are read in the Vatican. Later I learned that this was in fact how the Vatican found out. Here are the main passages in the letter:

Dear Bishop Calabresi:

I believe that in conscience I have no choice but to express to you my deep concern over some impressions spreading in public opinion which I believe demand urgent attention from you, from Vatican officials, from the executive commission of the bishops' conference and from the Holy Father himself.

Now that any contact between the pope and representative sectors of

Argentine society, and especially those that are directly suffering grave violations of their human dignity, has been eliminated, all that is left are official meetings with the leadership of the armed forces and with officials of the imposed government. Thus, a visit that was conceived as a gospel-oriented mission of peace to the Argentine people—to whom John Paul II's moving and frank letter was sent, not to the government—will become a political act. It therefore becomes necessary to make major efforts to change this situation.

In order to appreciate the risks involved in this trip, one must take into account the routine manipulation practiced by the military government, of which you are abundantly aware. In our country, it is obvious that there is no freedom of expression, and the media, especially radio and television, are subject to the dictates of government authorities and manipulation by them. The massive propaganda that is already being prepared, and the broadcast of the ceremonies themselves, with the members of the military junta given the most prominent positions, may completely undermine the meaning of the papal trip, and turn it into support for the military dictatorship and its bellicose ventures.

There are various indications that what I am warning against is already happening. I read that John Paul II has been declared an official guest. I realize that that was unavoidable. But the press also states that the administrative undersecretary of the ministry of the interior, Colonel Bernardo Menéndez, is coordinating the commissions that are organizing the visit. Is that not the church's role?, I ask. It has been the Office for Public Information of the presidency, not a church agency, that has published the schedule for this visit. It is going to set up a press office that will funnel news through the San Martín Cultural Center, thus monopolizing relations with the media.

One could reply that the Argentine Catholic News Agency will also be operating alongside the government agency. But will it be able to counteract, as it were, the flood of purposefully chosen images and messages? There is no guarantee here. The head of this agency, Miguel Woites, is well known for his consistent posture of praise for the military regime, and Cardinal Aramburu's instructions will not change this position.

The military authorities will strive to be conspicuous and appear on the television networks, which are beholden to them. Bishop Calabresi, you are as aware as I am of the style and rhetoric of our radio and television broadcasters and journalists. General Galtieri will welcome the pope and bid him good-bye at Ezeiza. The military junta and the whole government will be waiting for him at government headquarters. The junta will sit in the place of honor during the Mass in Palermo, at the invitation of the archbishop of Buenos Aires. I do not know what will happen at Luján, but I note that twenty-five hundred invitations have been distributed to limit the number of persons going into the basilica.

Have you as nuncio inquired who will serve as radio and television commentators during the ceremonies? What assurances are offered by the priests who will interpret their religious meaning? I have seen that at the top of the list of those preparing for these events is Father Raúl Rossi, whose unfortunate sermon on May 25 in the cathedral in the presence of the military junta places him directly in contradiction with the magisterium of the last four popes and with what John Paul II said as he bade farewell to the Welsh in Cardiff.

Moreover, there is the familiar tendency of a good number of bishops and especially Cardinal Aramburu to put themselves in a position of dependence on political power, as "state functionaries" rather than as "teachers of truth," to use John Paul II's words at Puebla.

There is still time to change these orientations. The May 17 letter to Bishop Jorge Novak of Quilmes to the executive commission of the bishops' conference is a useful warning on this same topic.

I think that by writing you this letter, impelled by the gravity of the situation, I am fulfilling a duty in conscience.

I never received a reply to this letter, but some of the points I raised were corrected.

THE VOICE OF THE POPE

In order to analyze the position taken by the popes in connection with the extremely grave human rights violations that took place in Argentina, I must make some prior observations.

The way the Roman pontiffs govern the worldwide Catholic Church is extremely complex. Of necessity, their observations must be very general in nature. It is the bishops in each area who have the responsibility of applying these teachings to specific situations. A pope cannot follow each step of a particular issue or a particular country, unless special circumstances make it advisable.

Moreover, the apostolic see is largely dependent on the information and assessments it receives from nuncios and bishops, and must keep its own statements and positions in line with the episcopal conferences. As an old saying puts it, "What comes from Rome is what is sent to Rome," thus indicating how the highest authority in the church is conditioned.

In view of all this, I believe the public statements made by Paul VI and John Paul II were clear. I do not know whether private efforts were made or what their nature might have been. The fact is that instead of using these statements to back up their own efforts to influence the situation, most of the bishops downplayed them or ignored them, as I will indicate.

The teachings of recent popes on the need to enforce human rights and their unconditional condemnation of disappearances, torture, and secret executions, provide a basis for a decisive kind of pastoral work that would include denouncing those responsible for such actions. The Bishops' Conference of Argentina did not do that. In fact, many bishops were in explicit complicity with the terrorist dictatorship as is apparent in their own statements.

Paul VI made the first Vatican effort in September 1976, when he accepted the credentials of Rubén Blanco, the Argentine ambassador. In a November 29 story, the Rome correspondent for the French paper *La Croix* noted "the unusual tension aroused" on this occasion. Omitting the normal diplomatic niceties, the pope made a brief response to the clumsy apology for the military regime delivered by the former Radical Civic Union Party congressman-turned-diplomat. He addressed only the Argentine people, stating that he was "in solidarity with your aspirations" and emphasizing the church's support for the promotion of "the dignity of persons." He went on to say that the disappearances and murders "are still awaiting an adequate explanation." Finally, warning the bishops, of whose shortcomings he was obviously aware, the pope pointed out that "the Argentine church should not hold onto any privilege. It should be content to serve the faithful and the civil community in an atmosphere of tranquility and security for all."[8]

Before going any further, it would be a good idea to consider the role played by Ambassador Blanco, a longtime leader of the Radical Civil Union of Arrecifes in the province of Buenos Aires, close friend of Ricardo Balbín [well-known chief of the Radical Party]—who gave him support—and an ex-president of the commission on education in the national congress. Betraying his democratic past, for over five years he devoted his energy to defending the crimes of the military dictatorship before the Vatican. The fact that his brother is Bishop Guillermo Blanco, then vice-rector and now rector of the Catholic University of Argentina, and that he has a sister in the Sisters of Mercy, was useful with reactionary sectors in the church in getting him appointed. This collaboration of his undermined his political future, but President Alfonsín, taking advantage of the confidence Blanco enjoys in military circles after such loyal service, appointed him to head the National Defense School. He boasted that this was the first time it had been headed by a civilian . . . *ma non troppo!* But Blanco cannot undo the past. There is no doubt that he lived it up for six years in a Roman palace at state expense, with innumerable visits from relatives and friends, cardinals and ambassadors.

The pope's remarks surprised and angered the military government, which felt confident that it enjoyed good relations with the church, given the attitudes of the Argentine bishops. For the bishops themselves, it was a warning. At first the bishops attributed the pope's tone to the influence of Argentine Cardinal Eduardo Pironio, who was close to Paul VI and was secretary of the Sacred Congregation for Religious Orders and Secular Institutes, a very influential post in the Roman curia.

In mid-1978 I was in Rome. I went to see Pironio, an old friend, with whom I had been corresponding. I also met with the person responsible for Argentina at the Secretariat of State, a Jesuit named Fiorello Cavalli. He enjoyed the confidence of Cardinal Agostino Casaroli, the secretary of state, who was then the under secretary. I missed the chance to speak with Casaroli himself by a matter of hours.

I gave both Pironio and Cavalli a detailed report about what was happening in Argentina with regard to human rights. Pironio seemed overwhelmed by the number of letters and accusations about disappearances he was receiving from his country. While we were talking, the day's mail was brought in, he opened it, and indeed there were several letters of this nature. I was with Cavalli for three hours. He listened carefully, took notes, and promised to pass a summary of what I had said to Casaroli and Paul VI, who was just a few meters away, he told me.

I was utterly frank, just as I am in this book. I did not hold back my criticism of the majority of the bishops, or my praise for the few bishops who were facing up to the situation in a gospel spirit. Referring to Archbishop Plaza, who had been in the Vatican a few weeks before, I expressed my puzzlement that he was allowed to continue in his post, scandalizing both believers and nonbelievers. I argued that his was a case of criminality. Cavalli did not even blink. Three days after I left Rome, August 6, 1978, while in San José, Costa Rica, I heard the news that Paul VI had died.

I came back convinced that Pironio had not done anything but anguish over the situation in Argentina and that he would not do anything. That attitude reflects his ambiguous and hesitant personality. Cavalli had a detailed knowledge of matters in our country and the role being played by each of the participants. He told me the bishops were sending contradictory reports, and he seemed willing to step in on the right side.

The death of Paul VI, the 33-day pontificate of John Paul I, and a new conclave, inevitably meant an interregnum. On October 16, Karol Wojtyla, was elected pope, taking the name John Paul II. On October 23, John Paul II, from the balcony of St. Peter's, spoke about Argentina in one of his weekly audiences. He addressed the Argentine bishops, asking them to "echo the distressing problem of disappeared persons in that beloved nation, wounding the hearts of many families and relatives." That mention of the situation, no doubt introduced by Cavalli, bothered the military government. When Cardinal Primatesta returned from Rome on November 13, he tried to downplay the importance of the statement, stating that the pope's observations "had been taken one-sidedly."

On August 30, 1980, in another discourse in St. Peter's square, John Paul II returned to the issue of the disappeared and the lack of respect for human rights in Latin America. He mentioned several countries, including Argentina, in the general framework of the "martyrology of Christians in our times," a martyrology, he concluded, "that cannot be forgotten." Finally, as I have mentioned in chapter 2, above, on May 4, 1983, the pope made an unmistakable reference to the military's "final document."

In January 1983, in the presence of the diplomatic corps and with the new ambassador from Argentina, José María Alvarez de Toledo, present John Paul

II issued a ringing call for peace, disarmament, and human rights. Speaking about the disappeared, he said, "The church cannot pass over in silence the criminal activity that consists in making a certain number of persons disappear without trial, leaving their families in cruel uncertainty."[9] Despite the obvious reference to Argentina when he mentioned those who "disappeared" without trial—that is, those arrested by the authorities—Cardinal Primatesta stated over radio and television that the pope had not been referring to our country.[10]

Both Paul VI and John Paul II addressed the Argentine bishops, urging them to act. That is normal in the context of the universal church. The pope cannot replace the bishops who experience—or should experience—what the Christians and non-Christians of their country suffer, and should apply the teachings and advice of the supreme pontiff to concrete cases.

However, despite these statements, included in speeches prepared with the help of his aides, I believe that John Paul II has never understood—or has not wanted to understand—the peculiar case of the arrested-and-disappeared in Argentina, who were annihilated by a terrorism that was deliberately set up by the armed forces who had taken over the state. This can be seen in his spontaneous expressions. When two of the Mothers of the Plaza de Mayo, Nora de Cortiñas and Angélica P. Sosa de Mignone, my wife, approached him during a public audience in St. Peter's square, John Paul II simply listened. Through the good offices of Cardinal Vicente Scherer, a group of members of the Mothers of the Plaza de Mayo managed to meet John Paul II in Porto Alegre, Brazil, on June 5, 1980. The pope listened to them, held their hands, and told them to have faith, patience, and hope. He said he had pleaded their case and would continue to do so. When John Paul II visited Buenos Aires it was impossible to arrange any meeting with human rights organizations. On the way back, in the plane, when reporters asked him if he had spoken about the issue of the disappeared, he said it was his understanding that things had improved, and said, "Now they try to give answers, whereas previously they didn't." He added that "the issue had been raised in private conversations, but he could not speak about that publicly. 'In any case, we have always tried to get information in the past, and we will continue to do so.' "[11]

On his frequent visits to our country, Cardinal Pironio has carefully avoided meeting with the victims of repression and with human rights organizations. On the other hand, he had time to meet with Videla and his successors. On a visit to Mar del Plata, on September 2, 1979, he said, twisting the truth, that "now Argentina is better understood in Europe. . . . Some persons are always looking for the negative side, . . . but the face of Argentina is seen in a very positive light."[12]

CHAPTER FOUR

Archbishop Plaza and Other Bishops

ARCHBISHOP PLAZA

Of all the members of the episcopacy, Archbishop Antonio José Plaza, who headed the see of La Plata until his retirement in 1986, is perhaps the one who most obviously and uninhibitedly has been identified with the military dictatorship and its methods of repression. He died in La Plata, August 11, 1987.

Plaza was unconcerned about episcopal collegiality and even flaunted his contempt for it. Every time the bishops' conference released a joint pastoral letter reaffirming Christian principles about the dignity of the human person, the archbishop of La Plata found a way to make it clear that he disagreed even though he had signed it.

This suggests that the tradition of releasing episcopal documents with the signatures of all the members of the group is in fact a mistake, for it gives the appearance of a unanimity that does not really exist. The consequence is that such texts are confused and ambiguous, with paragraphs contradicting one another, aimed at meeting divergent criteria.

No one need be scandalized by the fact that bishops have differing opinions. The fiction of unanimity comes from the notion of a monolithic church, in which the only role for the faithful is that of obedience. The New Testament shows a different church, one with a variety of gifts, in which the episcopal function is a service, and the ultimate judge for individual behavior is each Christian's conscience, as Cardinal Newman used to insist.

It would make better sense if collective pastoral letters on controversial issues were signed only by the majority in favor of a particular opinion. Members of the minority, or minorities, would also have a right to express their disagreements. With this kind of procedure we would have known clearly the position of the various bishops about the problem of human rights violations, with no fear of incorrectly lumping all the bishops together.

In the United States the bishops' conference has adopted the policy of publishing the drafts of pastoral letters on controversial issues, which have been prepared by a committee of experts, in order to find out what church members

55

think. Their observations and criticisms enrich the final text. That was what happened with the letters on nuclear weapons and the economy, and they had a significant impact on public opinion.

Bishop Justo Morón Laguna traveled to the United States at the invitation of the American bishops' conference. He reported:

> The bishops' conference of the U.S.A. is preparing a document on the church's social teaching and the U.S. economy. . . . I was quite surprised to see how they work with a freedom and openness that enables them to grow and become very familiar with the situation of their country. It is quite remarkable that they publish their drafts and receive criticism from all sectors [*La Razón*, May 26, 1986].

In ecumenical councils, proposals for formal documents are decided by majority vote, and the results of the vote count are published. There is no mystery about the names of those who vote. At Vatican Council I, a fifth of those present were opposed to taking up the dogma of papal infallibility and seven of the council fathers—whose names are known—withdrew rather than having to state their *non placet* on the final vote.

A DISCORDANT VOICE

Plaza's was the only episcopal voice raised to defend the military's self-declared amnesty a few months before leaving office. At that time, I published an article in *La Voz*, on September 3, 1983, offering a sketch of the archbishop of La Plata. I think it is worth repeating here, for many members of the clergy and laity in his archdiocese called to express their agreement.

> Archbishop Antonio J. Plaza of La Plata raises a discordant voice in our country. Besides Emilio Hardoy, he is the only one to publicly defend the law of self-amnesty.
>
> Hardoy, who benefited from the military coup of September 6, 1930, and was a member of congress by fraud in the 1930s, does so in terms that are cynical, but political. Plaza, on the other hand—and this is what is serious and scandalous—has sought to defend it from a religious viewpoint. He has said that the so-called law of national pacification, by means of which the criminals who currently occupy the seat of power grant themselves an amnesty, is a "gospel" norm. The fact is that Archbishop Plaza has never had anything to do with the gospel, even if he is a bishop in the Catholic Church. In the forty-five years that I have known him, I have never heard any phrase from him that had any connection with the teaching of Christ. An ambitious and politicking priest, he managed to get himself made bishop in 1950 by flattering behavior vis-à-vis Domingo A. Mercante, governor of the province of Buenos Aires, and was in charge of the diocese of Azul until 1955. After the coup that year, in an unfor-

tunate and (in)famous statement, he attributed the contemporaneous polio epidemic to sins committed by the government that had been overturned (and which had raised him to where he was). Obviously his theology was not well grounded.

In compensation for his support to the new power holders, he was successful in getting Mario Amadeo, minister under the imposed president, General Eduardo Louardi, to have him promoted to the archepiscopal see of La Plata. At that time the *patronato* system, incorporated in the national constitution, was still in effect, and presidents presented candidates to the pope for the episcopacy. Fortunately, this outdated system, the letter of which still remains in our fundamental law, was abolished through an agreement with the Holy See, worked out by Foreign Minister Miguel Angel Zavala Ortiz, during the constitutional presidency of Humberto Illia, and signed by the imposed president, Juan Carlos Onganía, in 1966.

For over twenty years, we Christians and our nation have been suffering under Plaza. In 1958 he aligned himself with Frondizi and his all-powerful advisor Rogelio Frigerio, and got many benefits talking poetically about free schooling and other more businesslike activities. Among other things, he convinced the Central Bank to allow a Uruguayan loan agency, the Banco del Este, to operate in Argentina. After being bought by Pérez Companc the name was changed to Banco Río de la Plata and today it is called the Banco Río. He bought all the shares of the Banco Popular de la Plata, which turned out to be a swindle, but he got out of it clean, because he was a bishop. He escaped the anger of General Camps—who has high words of praise for him in his book *Punto Final*—thanks to the services he rendered to the illegal and murderous repression, bringing accusations against students and even his own nephew, and accepting the post of chief chaplain of police in the province of Buenos Aires. That enabled him to receive a second salary and to enjoy a second automobile. In that role he used to visit the secret prisons where persons were tortured and shot to death. There is no evidence that he provided prisoners with any religious services, although years earlier he taught mystical theology in the seminary in La Plata, a discipline seemingly foreign to his personality and interests. Curiously, even mysticism benefited him: using the cloak of the great mystics Saint Teresa and Saint John of the Cross, for years he looted the Carmelite Fathers of whose order both saints were members.

However, Archbishop Plaza's mother lode has been education, which he has worked from the education commission of the bishops. In his lust for power, he dictated who should be appointed minister of education for the province of Buenos Aires and directors of supervision over private schools for the whole country. For years he finagled all kinds of legal and economic advantages throughout the various government regimes. To do so, he engaged in political intrigues. I recall how he pressed for Vice-

Governor Victorio Calabró to be allowed to remain in office when Perón forced Governor Oscar Bidegain to resign. His most recent exploit was getting a tax exemption through the offices of the minister of the economy, Raúl Salaberren Malgor, during the last military dictatorship.

Not losing a single minute, Plaza has taken sides with the Peronist candidate for governor in the province of Buenos Aires, Herminio Iglesias, who has publicly promised to appoint as minister of education the candidate proposed by Plaza. But Herminio is mistaken. In the Catholic Church of today, Plaza represents nothing but a muddy and preconciliar past, which is disappearing—sometimes too slowly, but nevertheless inexorably.

One example of Archbishop Plaza's contempt for the decisions of the bishops' conference and his collusion with the military dictatorship is the episode of the *Dios es Fiel* ("God is faithful") catechism by Sister Beatriz Casielo of the Sisters of María Auxiliadora in Rosario.

In late 1978 there was a noisy newspaper campaign led by *La Razón,* which was then the voice of the army's intelligence service, to convince the public that her textbook, which was widely used in Catholic schools, incited students to subversion. Concerned over the situation, the bishops' conference moved into action, but, without praising the book, declared that it "contains no erroneous statement nor any denial of Catholic teaching."

This opinion did not satisfy Archbishop Plaza, who in questions of Catholic orthodoxy trusted army officers more than his brothers in the episcopacy. On November 18, 1978, the archbishop of La Plata banned the book from Catholic schools in his diocese, and the minister of education in the province of Buenos Aires, General Ovidio Solari, took a similar measure with regard to his jurisdiction, which included several dioceses.[1] In response to some protests, the press secretary for the government of Buenos Aires province, Captain Jorge Cayo, categorically stated, "The bishops are no concern of ours. It's banned and that's all there is to it."[2] Plaza sent a letter, publicly thanking General Solari for his help.[3]

RECENT YEARS

As a result of what I have been describing, during the plenary assembly of the Bishops' Conference of Argentina, April 19–24, 1982, Plaza lost the presidency of the bishops' Commission on Catholic Education, one of his sources of power. Bishop Emilio Bianchi di Cárcano of the diocese of Azul replaced him.

In 1983, Plaza's open support for the candidature of Herminio Iglesias for governor of Buenos Aires, in exchange for control over the ministry of education, led to criticisms both inside and outside the church. In this connection *La Prensa* carried an interesting editorial on September 13, 1983, under the heading "Limits of the Church's Mission":

A news item we published on September 3 reported that a group of priests of the archdiocese are checking with one another to weigh the possibility of making a complaint to the nunciature or to the Holy See itself, in view of the problems and division created among the faithful by the fact that the archbishop of La Plata has announced that he is supporting the Peronist Party in this province and its gubernatorial candidate, who in all his statements to the press has stated that he is certain to win in the next election.

It is not only those priests, but also the archbishop of Bahía Blanca and the eight diocesan bishops in the province of Buenos Aires who share the same concerns about the statements the bishop has been making and his meetings with the Peronist candidate for governor. Even activists in the Peronist Party, themselves members of the Catholic flock, have felt the impact of the behavior of the archbishop of La Plata, and they have stated that the promise made to the bishop that the "candidate" he wanted would be made minister of education is a hasty exchange of favors.

Nothing we are saying has been denied, and thus we must recognize that we are witnessing a singular event, in which we have on the one hand a gubernatorial candidate negotiating favors and counterfavors with a member of the Catholic hierarchy of Buenos Aires, and we see the latter accepting a proposal, which means, on his side, proposing his own candidate for the post of minister of education in a possible future Peronist government in the province of Buenos Aires.

Both partners in the negotiations have gone beyond the boundaries of their proper functions. However, the attitude of the bishop is more serious, when he compromises the neutrality of the church to which he belongs, and in addition is failing to observe the moral commitment not to be involved in politics that he undoubtedly took on when he was made a bishop.

Under the heading "Cards on the Table," *La Nación* ironically commented on September 18, 1983:

Whatever criticisms the Peronist gubernatorial candidate for the province of Buenos Aires, Herminio Iglesias, may deserve from his adversaries—both inside and outside his party—no one can accuse him of hiding or dissimulating what he is doing. He has revealed himself as a man who speaks clearly, without evasion, one who likes to bare his thinking.

In this province it was the *vox populi*—it is not clear whether it was also the *vox Dei,* although from what follows one could think so—that for many years and especially during military governments, the ministry of education had to be occupied by someone who was approved by the Catholic Church, expressed, by reason of jurisdiction, by Archbishop Antonio Plaza of La Plata. In addition, Plaza has traditionally enjoyed, at least from 1958 to the present, significant weight in all educational questions on a national level, and numerous officials in that area have been mentioned as belonging to Plaza's circle. Moreover, Plaza was quite influential in drawing up the legislation on private education, which was decreed in that same year. He has sometimes been named as the one directly responsible for appointing state officials in the field of education.

Of course, everything was always on the level of what some individuals "said" or "knew," of rumors in different versions, of banquets put on by official bodies or of commentaries in those publications that were more aggressive politically or ideologically. This was never public in nature and no one could ever prove statements about the concrete influence of Archbishop Plaza in the area of education on both the national and the provincial levels.

Now, suddenly everything has changed and the cards are on the table. Now there is no reason for expressions like "they say" or "there is information that. . . ." Now there is no lack of "well-informed sources," so that "rumors or versions" are now worthless.

If Iglesias becomes governor of Buenos Aires, the church, through Archbishop Plaza's involvement, will be able to appoint the minister of education. . . . Herminio Iglesias has had no desire to hide anything or to keep his meetings with the archbishop of La Plata in the shadows, or to allow it to be said in the future that hidden influences were at work in the selection of the minister of education: in this matter he will do what Plaza says, or he will not do anything.

Those who continually proclaim that the openness of government activities is the mark of true democracy will have nothing to complain about. Nor will those who always want the public to know what is going on. However, some orthodox constitutionalists and some—many?—church-related individuals may perhaps complain. Both sides could argue that this confusion of powers favors neither the republic nor the church. In any case, everyone knows that some persons are never content.

Peronism lost the elections in Buenos Aires, largely because of Iglesias's candidacy. He did not become governor.

On December 30, 1983, the new government of the province of Buenos Aires, which had taken office on December 10, forced Archbishop Antonio José Plaza into retirement as general chaplain of the police. He had been appointed on November 11, 1976, when military dictatorship was in full swing. At his inauguration were present the commander of the I Army Corps, General Carlos Suárez Mason, and the head of police, Colonel (now General) Ramón Camps, whose roles in state terrorism are very well known.

When announcing the retirement, the minister of the interior of Buenos Aires, Juan Antonio Portesi, pointed out that besides his regular police salary, Plaza was being paid an extra 30 percent bonus for having a law degree—even though he does not have one. He also had a chauffeur-driven automobile and personal servants to take care of him. Doctor Portesi stated that "a considerable sum from province revenues was going to the archbishop."[4]

In 1985 Archbishop Plaza had to appear in penal court in La Plata to answer an accusation presented by his nephew Jesús Plaza, with the aid of lawyers from the Center for Legal and Social Research. The case was related to the arrest and disappearance of Juan Domingo Plaza, the archbishop's nephew and Jesús' brother. Jesús had met with the archbishop to express his fears the day before Juan Domingo was arrested. That fact makes Archbishop Plaza's behavior suspicious. Despite their family ties, he did not do anything to help his nephew. Several survivors saw the young man in the Navy Mechanical Training School.

At the hearing on October 3, 1986, of the trial against General Ramón Camps in the federal chamber, Eduardo Schaposnik stated that he had seen General Camps with Archbishop Plaza in the secret detention center located in the headquarters of the infantry division of the police of the province of Buenos Aires.

According to *La Nación* (May 21, 1985), Archbishop Plaza held that the trial of the former commanders then taking place was "revenge by subversive forces, and garbage." Once more in agreement with Emilio Hardoy, he said, "It is a Nuremberg in reverse, in which the criminals are judging those who defeated terrorism." Such expressions motivated Eduardo Barcesat, a lawyer for the Argentine League for Human Rights, to start legal action against Plaza for contempt. In his motion, Barcesat stated that Plaza was "clearly and unmistakably alluding to the National Chamber of Appeals for Criminal and Federal Correctional Matters, and to an important legal process taking place before that judicial court. The word 'criminals' refers unambiguously to those judges who are part of the nation's judicial system. Hence he petitioned that there be a trial, and that the accused be jailed preventively and his goods be seized.[5]

December 21, 1984, was Archbishop Plaza's seventy-fifth birthday. Article #401 of the Code of Canon Law states that diocesan bishops must present their resignation to the Holy Father when they reach that age. In his arrogance, the archbishop of La Plata never wanted to admit publicly that he had fulfilled this canonical prescription. However, he did send his resignation. For unexplained reasons, the pope did not accept it for over a year.

THE HONOR CONFERRED ON THE REVEREND MOON

On November 14, 1984, while Plaza was traveling in Europe, shortly before his seventy-fifth birthday, Nicolás Argentato, the rector of the Catholic University of La Plata, whose chancellor was the archbishop, awarded an honorary doctorate in New York to the Reverend Sun Myung Moon, founder and head of the powerful sect that bears his name. Because Moon was in jail for tax evasion in the United States, he was represented by his second in command, the Korean Colonel Bo Hi Pak.

The unprecedented spectacle of a Catholic university's conferring an honorary academic degree on Moon led to a loud outcry, but that did not bother Archbishop Plaza. The Holy See stepped in to cover up for him, declaring over Vatican Radio that "public opinion is amazed and saddened by the honorary doctorate conferred on Moon by the Catholic University of La Plata." The Vatican delegation to the United Nations stated that "with this event Argentato went against a decision made by his superior, Archbishop Antonio José Plaza of La Plata." Cardinal Primatesta, aware of the situation, was more hesitant, declaring from Rome that "as far as I know, I can state that Plaza has expressed his disapproval of what Argentato has done." In addition, the secretary of the Bishops' Conference of Argentina, Bishop Carlos Galán, said that giving this award "does not square with the name 'Catholic' as applied to that institution of learning."

Plaza has maintained an absolute silence on the question. He refused to make any statements when he returned to Argentina. Not only did he not express disapproval of Argentato, but he backed him and reaffirmed his trust in him as rector of the Catholic University until the moment he left the archdiocese. It has been his successor, Archbishop Antonio Quarracino, who had to replace Argentato with Father Gustavo Ponferrada.

As can be seen from this context, Archbishop Plaza arranged for, or approved of, the diploma award, and did not change his mind. The statement of the Vatican U.N. delegation was not true, and its only purpose was to keep up appearances.

The reasons for conferring the honor should be found in two facts: (1) a donation of $120,000 Moon made to the Catholic University of La Plata, which Doctor Argentato has acknowledged;[6] (2) common ends and activities uniting the powerful sect, Archbishop Plaza, and the Latin American military groups who hold, or have held, absolute power in the southern part of South America.

Before going any further, however, it would be well to recall the background of this sect. According to the material contained in his book *The Divine Principle,* the Reverend Sun Myung Moon, a Korean ex-monk born in 1920, believes:

> When he was 16 years old, Jesus revealed to him that he was the second Messiah. His mission was that of laying the groundwork for saving human beings, and then conquering a nation whose responsibility it would be to restore "the Kingdom of Heaven on Earth." Two thousand years ago the nation prepared and chosen was Israel, and today the chosen nation is the United States. However, foreseeing the possibility that the people of the United States might not fulfill its responsibility of following the Messiah, as was the case of the Jews with regard to Jesus, several alternative countries were sought. In 1965 the Reverend Moon traveled through forty countries on three continents. Argentina was chosen as "God's alternative land." That is why the Reverend Moon blessed the soil of the Colón square, located between Hipólito Yrigoyen, Rivadavia, Alem, and

the Casa Rosada. In 1975 he sent out the first mission and nine years later such missions are located in almost every province in Argentina.[7]

The official title of this sect, which was founded in 1954, is "Unification Church," or the "Association of the Holy Spirit for the Unification of World Christianity." That is the name by which it has been registered since 1980 in the Argentine National Registry of Worship, in the Ministry of Foreign Relations and Worship. Its number is 1,184 and its address is calle Vidal 2321 in the Belgrano neighborhood of the capital.

One worrisome aspect about the activity of this sect is the way its members recruit followers from among disoriented young persons, whom they isolate from their families and subject to genuine brainwashings, using psychological techniques to destroy the personality. They often take them to South Korea or the United States. An Argentine journalist, Alfredo Silletta, got himself into the "Moonies" in order to investigate their activities, which he describes in great detail in his book *La Secta Moon—Cómo destruir la democracia* ("The Moon sect: how to destroy democracy"):

The Moonies have economic power around the world, so much so that their assets in South Korea are around $200 million, invested in companies that produce titanium, machinery, weapons, ginseng tea, and other kinds of products. According to statements made to the *Washington Post* by Yoshikazu Soejima, the former director of public relations for the Japanese branch, in the last ten years $800 million have been transferred from that country to the United States. Obviously these are not donations from the faithful, but business profits and tainted money to be invested in the United States and elsewhere for both economic and political purposes.

Since 1980 the sect has intensified its offensive in the Southern Cone of Latin America with various trips by high leaders to Uruguay, Paraguay, Chile, and Argentina in order to set up branches of CAUSA International (Confederation of Associations for the Unification of American Societies), the sect's political arm, in our countries, and to set up news bureaus for its daily papers in the U.S.A., which are edited in New York and Los Angeles; one edition is printed in Spanish. Among the leaders they met were Presidents Alfredo Stroessner [of Paraguay] and Augusto Pinochet [of Chile], General Luis Queirolo, the head of the Uruguayan army, and in Argentina Admirals Emilio Massera and Armando Lambruschini and former unelected [Argentine] presidents Juan Carlos Onganía and Roberto Levingston. Their penetration into Uruguay is spectacular, and it is estimated that they have $60 million in investments, including a newspaper, a first-class printing company, banks, and the Victoria Plaza Hotel, the main hotel in Montevideo.[8]

In collaboration with the Argentine military dictatorship, the sect's New York paper, *News World,* in late 1979 published an interview with a woman who was allegedly the "mother of a subversive" who said she was in Uruguay because of threats from the Montoneros [Argentine guerrilla group in the 1970s]. The woman interviewed was Thelma Jara de Cabezas who in fact was secretly imprisoned in the Navy Mechanical School, as stated in a detailed account to the federal court during the trial of the former commanders. In her statement, Mrs. de Cabezas states that in September of that year she was taken to Montevideo with false documents so she could be interviewed by two U.S. reporters.[9]

July 13–17, 1980, CAUSA held a seminar in the Libertador Hotel in Buenos Aires, under the sponsorship of the Catholic University of La Plata. Moon's assistant, Colonel Bo Hi Pak, was there as were General Genaro Díaz Bessone and the former military presidents Onganía and Levingston.

On that occasion, Pak and Plaza referred to one another in their speeches. The former expressed his gratitude for "the inspired guidance and help of Archbishop Plaza, whom I sincerely admire and respect as a champion of God and of freedom in our age." Plaza answered stating that "we must confront Marxism in its ideology, ... Reverend Moon chose to challenge the cause of violence in the obsolete theory of Marxism. . . . We are emphasizing Colonel Pak's activity in his struggle against Marxism, but also in his counterproposal."[10]

Plaza was probably the connection for the trip to South Korea made by then chief of staff of the Argentine army, Jorge Arguindeguy, who went to Seoul with his wife and two colonels at the invitation of Bo Hi Pak.

In Paris, in February 1985, the political arm of the sect held a meeting of more than a hundred high-ranking military officers to analyze the situation in Central America. Those attending from Argentina were Generals Díaz Bessone, Osiris Villegas, and Mallea Gil, Admiral Fitee, and Brigadier General Martínez Quiroga.

During the first week of 1985 twelve former Latin American presidents, including Arturo Frondizi, met as a group with Pope John Paul II. There would be nothing remarkable about the news except for the fact that these ex-presidents had been brought together by AULA (Association for Latin American Unity), which is one of the two hundred civic organizations of all kinds that the Unification Church finances. Since then Frondizi has traveled to South Korea. It is not surprising to find such a connection in this former president of Argentina, in view of his present ideological and political position, but that they should have an audience with the Holy Father is surprising, given the characteristics, teaching, and background of this sect that venerates the Reverend Moon as the "second Messiah."

In mid-1987, and probably because of the denunciation appearing in my book—the Spanish version, published in October 1986—the Holy See let it be known that the papal audience with the former presidents had been granted without awareness that they had been brought together under the auspices of the Moon sect.

SOME QUESTIONS

With the foregoing information, I have tried to show, within the limits of this work, the posture and role of the archbishop of La Plata with regard to the state terrorism implanted by the military dictatorship.

However, this analysis has led me to present a broader picture, which raises some questions.

An editorial writer in the magazine *Criterio* also has questions:

It should be acknowledged that many Catholics do not feel comfortable in the church today. What they observe is that behavior judged reprehensible on the part of different sectors in the church is not treated with equal fairness. The severity of the measures taken against Father Boff, for example, stands in contrast with the leniency with which Archbishop Marcinkus's "errors" in the notorious case of the Banco Ambrosiano has been treated. In our country there is the impunity with which the authorities of the Catholic University of La Plata gave an honorary doctorate to the head of the Moon sect. A kind of ecclesiastical neoconservatism is oversensitive to the deviations of the left, while it turns a blind eye when some religious institutions obviously fail to adhere to Vatican II.[11]

I wonder how it is possible that for so many years the head of one of the main archdioceses in the country could act in the manner I have been describing, against the teaching of the gospel and the norms of the church, causing true scandal—and the Holy See and the bishops' Conference did not step in to solve the problem. I will be told that each bishop is responsible solely to Rome. That is true, but collegiality makes its demands and sets limitations. The bishops who were concerned to defend human rights accepted those demands and limitations, whereas Archbishop Bonamín and other colleagues disdainfully ignored them, as we will see below.

I do not understand why Plaza's resignation had to wait until his seventy-fifth birthday, and even less why the pope waited a whole year before letting it be known that the resignation was accepted. If the decision had been immediate, we would have had the impression that it was a gesture of disapproval. I feel inclined to accept the opinion of some experts who believe Plaza enjoys the protection of certain groups in the Vatican.

In any case, social sanction has made itself felt both inside the church and outside. There was utter silence around Archbishop Plaza's retirement. I have not seen the news refer to a single homage or farewell, not even a Mass, as normally happens. There may have been some fanfare—I do not live in La Plata and I cannot say for sure. However, I am an avid reader of newspapers and magazines, and I have not seen a single such news item. By contrast, the inauguration of his successor, Archbishop Antonio Quarracino, received wide coverage.

OPINIONS OF THE BISHOPS

It would be both wearisome and impossible to attempt to analyze the position each bishop in our country took with regard to human rights violations, whether they condemned state terrorism, and how they provided pastoral care for victims.

I will limit myself to reproducing a collection of expressions and attitudes that in my judgment prove that there prevailed among the bishops a political option in favor of the military regime at the cost of the demands of witness to the gospel.

Let me begin with Archbishop Plaza of La Plata. In May 1977 he said in a speech in Buenos Aires:

> Malevolent Argentinians who leave our country are organizing against our country from outside, supported by the forces of darkness, and they spread news, and from outside carry out campaigns in combination with those who are working in the shadows within our borders. Let us pray that the arduous labor of those who govern us spiritually and temporally may be successful. Let us be children of a nation in which the church enjoys a kind of respect that does not exist in all countries under the curse of Marxism.[12]

Note the adverb "spiritually." To Archbishop Plaza—openly contradicting Catholic teaching—the spiritual sphere belongs to the military government, as he made clear in the case of the prohibition of the book by Beatriz Casiello, previously mentioned. His main concern is that the church enjoy respect—that is, privileges—in contrast to the way things are in other countries, "under the curse of Marxism."

In August 1978, Plaza, replying to a letter from Amnesty International, stated that "there are no political prisoners in Argentina."[13] A few weeks earlier, upon returning from the Vatican, he bewailed "the present campaign of detraction" aimed at Argentina, "which has support from the forces of the left." He said that the Holy See was now showing greater understanding of the situation in Argentina, and he expressed his hope that the reporters who would be coming for the world soccer championship would get a better view of things.[14]

In some cases, bishops have utterly forgotten their pastoral duty and expressed their opinions with an incomprehensible violence and blindness. Such is the case of Bishop Carlos Mariano Pérez of Salta, now retired. In January 1984 he went so far as to say, "The Mothers of the Plaza de Mayo must be eliminated." No doubt, in the spirit of the gospel, he had in mind using a gas chamber. Moreover, "he opposed putting the military on trial and punishing them, said that the organizations that defend human rights in our country belong to an international organization, and he believed that digging up anonymous bodies is a disgrace for society." [15]

The 1979 visit of the Inter-American Commission on Human Rights (ICHR) of the OAS irritated many bishops. I believe a number of factors were involved in this reaction, starting with ignorance. The bishops give the impression that they do not know that this commission is part of the Organization of American States, of which Argentina is a member, and whose intervention it is obligated to accept by treaties it has signed. They have not the slightest idea of the role played by such organizations in protecting human rights, a role that the Holy See has frequently praised. They imagine that the commission is a group of enemies of the Argentine regime, not an impartial body made up of independent jurists.

In addition, we must note their narrow and flag-waving mind-set, shaped by the ideology of national Catholicism. The most decisive factor, however, is clearly the alliance of the bishops with the military regime, which they feel obligated to defend without seriously analyzing the situation.

In their statements, some of them, such as Bishop Octavio Nicolás Derisi, rector of the Catholic University of Argentina and auxiliary bishop of La Plata, combine a primitive mentality, derision of the victims of state terrorism, and flattery toward state authorities. "I believe the ICHR should not have come," he said in September 1979:

> The government very generously allowed them. Thus, I also respect the commission, but there was no reason why a foreign commission should come to examine us. I believe that the government is now doing things well and all this was unnecessary. In any case, now that the commission has come, I pray to God that they may be objective and not be influenced by those who have created this problem in Argentina: the families of those guerrillas who engaged in killing, kidnaping, and robbery. [16]

As in all his statements, Derisi here shows his foolishness, incompetence, and dishonesty:

> I sincerely believe that Argentina is one of the countries where things are most peaceful and where human rights are most respected. There are prisoners now, but they are in jail for crimes, according to the government, and in any case, they are there in accordance with the provisions of the law and the constitution. As far as I can see, in Argentina today there is no jailing, killing, or abuse of human rights anywhere. If a particular case happens . . . we are human beings, but I am not aware of such a situation. Anyway, I have come from Europe and I can assure you that things are calmer in Argentina. In Argentina a woman can feel

safe walking the street at night. I would say that human rights are substantially defended in Argentina.[17]

In a survey made by the magazine *Somos* on the visit of the ICHR, Bishop Derisi repeated the same arguments, adding a touch of intellectual vanity with his supposed knowledge of philosophy:

I prefer to speak of the rights of the human person rather than human rights. There are certainly those who talk a lot about the issue. But does a country like the United States, where there were a million abortions in one year, have the right to become the judge?[18]

Once more, we see confusion about the ICHR, most of whose members are Latin Americans. Moreover, it is not at all clear why the fact that there are abortions in the United States—just as there are in Argentina—makes it legitimate for our armed forces to abduct, torture, steal, and kill.

I am not going to outline at length Bishop Derisi's intellectual and moral qualities; this is not an appropriate occasion. That occasion will come. I want to remain within the limits of my topic and indicate the despicable role Derisi played during the dark years, going so far as to denounce. Reading the paragraphs I have transcribed is enough to reveal his servility toward those who hold power and his calumny toward the pursued and the victims. When my daughter was arrested, I wrote to him for help. In his reply, he said he could not do anything. The fact is that he did not *want* to do anything, for the fact that he was on the side of the government got him a good deal of influence, which he used to obtain material advantages.

Archbishop Idelfonso María Sansierra of San Juan, now dead, stated that "the ICHR has a political aim. It should be concerned about other countries where human rights are violated openly. We should defend our sovereignty, and if the commission goes further than it should, the government should exercise its sovereign rights and declare the mission ended."[19]

Archbishop Sansierra was one of the most reactionary and ignorant of all our bishops. With no touch of shame he said, "human rights are observed in Argentina." He also said that "they are suspended in wartime."[20] Where in the world did Archbishop Sansierra study moral theology? He apparently believed that if war should break out—which was not the case with us—it would be legitimate to torture, murder prisoners, steal, and rape women! His statement openly contradicts the teachings of the church, and makes plain the murderous passion that inspired him. Once, when speaking with persons who were complaining about the fact of political prisoners, he said, "I also go to the prison and I never stay there. They always let me leave."[21]

Another example of someone who would change the church's teaching was Archbishop Guillermo Bolatti of Rosario, a representative of the integralist wing, who also is now dead. He said that "every country should watch over human rights." He meant putting the sovereignty of the state over basic rights including freedom of conscience, which has been repeatedly condemned by popes and councils. "Foreigners [the ICHR] should not come to tell us what to do. I imagine the ICHR interview with Primatesta will be positive, because they will be able to receive some clarification about the situation in Argentina, which is distorted in other countries, especially in Europe."[22]

On another occasion, according to *La Opinión* (October 8, 1976), Archbishop Bolatti expressed an idea I have myself heard many bishops express: "If this [military] government collapses, the next one will be Marxist." This is an absurd fear in a country whose combined Marxist political parties garner only 1 percent of votes in an election. And yet it was one of the reasons for episcopal support of the genocidal dictatorship!

Bishop León Kruk of San Rafael said that "the ICHR visit does not mean that our sovereignty is being overthrown, for it is coming here at the invitation of the government," although he expressed his doubts about whether its "conclusions would be accurate."[23] Curious regalist bishops, who are more concerned about the sovereignty of the state than about whether the gospel is being observed! Further on, we will see the root of this worldvision.

A few days before the arrival of the commission I was close to an episode that confirms the preconception one has of the bishops. I went to Córdoba with an ICHR official to look for some place that did not belong to the state, where commission members would have freedom and a climate of trust in which to hear the accusations of family members of the victims of human rights violations. It was not easy, given the prevailing fear. The woman representing the commission, encouraged by the cooperation it had found in other countries, thought of using a Catholic church, and so we asked for a meeting with Cardinal Raúl Primatesta. Because he was out of the city, his auxiliary, Bishop Estanislao Karlic, now archbishop of Paraná, met with us. He listened attentively and said he would pass our request to the cardinal. We had a long conversation. I took advantage of it to explain how serious the situation was and how urgent it was that the church become involved. The next day Karlic phoned us in Buenos Aires to let us know that Cardinal Primatesta had decided not to provide any church or any church building for interview purposes, because he did not want to take a stance that could be considered critical of the government. . . . The same thing happened to the request we sent to Bishop Blas Conrero of Tucumán, who based his own decision on Primatesta's. Obviously this was one more explicit failure to carry out pastoral responsibility due to servility toward the state.

The ICHR report on the situation of human rights in Argentina says, "On Wednesday, September 12 [1979], at the headquarters of the bishops' conference, the ICHR met with the cardinal primate of Argentina, the archbishop of Córdoba and president of the Bishops' Conference of Argentina, who gave his views on the situation of human rights in Argentina and exchanged views with members of the ICHR."[24] Subsequently, talking with members of the commission, I found out that Cardinal Primatesta made only vague statements aimed at justifying the position of the armed forces.

The accusations of human rights violations in Argentina exasperated some bishops. Bishop Bernardo Witte of La Rioja said there was a campaign of defamation, and Bishop Rómulo García of Mar del Plata called them "campaigns dreamed up and organized by persons who deny freedom."[25] In that description, which was certainly calumniating, he was referring to the victims' families, the human rights organizations in the country, and international organizations. Bishop García refused to let the relatives of the arrested-and-disappeared meet in a church.

The high-level prelates pluck other strings when they defend the armed forces. Archbishop Quarracino has insisted that a "law of letting bygones be bygones" should be passed, although he has never explained how it might work.[26] Cardinal Aramburu inclines toward an amnesty.[27] Cardinal Primatesta, with questionable theology, says that forgiveness is proper to human beings and justice is proper to God, thus excluding the possibility of penal sanctions for the criminals responsible for state terrorism.[28] By this criterion the Italian government should have immediately freed the Turkish citizen who gravely wounded Pope John Paul II.

I do not want to abuse the reader's patience with similar quotes. I recall expressions of this sort from Bishop Rubén Di Monte of Avellaneda, Archbishop Jorge Mayer of Bahía Blanca, and Bishop Emilio Ogñenovich, then his vicar general and now bishop of Mercedes, with whom I had a difficult conversation on a trip to this southern city; Bishop Horacio A. Bózzoli, then the auxiliary bishop and vicar general of the archdiocese of Buenos Aires and now archbishop of Tucumán; Bishop Pedro A. Torres Farías of Catamarca; Bishop Jorge Manuel López, then of Corrientes and now the archbishop of Rosario; Bishop Elso Desiderio Collino of Lomas de Zamora, who was willing to fly to Paris to celebrate a Mass requested by the Argentine embassy, which Archbishop Marty of that city refused to celebrate; Bishop Manuel Guirao of Orán, subsequently made archbishop of Santiago del Estero; Bishop Italo Di Stéfano of Presidencia Roque Sáenz Peña, now archbishop of San Juan; Bishop Jorge Carlos Carreras of San Justo, who thinks defending human rights is the same as being a communist; Bishop Juan Rodolfo Laise of San Luis, one of the most stone-age among all the bishops; and Bishop Adolfo R. Arana of Santa Rosa, son of an army general—he has the same mind-set as his father.

The fact that the bishops and the military shared objectives was expressed by Admiral Emilio Massera in one of his most cynical replies:

> When we act as a political power, we continue to be Catholics, and Catholic priests who act as a spiritual power continue to be citizens. . . . However, because we are all acting out of love, which is the underlying basis of our religion, we have no problems, and our relations are excellent, as befits Christians.[29]

Isabel Perón greets Bishop Tortolo

Bishop Tortolo, followed by members of the first junta of the military dictatorship; (right to left) Massera, Videla, and Agosti

(left to right) Viola and Videla, among others; Bishop Bonamín applauds

The junta receives the "evangelical message;" (right to left) Galtieri, Lambruschini, and Graffigna

Military vicar, Bishop José Miguel Medina

A military chaplain, reading from Lives of the Military Saints

Cardinal Aramburu, part of the military dictatorship's public image

Aramburu, Viola, Galtieri, and Graffigna, behind the bayonets (right to left)

Papal nuncio Pio Laghi, Cardinal Primatesta, and two members of the dictatorship, enjoying a friendly toast

Father Christian von Wernich

Cardinal Aramburu repeating his assertions of "lack of proof" about the disappeared

G. LOIACONO

A fruitless wait: families of the disappeared gather at the gates of the Argentine Episcopal Conference

Bishop Jorge Novak

Bishop Jaime de Nevares

Father Antonio Puigjané and the Mothers of Plaza de Mayo

A demonstration of human rights: (left to right) Adolfo Pérez Esquivel, Father Luis Farinello, Eduardo Pimentel, Bishop Jaime de Nevares, Bishop Jorge Novak, and Bishop Federico Pagura

Father Carlos Mugica, carrying on his pastoral work in slum areas, before he was gunned down in the street

Adolfo Pérez Esquivel, winner of the Nobel Peace Prize

Memorial service for Christian victims of the repression; Bishops Jorge Novak and Federico Pagura preside

The murdered Pallottine fathers and seminarians, executed in their house by police

Bishop Angelleli in his daily work with the poor

Bishop Miguel Hesayne, paying tribute to Bishop Angelleli on the tenth anniversary of his murder by the dictatorship

CHAPTER FIVE

The Weight of History

CONCLUSIONS AND QUESTIONS

Both the individual attitudes of most bishops and the influence of the top leadership of the bishops' conference were decisive in determining the position they took as a body toward the state terrorism set up by the military dictatorship. As previously noted, the Argentine bishops made a purely political option. They aligned themselves with temporal power, rejecting the witness of the gospel, which demands that crimes be denounced, those responsible be accused, and the victims actively helped, even at the risk of persecution. The bishops knew the truth and they hid it in order to aid the military government. Faced with a choice between God and Caesar, they chose Caesar.

In his opening address at Puebla, Pope John Paul II said:

As pastors, you keenly realize that your chief duty is to be teachers of the truth: not of a human, rational truth but of the truth that comes from God. That truth includes the principle of authentic human liberation: "You will know the truth, and the truth will set you free (John 8:32). It is the one and only truth that offers a solid basis for an adequate "praxis." [1]

Further on, he stated:

Those familiar with the history of the Church know that in every age there have been admirable bishops deeply involved in the valiant defense of the human dignity of those entrusted to them by the Lord. Their activity was always mandated by their episcopal mission, because they regarded human dignity as a gospel value that cannot be despised without greatly offending the Creator. [2]

It is not out of opportunism or a thirst for novelty that the Church . . . defends human rights. It is prompted by an authentically evangelical commitment which, like that of Christ, is primarily a commitment to those most in need. [3]

71

The political effects that derive from defending human dignity are a result of the message of Jesus, who came to announce the good news "to the poor" (Matt. 11:5) and to "bring forth justice to the nations" (Isa. 42:1). Hence, the fast that the Lord desires is "releasing those bound unjustly, untying the thongs of the yoke; setting free the oppressed, breaking every yoke; sharing your bread with the hungry, sheltering the oppressed and the homeless" (Isa. 58:6–7). That is why the Lord "has confused the proud in their inmost thoughts. He has deposed the mighty from their thrones and raised the lowly to high places. The hungry he has given every good thing, while the rich he has sent empty away" (Luke 1:51–53).

Merely repeating Christian principles as the bishops limited themselves to doing, is not enough, "Modern persons," Pope Paul VI observed, "listen more willingly to witnesses than to teachers, and if they listen to teachers, it is because they are witnesses."[4]

With its message of integral human liberation, the gospel demanded that the military regime be condemned, because it was assaulting the dignity of the human person by means of state terrorism, and because its political, social, and economic thrust meant subjugation and misery for the bulk of the Argentine people.

THE REASONS FOR THE BISHOPS' OPTION

What caused the bishops to take this stance, one that is incomprehensible after Vatican II, the Medellín documents, and Paul VI's exhortation on evangelization in the modern world? I have been asked that question dozens of times, especially in other countries. I will try to answer it in the following pages.

Those who most insistently ask this question are Catholic bishops and priests in other countries, where our bishops have been quite discredited. During that period several episcopal conferences wrote to their counterpart in Argentina, urging it to fulfill its gospel mission. On my travels, I have read some of their responses signed by the secretary general of the Argentine conference, Bishop Galán. They make obvious both the bishops' annoyance over this "meddling" and their complicity with the regime.

HISTORICAL CONDITIONING FACTORS

The Argentine church was born yoked to the state by reason of the *patronato* ("patronage") of the Indies, and it remains both legally and ideologically under the conception that originally inspired it.

The basic elements of *patronato* can be found in Alexander VI's famous bull of May 4, 1493, which gave to the Catholic kings of Spain and Portugal newly discovered lands in other parts of the world, and those yet to be discovered. A similar document, *Universalis Ecclesiae,* published by Julius II on July 28,

1508, further developed the legislation and was incorporated into the Laws of the Indies.

Of course *patronato* was not a new institution in the history of the Catholic Church. It had existed in Europe, in various forms, since the Middle Ages, and its concessions to temporal power were broadened with the consolidation of absolute monarchies during the Renaissance. It remained in force until the beginning of the twentieth century, and disappeared only during the next few decades, although some of its principles can still be found in the 1953 Spanish concordat between Pius XII and Franco. In most Latin American countries it ended with the separation of church and state.

As Father Gómez Zapiola observes,

> By means of this and other bulls, the Spanish crown obtained comprehensive powers extending from the appointment of bishops to setting up a village hospital; from building a cathedral to dictating how a tabernacle should be illuminated; from authorizing or prohibiting missions to setting up a religious fraternity; from withholding a papal bull not approved by the Council of the Indies to granting authorization to preside over the election of the provincial in the chapter of a religious order; from authorizing and presiding over councils and synods to prohibiting bishops from ordering excommunications without careful consideration. The legal organization of this whole mechanism is found in Book I of the 1608 Collection of the Laws of the Indies.[5]

The crown collected tithes and took charge of supporting the clergy. Offices and benefices were granted in Madrid, and thus there was no direct communication between bishops and Rome. Because of bequests and pious foundations, the church, and particularly religious orders, had considerable wealth, but that did not make the church independent, because legal prescriptions were so detailed. Bishops were appointed by the king and presented to the Holy See to be invested. Only then was a bishop consecrated.

This dependence of the church on the state became more rigid after 1700 with the establishment of the Bourbon dynasty, which brought in royalism from France. Toward the end of the eighteenth century and during the period of the emancipating revolution, this was the prevailing doctrine among bishops, royalty, theologians, jurists, and the clergy.

Under the influence of the Enlightenment, progressives during the era of Charles III, such as the viceroy Vértiz and Bishop San Alberto, were fervent royalists. This system lasted after independence and it had its devotees until the beginning of this century.

From the very beginning, in 1810, the [postindependence] junta took on the rights and obligations of *patronato* and intervened in religious matters. One of its first acts was that of declaring vacant the episcopal see of Córdoba, which Orellana had occupied without following any of the procedures laid out in canon law. Faced with a conflict over how to replace the seat vacated by Magistral in the cathedral church of Buenos Aires, the junta decided to consult two famous canonists in Córdoba, Gregorio Funes and Juan Luis de Aguirre. Their separate opinions, signed September 15, 1810, agreed that *patronato* was a prerogative attached to the *sovereignty* of kings, not their *persons*. Hence it should be regarded as having passed on to the independent national government.

Since then, all constitutions, both proposed and accepted, including the one in 1853, and the present one (excepting only the provisional statute of 1815) have maintained *patronato* and its counterpart, the maintenance of Catholic worship by the state. *Patronato* is present in the constitutional initiatives of 1813, in the provisional rule of 1817, in the constitutions of 1819 and 1826. Successive legal opinions, and especially the well-known *Memorial Ajustado* of 1834, develop the doctrine in a direction that favors its maintenance. The central issue was appointing bishops and other ecclesiastical officials, a right claimed by the state.

Contrary to the predictions of the Voltaireans of the previous century, the nineteenth century witnessed a significant renovation in the Catholic Church and a strengthening of papal power. The Holy See decided to reclaim its authority to appoint bishops and opposed *patronato,* at least in Latin American countries. The same position, called Ultramontanism, took hold among the clergy, whose training became more systematic and was largely centralized in Rome.

As a result of this evolution, the question of whether *patronato* should continue in effect became a source of conflict between the Holy See and governments. With governments insisting that they had inherited the faculties conferred by the popes on the Spanish monarchy, both sides compromised and reached a modus vivendi: the state continued to propose names of bishops, usually after confidential negotiation, and in appointing them the pope omitted any mention of their presentation by the government.

These problems came to a head when Gregory XVI attempted to restore the Catholic hierarchy [many sees were left vacant during the Independence struggle] by appointing bishops by himself, ignoring *patronato*. He did that in 1832, designating Bishop Mariano Medrano as bishop of Buenos Aires. However, the governor of the province, appealing to the legal opinions in the *Memorial Ajustado,* held that *patronato* was still in force. He allowed the bull to take effect only in 1834. Similar problems arose in the appointment of bishops for the dioceses of Córdoba and Salta, and in creating the diocese of Cuyo. Government authorities were actively involved.

Governor-dictator Juan Manuel de Rosas (1829–1832, 1835–1852) firmly upheld *patronato,* following the advice of Dalmacio Vélez Sarsfield, which issued in his well-known work *Public Ecclesiastical Law.* Rosas collaborated with the church but he kept it under rigid control.

Pope Gregory XVI in his encyclical *Mirari Vos* (1832), and Pope Pius IX, in his famous *Syllabus* (1864), were opposed to interference by civil authority in ecclesiastical matters, and opposed to separation of church and state. That led to the condemnation of the movement led by Montalembert and others within Catholicism. This movement invoked the formula, "a free church in a free state." As evidence of how fruitful this approach would be, they pointed to the example of the United States.

The general constituent congress of 1853 chose a compromise solution. It refused to declare Catholicism the state religion, and discontinued the immunity of the clergy from civil law, and the requirement that government employees profess Catholicism, as proposed by deputies Leiva, Zenteno and Manuel Pérez. It did not go as far as separation, however, opting instead for the *patronato* system, which involved a form of state control. For its part, the state was obligated to maintain "Roman Catholic apostolic worship" (article 2), and the president of the country had to be a Catholic (article 76).

Article 86 of the constitution includes among the powers of the president of the republic the exercise of "national *patronato* in the presentation of bishops for cathedral churches, following the proposal of three names by the Senate" (clause 8). It also confers on him the right to accept or reject "the decrees of councils and the bulls, briefs, and rescripts of the pontiff in Rome, in accordance with the Supreme Court; when the provisions are general and permanent, a law is required" (clause 9).

In listing the powers of the congress, article 67 states that it should promote the conversion of Amerindians to Catholicism (clause 15); "approve or reject . . . concordats with the Apostolic See and arrange that *patronato* be exercised throughout the Nation" (clause 19); and "allow other religious orders besides those already present to enter the territory of the Nation" (clause 20).

In the constitution these provisions coexist alongside freedom of worship, which was established by article 14, a principle that the Catholic Church did not admit at that time.

It is interesting to note the origin of the religious requirement for being president. In the April 29, 1853, session of the constituent assembly, Father Lavaysse, a deputy representing Santiago del Estero (who had voted in favor of freedom of worship and against the imposition of a state religion), requested that "there be added to the requirements for being president or vice-president that of belonging to the Roman Catholic and apostolic communion, based on the provision in the proposed constitution that grants to the executive the rights of national *patronato* . . . and that have to do with approving bulls, briefs, and rescripts from the Holy Father."[6] The requirement was accepted by the commission rapporteur and drafter of the constitution, Gorostiaga, and approved by the congress.

The power to present bishops to the Holy See to be appointed and consecrated was exercised uninterruptedly for over a century by both constitutional and dictatorial governments until the signing of an agreement on October 10, 1966, approved as law 17,032 of the Onganía government. This agreement, proposed during the constitutional Frondizi presidency, was negotiated during the elected presidency of Illia by his minister of foreign relations and worship, Miguel Angel Zavala Ortiz and was scheduled to be signed the day of the coup that deposed that government.

Despite the precarious nature of the church-state modus vivendi, there were few conflicts, considering how long the period lasted. Prudence prevailed on both sides. Normally, they came to an agreement over candidates in confidential meetings. There were memorable episodes during the first presidency of Roca, who had Clara, the vicar general of Córdoba, removed, and Bishop Risso Patrón of Salta suspended as though they were civil servants, government officials. Matters did not get out of hand, because the Córdoba vacancy was filled almost immediately and Risso Patrón soon died. During the 1920s when President Marcelo T. de Alvear insisted on having Bishop Miguel de Andrea made archbishop of Buenos Aires and Rome refused, the see remained vacant for a number of years.

The 1966 agreement, which is of a concordatlike nature, suppresses *patronato,* which had become an anachronism and was annoying not only the Holy See but state officials as well, forced to be involved in appointments that, as things are seen today, should be the exclusive concern of the church. The first article of the agreement states that "the Argentine state recognizes and guarantees the Roman Catholic apostolic Church the free and full exercise of its spiritual power, the free and public exercise of its worship, and jurisdiction in the sphere of its own competence for attaining its specific ends." Subsequent clauses establish that the Holy See will be able to create, set up, or suppress ecclesiastical jurisdictions, and that it has the authority to appoint archbishops and bishops.

The fourth article of the agreement eliminates the president's authority to approve papal documents and allow them to be implemented within the country. This norm is incompatible with freedom of expression and contemporary modes of communication, and was in fact being ignored. It recognizes "the Holy See's right to publish in the Argentine Republic its decisions on the governing of the church and to communicate and correspond freely with the bishops, the clergy, and the faithful in matters connected with their noble ministry, just as they can do so with the Apostolic See."

The 1966 agreement nevertheless retains lingering elements of royalism, due to state involvement in maintaining dioceses. These elements should be eliminated during the next constitutional reform, in the course of working out a healthy and friendly separation of church and state. The agreement states:

> Before proceeding to appoint archbishops and residential bishops, prelates, or coadjutors with right of succession, the Holy See will convey to the Argentine government the name of the person chosen so as to find out whether there are any objections of a political nature against him. The Argentine government will answer within thirty days. When such time has passed, the government's silence will be interpreted as signifying that there are no objections to the appointment. Such communication will be carried out in the strictest secrecy.

Patronato has been eliminated, but not all government involvement in the appointment of bishops. The possibility that military regimes might have objected to the appointment of bishops who were critical of human rights violations and to their overall authoritarian policies cannot be discounted. Even if the Holy See would have attempted it—and it was not likely—I am persuaded that during the period of military dictatorship, from 1976 to 1983, it would have been impossible to appoint to the episcopacy a priest who had been outstanding in defending the dignity of the human person and in the people's struggles. We have here a constraint that no priest interested in becoming a bishop will fail to take into account.

There are important practical consequences to the agreement. I concur with Father Fernando Storni, S.J., who holds that inasmuch as the president is no longer the protector of the Argentine church, the constitutional requirement of membership in the Catholic Church no longer makes sense and is not binding. Such an interpretation is obvious in the light of the proposal of deputy Lavaysse during the general constituent congress of 1853, noted above. The same could be said with regard to support for Catholic worship, although that involves a wider problem, which I will deal with next.

In concluding this historical sketch, the important point I want to highlight is the longstanding tradition of subjection to the state that lingers among the Argentine bishops and influences their decisions. This subjection favors alliance when a government and a hierarchy are in ideological agreement, as has generally been the case with military regimes, which normally take the position of defending the interests and privileges of the church. The pluralism that accompanies constitutional governments, like the present one, has the effect of exposing the position of bishops who foster procoup and antidemocratic movements. This question, however, will also require separate treatment.

MAINTAINING WORSHIP

As I have said, the second article of our national constitution declares that "the federal government maintains Roman Catholic and apostolic worship."

There has been discussion over whether this clause refers only to economic support or demands a broader interpretation. I believe the latter position is more correct, but that is not what concerns me at this point. I should like to determine to what extent the economic support given by the state to the Catholic Church—specifically to the bishops—may have had an influence on the decisions that led to whitewashing the crimes of the military dictatorship.

The problem is complex and necessarily entails a consideration of various little-known and little-studied aspects. In place of serious analytical studies, what we have are defensive writings or sectarian and sensationalist critiques.

As a result of the *patronato* system during the Spanish colonial period, the expenses of the ecclesiastical superstructure and in particular the salaries that went along with offices and benefices were paid by the royal treasury, which collected the tithes destined for the church. Pastors also received stipends for various services and collected other fees. Bishops, and especially religious orders, owned income-producing property in both the cities and the countryside.

Many of these resources financed works that benefited the population, such as hospitals and schools.

In 1767 Charles III ordered that the Jesuits be expelled and their considerable wealth expropriated. After independence, Bernardino Rivadavia, the all-powerful minister of government for the province of Buenos Aires, in 1822 ordered a reform that entailed confiscating the goods of the church in the Buenos Aires region and of most religious orders. In compensation, the state reaffirmed its commitment to maintain worship. This measure was imitated in a number of other provinces. Tithes were eliminated.

This measure was taken when the see of Buenos Aires was vacant and there were no relations with Rome. One part of the clergy was opposed, but another part, whose mind-set was more royalist, supported it. As a result, the church became even more dependent on the state.

Among the properties confiscated were several large tracts of land in the center of the city—the lands around the cathedral today occupied by the city government, the Recoleta cemetery, the Casa de la Moneda, Avellaneda park, Chacabuco park, the military hospital—and a dozen large estates in the rural areas of the province, including those belonging to the sanctuary of Nuestra Señora de Luján. Their value today would be astronomical.[7]

Such episodes have been inevitable in all those countries where the church acquired excessive economic power by accumulating donations. These constituted what was regarded as mortmain during the Middle Ages in Europe. In our case, confiscation was justified by the second article of the constitution and by the obligation to support Catholic worship.

CONTRIBUTIONS TO DIOCESES

After taking office in Paraná in 1854, President Justo José de Urquiza worked persistently to renew relations with the Holy See and to have episcopal vacancies filled and new dioceses created. For this purpose and in order to train the diocesan clergy, he guaranteed economic support from the state, in accordance with the norms laid down in the general constituent congress.

In this connection, there was a series of diplomatic missions, among which we may mention the sending of Alberdi and del Campillo to Rome and a visit to Buenos Aires by Marino Marini, the apostolic delegate of the Holy See to the government of the Argentine Confederation.

As a result of these efforts, the bishops of Salta, San Juan, and Córdoba were canonically installed, and the diocese of El Litoral was set up. These measures and consequent budgetary provisions were put into effect by means of a series of laws. Two of these laws are important insofar as they were in effect up to the 1976–1983 military dictatorship, with budgetary modifications to take into account increases in the numbers of bishops and changes in currency. They are law 176 of 1857 and law 186 of 1858. The former laid down the annual amounts to be given to cathedral churches and chancery offices, and the latter provided for maintaining seminaries. Between 1855 and 1888 there were other legal regulations that further developed legislation with regard to the jurisdiction, installation, and support of bishops and creation of further dioceses: laws 28 and 49 of 1855, 85 and 99 of 1856, 116 of 1864 (numbering began anew in 1862), 597 of 1873, 982 of 1879, 1406 of 1884, 2246 of 1883, and 2302 of 1888.

Law 186, passed on September 7, 1858 (which was set aside by the military government, as I will explain below), states that "for every cathedral church in the Argentine Confederation, those now existing and those that will be set up in the future, there will be a Conciliar Seminary financed by the national Government." This decree was promulgated by President Urquiza, and authenticated by the minister, Santiago Derqui.

Along the same lines, President Bartolomé Mitre, by means of a decree on February 15, 1865, founded "a house of studies called the Conciliar Seminary of Buenos Aires for young men who feel inclined toward an ecclesiastical career."[8] The resolution stipulated that the bishops would propose to the government for its approval a plan of studies and internal regulations as well as the names of employees and teachers to be appointed. There was resistance to such control and it fell into disuse. The resolution took into account money for buildings, salaries, and scholarships for poor students.

As I have noted elsewhere, President Domingo Sarmiento complemented this initiative by founding a teachers' college, a military college, and the naval college:

> [These four institutions] were characterized by the way they recruited their students at a very young age and gave them a rigid and closed education, which led to honorable but poorly paid careers, except at the higher levels, and little participation in economic and political decision-making. Candidates came from the impoverished masses of the rural areas and from the middle classes. . . . Teachers, military officers, and priests were schooled in institutions with a strong espirt de corps so as to play roles that were necessary but subordinate, and under state control. Thus, recognition was given to the social functions of religion for instilling morality into the popular classes and holding them in subjection, and the teaching given in seminaries was supervised.[9]

In accordance with the lines laid down in this political design, which was successful, leadership groups were to be trained in national schools and the university.

The bishops have remained dependent on state financial support up to the present. For many years the first concern of bishops in new dioceses was getting the government to put up a building for their residence and chancery office and another for the seminary. I witnessed what happened in Mercedes, in the province of Buenos Aires, where I lived, and I am aware of other cases. The unending and competitive appeal for money was one of the reasons President

Juan Perón formed a negative image of the Catholic hierarchy and prompted him to attack it and try to divide it.

During the 1976–1983 military dictatorship this dependence reached its high point. By receiving a salary and a privileged kind of retirement pension, bishops were held in check. Such an attitude contradicts the teaching of the Vatican II, and the only way to explain it is the close connection between the military and the bishops, and the preconciliar mind-set of the latter. According to the Constitution on the Church in the Modern World, approved by Paul VI and the council fathers on December 7, 1965:

> [The church] does not lodge her hope in privileges conferred by civil authority. Indeed, she stands ready to renounce the exercise of certain legitimately acquired rights if it becomes clear that their use raises doubt about the sincerity of her witness or that new conditions of life demand some other arrangement.[10]

In the light of the conciliar teaching, there is no doubt that increasing economic privileges, as legitimate as they might be regarded, blocked the Argentine bishops from witnessing to the gospel with regard to the crimes of the military government. The least bit of pastoral clear-sightedness should have made the bishops aware that this was not the moment to be negotiating, with the cock crowing, in order to get concessions, when the clear purpose of those concessions was to keep the bishops quiet.

On February 25, 1977, when state terrorism was in full swing, President Videla signed law 21,540, according to which:

> Archbishops and bishops, with jurisdiction over archdioceses, dioceses, prelatures, or exarchates of Roman Catholic and Apostolic Worship, and the Military Vicariate of the armed forces, who cease functioning in such positions for reasons of age or disablement, will receive for life a monthly payment, equal to seventy percent (70%) of the pay of a first-stage federal judge in the General Government Budget [article 10].

Article 2 provides the same kind of benefit, set at 50 percent for auxiliary bishops. As is well known, according to the new Code of Canon Law (article 401), bishops are obliged to resign at the age of 75.

As I noted in chapter 2, above, the bishops and the government of Argentina were worried about the General Conference of the Latin American Bishops that began in Puebla, Mexico, on January 28, 1979, in the presence of Pope John Paul II. Both the bishops and the government were afraid that at the Puebla meeting there would be criticisms and statements that might affect them. Accordingly, the bishops chosen to represent the national hierarchy were all close to the dictatorship. The latter very thoughtfully paid the expenses of their trip to Mexico. In addition, shortly before the meeting, President Videla sent to the so-called Commission for Legislative Advice a bill similar to the one just mentioned, providing that a salary be paid to each resident bishop and his auxiliaries.

Present at the Puebla conference with a right to speak but not to vote was the well-known political scientist, Carlos Alberto Floria, who was then president of the dead-letter Justice and Peace Commission of the archdiocese of Buenos Aires. In a class lecture he gave at the University of Belgrano on July 19, 1979, a transcript of which I have before me, during a course on security taught by General José T. Goyret (ret.), who was occupying the Chair of Argentine Thought, Floria spoke about the participation of the Argentine bishops. The title of the lecture was "National Security from the Perspective of the Puebla Document."

The bishops' document takes up the ideology of collective or national security seven times, vigorously defining and condemning it. In the course of a wide prior debate in the assembly, the various situations in different countries were analyzed. During the question period following Floria's presentation the following dialogue took place:

Question: Was any country taken as a paradigm of the abuses committed in the name of national security as an ideology?

Floria: The country that most had in mind in those terms was Brazil. We didn't come off very well; the assembly didn't spend a lot of time discussing Argentina.

Question: Why was national security considered an ideology in Brazil?

Floria: For the Brazilian bishops, the form in which the doctrine of national security is expressed in Brazil is that of an ideology.

Question: What was the opinion of the Argentine bishops on the ideology of national security in Argentina?

Floria: The opinion I recall was that for the Argentine bishops national security was not an ideology but a problem. They did not think that the Argentine military had been educated in terms of a military indoctrination that might introduce a kind of ideologization of national security.

What the Argentine bishops said, as recorded by Floria, is untrue, and its only purpose was to defend the military dictatorship. It is not within the scope of this book to study the impact of the ideology of collective security on the mind-set and practice of the armed forces of our country, but the question has been studied enough, and is obvious to any observer. Prudently—this was 1979—Floria did not offer an opinion, and it is clear from what he said that he did not dissent from what the bishops said at Puebla although he could have done so.

At the end of Floria's class, General Goyret stated that he agreed with the position of the bishops:

I want to state that in Argentina there is no ideology of national security. . . . There is no ideology of national security in Argentina, even though in other countries studies may be published that include Argentina within a vast current of national security doctrine, which in fact would include almost all governments in Latin America.

Naturally, Goyret, who puts on the air of an intellectual, did not deign to provide any proof for such a sweeping statement, which is contradicted both by the way things are, and by what the armed forces say. What he said has the same level of certainty as another statement by him, also made at the University of Belgrano at the time of the Malvinas/Falklands conflict: "With my authority as a strategist, I am able to state that the Argentine forces that have occupied the islands cannot be defeated."

After the Puebla meeting, when President Videla was satisfied with the performance of the Argentine episcopal delegation, he approved law 21,950, dated March 7, 1979. An introductory passage, signed by Minister of the Economy José A. Martínez de Hoz, and Minister of Foreign Relations and Worship Carlos W. Pastor, explains that up to this point the maintenance of Catholic worship had been financed by lump sums paid to chancery offices, but:

By means of the system now being initiated the bishops will be given a monthly payment that will enable them to live in reasonable circumstances, without having to make use of the scarce resources of the dioceses, similar to the way the present system of the Military Vicariate functions. This measure affects approximately seventy bishops, both residential and auxiliary.

Article 1 of the body of the law provides that "archbishops and bishops with jurisdiction over archdioceses, dioceses, prelatures, eparchies, and exarchates of the Roman Catholic and Apostolic Worship will enjoy a monthly payment equal to 80 percent of the salary set for a first-level federal judge, until they cease those functions." Clause 2 orders a similar benefit of 70 percent for auxiliary bishops and the secretary general of the bishops' conference.

By way of a news item published by the religion reporter for *La Nación,* I understand that three diocesan bishops have refused to accept this payment.

In their haste to settle economic matters before the constitutional government was set up, the bishops managed to get an equally unfortunate change in the system for maintaining seminaries set up by the old law 186 of 1858. The new element involves making seminarians government employees. The norm approved by law 22,950 (October 25, 1983), which bears the signature of the unelected President Reynaldo Bignone, stipulates:

The national government will contribute to the training of the diocesan clergy, for which purpose residential bishops and those who function canonically as such will receive for each student of Argentine nationality in a Major Seminary that pertains to the proper ecclesiastical jurisdiction, a monthly support payment equivalent to the amount given to Category 10 in the Scale of Civilian Personnel in the National Civil Service [article 10.].

Article 2 confers the same benefit on provincial superiors in the following religious orders that antedated the constitution: Mercedarians, Dominicans, Franciscans, Jesuits, and Salesians.

When the bill was approved by the Commission for Legislative Advice, I published an article headed "Favors Repaid, Sidestepping Tough Discussion," in *La Voz* (October 10, 1983) drawing attention to its content. So as not to repeat myself here, I will quote only a few paragraphs:

> In announcing the conclusion of the Commission for Legislative Advice, the group's spokesman, Colonel Carlos Juan Frandini, pointed out that the initiative consists in providing Catholic seminarians with a monthly payment equal to that received by tenth-level civil servants.
>
> I do not know how the bill came about, but I suppose it is the result of negotiations between the military government and the top leadership of the episcopacy.
>
> It is striking that this payment is being approved during the final days of the military regime. One has the impression that it is a return payment for favors given, and particularly for the bishops' silence with regard to the so-called amnesty law, which the rest of society has unanimously condemned. The idea has been to avoid having the matter discussed in congress, for that would prove embarrassing.
>
> This give-and-take between bishops and government authorities is repugnant to the Christian conscience and is unacceptable. It compromises the church and detracts from its autonomy and credibility.

Three days before constitutional government was reestablished, the military regime thought that the cardinal archbishop of Buenos Aires, Juan Carlos Aramburu, who had remained unalterably aligned with the regime, did not have a residence in keeping with his dignity. Wasting no time, the unelected mayor, Guillermo del Cioppo, dug up an old petition from the archbishop and by means of ordinance 39,732 (December 7, 1983), ordered a payment of eight million Argentine pesos. In the prefatory clauses it is noted that the city government had demolished a building that had belonged to the archdiocese (where the present municipal building stands) without paying any compensation.

This is one more absurdity. As I will explain below, contrary to what many think, the Argentine church is not rich. However, the archdiocese of Buenos Aires has more than enough buildings to provide a house for the archbishop, who should live modestly in a place that everyone knows about, and available to the faithful, who at present do not know how to find him. The era of pomp and episcopal palaces is over. The Puebla document (#666) states that "the lifestyle of many pastors has grown in simplicity and poverty, in mutual affection and understanding, in closeness to the people, openness to dialogue, and shared responsibility!''—but certainly not in the archdiocese of Buenos Aires!

Plundering the state and thus sacrificing independence has been a constant in Archbishop Aramburu's way of governing the church. The other constant is isolation and lack of communication with society. He never met with organizations defending human rights, which he calls "communist." Even priests of the diocese are referred to regional vicars and are obliged to arrange an appointment. Presbyteral councils and pastoral councils, laid out in the new Code of Canon Law as a result of Vatican II, exist on paper only. And to think that when I was young I used to criticize Cardinal Santiago Luis Copello for his authoritarianism! At the old chancery office facing the Plaza de Mayo during siesta time he used to receive anyone who wanted to see him, with no need to make an appointment! Even though he did not know me, I went to see him several times with proposals or complaints. To get to see him, you only had to sit down in the waiting room. He usually did not settle anything, but at least he listened patiently and said some words of understanding.

The archbishops used to live in the chancery office building next to the cathedral until Peronist groups burned it down on June 16, 1955, as a reaction to a bombing that had taken place that day. With government funds, the building has been rebuilt just for offices. Meanwhile the chancery office was set up in a building owned by the government where President Ortiz once lived. It seems that this building has been permanently transferred to the church, and is being remodeled for the use of the bishops' conference, which presently occupies a house donated by Don Enrique Udaondo. The remodeled building was inaugurated during the visit by Pope John Paul II in May 1987.

I have never gone into the new chancery office but I went to the old one several times, in unsuccessful attempts to meet with Cardinal Aramburu. Acting as receptionist was a corporal in the federal police. This initial reception at the offices of a bishop bespoke its own symbolism. I once read the following slogan painted on a wall in Buenos Aires: "If Jesus Christ came back to earth, Aramburu would turn him over to the state intelligence service."

CONSTITUTIONAL REFORM

The next reform of the constitution will have to bring about the separation of church and state. I believe this can be done in harmony with the Catholic Church, along the lines of the principles of religious liberty approved at Vatican II.

I think readers will agree that the constitutional articles and paragraphs quoted at the beginning of this chapter should be eliminated. But there is no need to fall into the stupidity of making legislation as though the Catholic Church and other religious confessions did not exist in Argentina. I do not think there is any reason to change the preamble or the invocation of "God, source of all reason and justice," found there.

In this connection I think the 1978 Spanish constitution provides a good model. After guaranteeing religious liberty and stating that no confession is to have official status, it states, "Public authorities will keep in mind the religious beliefs of Spanish society and will maintain cooperative relationships with the Catholic Church and other confessions." The text of the 1984 concordat between Italy and the Vatican, mentioned above, would also be applicable.

This would open a broad field for collaboration in areas of common interest such as culture, education, health, welfare assistance, the young, and so forth.

FINANCING PASTORAL WORK

In the passage already cited, Vatican II teaches:

The Church herself employs the things of time to the degree that her own proper mission demands. Still she does not lodge her hope in privileges conferred by civil authority. Indeed, she stands ready to renounce the exercise of certain legitimately acquired rights if it becomes clear that their use raises doubt about the sincerity of her witness or that new conditions of life demand some other arrangement.[11]

Paul VI adds, "It is . . . primarily by her conduct and by her life that the Church will evangelize the world, in other words, is, by her living witness of fidelity to the Lord Jesus—the witness of poverty and detachment, of freedom in the face of the powers of this world, in short, the witness of sanctity."[12]

In this doctrinal and political context, the Argentine bishops should have given up state support for Catholic worship years ago, and thus recovered their "freedom in the face of the powers of this world."

It would be a very intelligent action on their part to do so now, taking into account the experience they have undergone. They would be taking the initiative themselves, before any reform of the constitution, which will most certainly eliminate the religious clauses from the constitution. Such a gesture would create the conditions for a peaceful and cordial separation of church and state, by avoiding conflicts and polemics, and paving the way for future collaboration. We would then have the only kind of system compatible with contemporary society and the guidelines laid down by Vatican II.

The idea is not new, although the lack of freedom for expression and creation in the Argentine church has kept it from being expressed for many decades. In his excellent study *Doctrina y Ejercicio del Patronato Nacional* ("Doctrine and exercise of the national *patronato*"), unfortunately never reprinted, Faustino J. Legón proposed it as long ago as 1920. This illustrious but ignored jurist, under whom I studied in the Department of Law and Social Sciences at the University of Buenos Aires, wrote:

Separation [of church and state], which could be necessary under certain circumstances, need not be punitive or unpleasant. In fact it could even

be advantageous for governing the church and desired by the bishops.
. . . And I believe it might help the church achieve more respect and
extend its influence, for there is no doubt that the *patronato* system is a
real hindrance in ambiguous situations, and does not help the church in
the area that should be its strong point—the inspiration it provides by
means of the teachings and moral precepts with which it has been entrusted. Being liberated from these bonds has always led to a beneficial
reaction, a new flourishing: I am thinking of the example of France. In
South America, both Brazil and Uruguay furnish compelling arguments.

For canonical orthodoxy the problem can be solved in terms of economic separation [of church and state], which the congressional deputy
Gustavo Martínez Zuviría, of the Progressive Democratic Party, recently
proposed in the Argentine parliament. The process of disconnection would
be a settling of accounts: the government would cease supporting Catholic worship and would compensate the church for the property and income it lost through civil governments. Such an arrangement would be
fair and reasonable, but should it prove impossible, the church should
still loosen its ties with the state, and give up its efforts for repayment.[13]

A great deal of water has gone under the bridge. Today it is preposterous
for the church to expect to be compensated for what the Rivadavia government
confiscated in 1822. After what has been made known in this book, is it too
much to ask of the Holy Spirit that the bishops be inspired to make an intelligent decision and give up government subsidies for worship? I am convinced
that the gains in the credibility of the gospel message would be immense.

Church-state separation was brought about amicably in Chile and Brazil, in
1924 and 1889, respectively. Those two episcopacies gained in their selfless
defense of human dignity and their defense of the dispossessed. This confirms
my point.

In Argentina democratic political sectors favor a constitutional reform that
would make the church independent of the state and would make it possible to
cancel the October 10, 1966, agreement mentioned above. Such a measure
would do away with a vestige of *patronato* that enables the government to take
part in establishing new dioceses and to object to the appointment of bishops.

The Catholic Church, for its part, no longer condemns separation of church
and state as it did in proposition 55 of the famous *Syllabus* of Pius IX (1864).
A practical application can be seen in the change in the Lateran treaties made
by the Italian government and the Holy See on February 18, 1984, with the
signatures of Cardinal Agostino Casaroli and the socialist prime minister, Bet-
tino Craxi. Article 10 of the new concordat stipulates: "The Italian Republic
and the Holy See reaffirm that the state and the Catholic Church are independent and sovereign, each one in its own order, and they pledge to fully respect
this principle in their relationships and mutually collaborate in promoting human values and the good of the nation."

Obviously such a change would force the Argentine church to rethink its economic bases of support. This topic is generally taboo. The issue involves four categories of government-to-church payments. In order to explain my ideas clearly, I will have to treat them one by one.

The first is the direct support of Catholic worship, which is included in function 1.60 of the budget for the administration of the nation. Contrary to common opinion, this payment is small. In the national budget for 1985 it amounted to 2.312 million *australes* out of a total of 8.612 billion *australes*—that is, less than 0.27 percent [the Argentine unit of currency was changed from the *peso* to the *austral* in 1985]. That included the office expenses of the ministry of foreign affairs and worship, support for dioceses and diocesan seminaries, as well as a few other categories such as those involved in constructing and repairing buildings. I do not know whether postal and transportation expenses are also included in those figures. With rare exceptions, parishes and religious congregations, which bear the burden of pastoral work, do not receive payments from the state. Law 22,262 of 1980, approved by the military government, grants a subsidy to parishes in border areas. There are about 140 of these and in 1986 they received 120 *australes* a month. In addition, some chaplaincies in old churches in Buenos Aires receive such payments.

This situation is not new. In his work quoted above, Legón pointed out:

In its 1919 budget the State limits itself to paying chancery offices and seminary staffs, plus some scholarships, but the vast network of parishes, where most worship takes place, do not receive any aid.[14]

Thus, it is clear that it is the bishops who are yoked to the state. This situation is a product of the historical development I have sketched out, but it is a reality. It explains why the bishops are terrified that they might have to face a situation in which they would not have at their disposal the resources to which they have become accustomed for their own personal expenses, office expenses, and maintaining the seminaries that provide continuity to their mission. This fear of losing a source of income—a needless fear, for there are other solutions, as I will explain—turns them into courtiers during dictatorial regimes and coup supporters during democratic regimes.

What I propose is that the church give up every bit of support for worship and that the secretariat of state for worship, in the foreign ministry, be abolished.

The second contribution of the state to the church's activity, and by far the most important, is what is given to private Catholic schools. In the Argentine system, based on laws 13,047 (1947), 14,395 (1954) and 14,473 (1958), the state pays the salaries of administrators, teachers, and other employees in the schools. It is regulated by decree no. 15 of January 2, 1964, which stipulates percentages: from 40 to 80 percent of the salaries in schools that charge tuition, and up to 100 percent in schools that are free. Private universities do not receive state support nor do schools with high tuition. In 1978 free private schools amounted to 62.9 percent of the total. Only 6.1 percent of schools charging tuition did not receive state support.[15]

Strictly speaking, this is not support of worship or maintenance of the church. These payments go to confessional schools of different faiths and nonconfessional ones alike. The issue is not religion, but educational policy. Doctor Héctor Félix Bravo has devoted copious study to the economic side of the question.[16] I am not aware of any research that would enable one to determine the percentage that goes to Catholic schools, which account for 80 percent of the total, and number about two thousand when all levels of schooling are included.

In this area I do not think the state should make any change. That is also what most Argentinians feel. I think that both religious and lay persons are doing very good and progressive educational work and that it should be encouraged and improved. During the 1976–1983 military dictatorship, private Catholic schools were under suspicion and suffered the harassment of state terrorism, as I will explain in detail later on. The Catholic Church has an instrument that has been effective in improving its school system, the Higher Council of Catholic Education (CONSUDEC), which publishes an excellent bulletin every two weeks. This work has gone forward, despite the objectionable guidance given by the bishops, over which Archbishop Antonio José Plaza maintained a monopoly for years.

The third issue is that of chaplaincies. I think we must make a distinction between military, police, and prison chaplains, and those who work in charitable and other agencies. Military, police, and prison chaplains should simply be discharged. They can return to their orders and congregations or join the diocesan clergy, where they are needed. The state would be freed of an economic burden, and the church will benefit from their work. This does not mean that soldiers, police, and prisoners would be left without spiritual care. On the contrary, parish priests and religious would be able to take care of them without being held to a double loyalty. When such care must be full-time, as in the case of remote bases or on ships, it would be proper to budget some payments for their support. The situation of hospital chaplains and chaplains in similar situations is different and should be analyzed in accordance with the needs of those cared for.

In mid-1986, when the situation in the National University at Salta returned to normal [the military government had intervened directly in the universities], there was a conflict with the diocese when the chaplaincy, filled during the dictatorship, became vacant. It is clear that there was no rational need for this post, which was in fact a sinecure. The church should be concerned about pastoral work in the university, but government-paid chaplains are not the answer. On the contrary, what is needed are committed priests and lay Christians, involved in the tasks of education and worship, who act freely and on their own. Naturally, they should have the same access to the university as do members of other organizations.

Finally the state at the national, provincial and municipal levels provides subsidies to different church or church-related bodies or centers that carry out useful social or cultural activities. There is no way of calculating the money involved, which changes every year. There are innumerable opportunities for church-state cooperation in this area, and they should continue. The church is facing problems that will become more aggravated with time, and it cannot solve all these problems by its own means, which are necessarily limited, and designed for pastoral work. That is the case in the preservation and restoration of old churches that are of architectural and historical interest. Here it is proper for the state to step in. In the case of charitable activities and those that benefit the public, to deny the church resources would be a mindless and unjust attitude, one unacceptable in a democracy. In this area church-related institutions generally do effective work. In the course of his well-known conversations with Frei Betto, Fidel Castro has said:

> Here [in Cuba] there are religious orders working in hospitals and in homes for the elderly. . . . There is an institution in Havana where they are doing very difficult work with children who have birth defects. . . . I really have a great deal of admiration for the work the sisters are doing. . . . We are very happy to help such institutions.[17]

When I was rector of the National University of Luján, I proposed that the pipe organ in the National Basilica—there is no other like it in our country—be restored, preserved, and used for cultural as well as religious purposes. Like many other similar projects, it was interrupted by the 1976 coup.

What I have been saying leads to another question of a general nature. How can the church's pastoral activity be financed without state resources and without depending on a few persons who live from investments or powerful business interests? In other words, how can we change the present method without getting into something worse, as sometimes happens?

Leonardo Boff has clearly summed up this matter and the new path it opens up:

> Latin America was missionized from within a definite model of the church—namely, that of *patronato*. According to this model, the church is present in the world by virtue of a pact or treaty with the state that provides for all the needs of the church and guarantees its existence. There is, therefore, a relationship between two hierarchies, one civil and one religious. Church, in this sense, is synonymous with hierarchy. With the end of colonial rule and the birth of independent republics, the church adjusted this model, adopting a new variant. The church then allied itself with the dominant classes that controlled the state, organizing its work around those classes.[18]

For Boff, a new model is provided by the Christian base community:

> [The Christian base community] is more than an instrument by which the church reaches and evangelizes the people; it is a new and original way of living the Christian faith, of organizing the community around the Word of God, around the sacraments (when possible), and around new ministries exercised by lay persons. There is a new distribution of power within the community; it is much more participatory and avoids centralization and domination. The unity of faith and life, of gospel and liberation, is given concrete form without the artificiality of institutional structures. It gives rise to a rich ecclesial sacramentality (the entire church as sacrament), with great creativity in its celebrations and a deep sense of the sacred—all belonging to the people. A true "ecclesiogenesis" is in progress throughout the world, a church being born from the faith of the poor.[19]

This will be a church that acts, not *for* the poor, but *from* the poor—and ultimately, a poor church.

However, this poor church must find ways to pay for its many activities and projects, and to support its pastoral ministers, albeit modestly. If it is not to be dependent on large contributions—from the state or the wealthy, who may tyrannize and corrupt it—this support must come from the faithful, with efforts made to have such contributions be in accordance with each one's possibilities—thus something like the ancient custom of tithing—and not have the church look like a "business" in which believers pay for a service (baptism, confirmation, eucharistic liturgy, marriage, funeral, catechesis).

The problem is not easy to solve. In our country it is complicated by the fact that most Argentinians believe all priests are paid by the state, due to article 2 of the constitution, which makes the government responsible for supporting Catholic worship, and which, for better or worse, is recited in schools. Given this belief and other factors I will mention below, the contributions of Catholics who have sufficient incomes to support their church is ridiculously low in our country.

Hence, I believe that if the bishops were to publicly and solemnly give up the money the state allocates for worship and for the military, police, and prison chaplaincies, and were to simultaneously ask for support from the faithful in order to live in gospel poverty and independence, the effect would be spectacular. In addition, it would be intelligent to do so, for it would anticipate events. How much better off the Christian faith would have been if Pope Pius IX on his own had given up the papal states and thus paved the way for the unification of Italy! A few years before Garibaldi's entrance into Rome in 1870, the minister of the kingdom of Piedmont, Camilo Cavour, had offered the papacy practically the status of the Vatican State that the papacy finally accepted in 1929.[20]

A church like ours should not really need aid from Catholic communities in other countries, such as those that many dioceses receive from the German foundations, Misereor and Adveniat. On the contrary, our country should aid Christian groups in poorer countries.

In comparative terms, the Argentine church is not rich, although there are dioceses—Buenos Aires and La Plata—and congregations—the Salesians—that have significant capital investments. Dioceses and parishes in the interior do not have enough to enable them to undertake any large project, and they have to be content with just getting along.

Some other requirements will have to be met, in addition to publicly giving up state support, if the problem of financing pastoral work is to be solved. The first is to publish financial reports. The church, especially in Latin countries, has a tradition of secrecy about how money is managed and this has been very harmful. Contributions decline when there is no way of knowing how they are spent, especially today when many lay persons have a legitimate aspiration to participate. Secrecy creates the impression of great wealth, which is often not the case. Every diocese, every parish, every order and congregation, every religious institution ought to regularly publish its balance sheet, so that contributors may know about, supervise, and participate in the use made of funds. The salaries and expenses paid to pastoral ministers, starting with the bishops, would be published in such accounts.

The second measure that should be taken is the establishment of commissions, preferably of lay persons, whose names would be made public, who would act as administrators of ecclesiastical property. This would enable the clergy to devote itself freely to its ministry and would eliminate the risk of its being deceived by unscrupulous manipulators, something that happens rather often. It is legitimate for the church to make investments, in order to ensure a steady income, but such investments should not be of a speculative nature, and they should be publicly known.

In this connection, a *Criterio* editorial hits the nail on the head:

In our judgment, and based on the conviction that the true wealth of the church is in its members, not in its property, there are two principles that should prevail in the economic organization of pastoral work. The first is that in principle every community should finance its own needs, and the second is that there should be a vertical and horizontal sharing in goods, so that what is collected at the base contributes to support hierarchical services, and prosperous communities aid poorer communities.[21]

As a Catholic and Christian I have suffered this problem personally. In 1948, if I recall correctly, my wife and I were expelled from Catholic Action in the parish of Our Lady of Luján, in the city of Luján, because we objected to the business dealings of the pastor, Armando Serafini, and the bishop, Anunciado

Serafini (unrelated). Monsignor Adolfo Servando Tortolo was the bishop's vicar general.

Since that time, I have contributed only to churches that provide accounts of how their money is used, and I do not contribute at the basilica of Luján, even though I often go there.

CHAPTER SIX

Ideological Influences

IDEOLOGY

In addition to the historical elements examined in the previous chapter, there is one more factor that has been at work, influencing the attitude of most of the Argentine bishops, and that is their intellectual training.

One can detect two very closely connected currents in the minds of most of the bishops: integralism and the ideology of national Catholicism. Both ideas are present in pastoral letters, sermons, and public statements. They are still present despite the changes in the church and the advent of new postconciliar models, including the church as sacrament of salvation and the church rooted in the poor. This last model arose in Latin America.[1]

A study of the doctrinal and pastoral evolution of the Argentine Catholic church does not fit within the scope of the present work. That is something yet to be done, but I cannot undertake it at this point, for it would draw me away from my central objective and would occupy disproportionate space. Hence, I will limit myself to briefly laying out a simple framework and indicating its impact on the problem we are dealing with.

Integralism is the basic doctrine, and the ideology of national Catholicism is an offshoot. They do not mean exactly the same thing, although in practice they become mixed together. In fact, besides amounting to a theologico-political position, both constitute a common form of expression and action, an attitude, a mind-set, as one Spanish researcher has put it.[2] It is a mind-set that appears—consciously or unconsciously—in many statements by our bishops and of course in their daily practice, although they superficially try to adapt to the formulas adopted by Vatican II, with which this mind-set is in fact incompatible. As *Criterio* editorializes:

In their document "Church and National Community" [1981] our bishops have recognized that Argentine society is pluralistic. However, we are also aware that not everyone who signs a document is fully aware of its consequences—as the experience of Vatican II attests. It is also clear

93

that a sufficient period of time must pass for the comportment of the church community to adapt to the new perspectives opened up by an updated reading of the "signs of the times". Accepting the fact that Argentina is a pluralistic society means giving up the model of "Catholic Argentina" and the kinds of expression that align Catholicism with a mythical and indefinable "national way of being."[3]

Integralism regards the church as a perfect society in the sense that it has its end in itself, an end not subordinated to any other end, and that it must assure itself of the means to accomplish that end, either directly or by acquiring those means from others, usually the state. The church is seen more as a juridical institution than as a mystery of faith or sacrament of salvation blazoning the good news.

For integralists, the most desirable situation for the church is that found in the "Catholic state." This leads to idealizing some periods of history, especially the European high Middle Ages, when ecclesiastical power permeated the whole social structure and held state power under its influence.

Integralists blame the destruction of this ideal society on philosophical nominalism, the Reformation, Cartesian philosophy, and the French revolution with its slogan of liberty, equality, and fraternity. The French revolution led to liberalism, which gave birth to all the other modern errors: socialism, anarchism, communism, indifferentism.

Integralism prefers everything to come by authority from above, and mistrusts human nature and procedures that use the data of experience to build up truth. Yves Congar has noted that the integralist condemns every shade of modern thought and accentuates an image of ecclesiastical glory, rather than that of an earthly church made up of sinning and erring human beings, a church that is not yet the kingdom of God announced by Jesus, to which we are called through conversion. In the integralist framework, there is no understanding of salvation history, the history of humankind advancing through the contradictions of sin toward the kingdom of God. In the integralist vision, solutions to political and social problems are like mathematical theorems, unchanging principles to which human beings must bow down.

Cardinal Suhard said that integralism does not accept adaptation of the expression or formulation of faith, for it a priori rejects evolution, which is the law of history, a law valid for the church as well. Tactical integralism and moral integralism have in common a contempt for the world, the kingdom of sin and error, which must be opposed by pitting one bloc against the other.

A detailed analysis of sermons, homilies, episcopal documents, newspapers, and Catholic literature in general would enable one to appreciate how heavily the integralist tendency weighs over Argentina, even though Vatican II dealt it a rough blow. The council silently abrogated encyclicals and condemnations such as the *Syllabus* of Pius IX (1864), of which there is little or nothing left. Although the influence of the council can be seen in episcopal statements like "Church and National Community" (1981), the integralist attitude continually rears its head, indicating that it is alive in the minds of many of our bishops. It was clearly present in the arguments and means used during the antidivorce campaign in mid-1986, whose high point was the mass demonstration in the Plaza de Mayo, called for by the archbishop of Buenos Aires and other bishops of the metropolitan region.[4]

A variant of integralism is the ideology of national Catholicism, which is very strong in our midst. Starting with the idea that Christianity ought to embrace social structures, Catholicism here becomes a kind of national religion. Religion and Fatherland—both capitalized—are mixed together, just as used to be the case with Religion and King. If one does not accept Catholicism and its devotions, and especially Marian devotions, one is a reprobate Argentinian. Many incidents in history are used to support this symbiosis of religion and superpatriotism, which reduces Christianity to the level of an ideology.

National Catholicism does not lend itself to the real situation of our country and is a corruption of Christianity. It is a legacy from Spain, where for historical reasons Catholicism was a national ideology for many centuries. Efforts to preserve it constitute a social, political, and religious absurdity. From my adolescence I recall an extreme expression of national Catholicism. In a procession at Luján, where I lived, a visiting priest said over the loudspeaker, "The Argentinian who does not revere the Virgin is a traitor to our country and deserves to be shot in the back."

Such currents of thought are connected with the so-called Catholic nationalism of Charles Maurras (1858–1962), the French writer and politician who created *Action Française* and promoted a promonarchy and antidemocratic movement that regarded Catholicism as one of the pillars of French nationality. Personally, Maurras was an agnostic and his doctrine was condemned by the Holy See in 1926. His ideas have made themselves felt in Argentine nationalism, which merges into national Catholicism.[5]

For the most part our bishops have not disentangled themselves from integralism and they often reduce Catholicism to the level of a national ideology.

This underlying set of ideas conditioned the reaction of the bishops to the military dictatorship. How were they going to stand up to a regime that in their eyes appeared to be one essential element of "the Catholic State," protected the church and was ready to eliminate heretics and enemies of the faith? It was a new alliance of throne and altar. The armed forces—whatever the personal conviction and moral behavior of officers—regarded Catholicism as an element that bound the nation together and an instrument of social control. The armed forces stood in agreement with national Catholicism.

For many bishops the continuation of the military regime was reassuring, for it enabled them to keep up the fiction of living in a nominally Catholic country and allowed them to use the power of the state to exert their influence. Return to a constitutional system suggested a leap into the void. Integralism and national Catholicism are opposed to pluralism and democracy, which the bishops have a hard time getting along with, for they regard both of them as stepping stones on the way to communism. Alfonsín is the "Great Satan," as he is represented on the cover of *Cabildo* magazine, and a democratic regime is linked with promiscuity, pornography, divorce, drug addiction, abortion, and delinquency among the poor.

At a Mass celebrated for FAMUS on August 2, 1986, Father Manuel Beltrán accused government leaders of being "responsible for and accomplices of the unleashing of anticlericalism." "They know about and are quite familiar with the increase of drugs, delinquency, and pornography."[6]

During the dictatorship, when some bishops were pressured to defend the dignity of the human person, they used to answer, "We can't do that because if this government falls, it will be replaced by communism." This fear was partly what held them back. Today some Argentine bishops are convinced that constitutional government is irreversibly heading in that direction.

COMPLICITY

Another factor at work in the attitude of the bishops was their ignorance and mediocrity. The few notable exceptions kept silent.

Those whom Jesus chose to be his apostles were humble men who had not been to school but they were adults who had their own vital experience. After an intensive training that did not separate them from the people, they went forth as witnesses of faith, calling others to conversion, with no concern for temporal authorities, who indeed were hostile to them.

In Argentina things are different with the successors of the apostles. Some years back, Enrique Tierno Galván pointed out that the bishops in Spain were influential in government and politics—but not in religion. Some things are changing in our homeland, but that observation remains valid here, with some outstanding exceptions.

The bishops' perception of things is faulty, a perception tinted with prejudices, ambiguities, and apprehensions. They listen only to those who reconfirm their biased way of seeing events and individuals. Moreover, it seems that their habits do not include reading or listening to eyewitness accounts. I have already pointed out that Cardinals Aramburu and Primatesta refused to meet with human rights organizations and the families of the disappeared. The same was true of other bishops, whose duty it was to have firsthand information on what was happening. The intelligence services of the armed forces were their only source of information.

Archbishop Ildefonso Sansierra of San Juan tells us about the 1977 assembly of the bishops:

At the initiative of the president of the nation [Videla], the bishops' conference met with Generals Viola [army chief of staff], Jáuregui, and Martínez [in charge of the intelligence services], who gave us a full report on the present situation of the country in the context of the defensive and offensive efforts being made to deal with the subversive guerrilla war that has been forced on us from outside and inside our borders. . . .

After the generals' presentation there was an exchange of ideas in a climate that was truly Christian and patriotic.[7]

What else could be expected when the bishops' only source of information was those who designed and carried out state terrorism, and when they fraternized with them and adopted their language?

A minimal level of responsibility would have demanded that the bishops invite human rights organizations to present their viewpoints. By so doing, the bishops would have been in a position to come to a founded judgment.

In Buenos Aires and Córdoba the two archbishops cut a pathetic figure. Except for formal occasions and protocol ceremonies, they are not public figures. They are part of the state/ecclesiastical structure, but have no spiritual, intellectual, or moral impact. Their speeches—read by no one except those of us who force this burden on ourselves—are a jumble of words deliberately obscure and ambiguous, disconnected from reality. They frequently quote the pope—in order to avoid any responsibility for giving their own opinions.

With the bishops the armed forces used a kind of blackmail that was effective due to the bishops' timid dispositions, and it helped paralyze them. The military spoke about the alleged involvement of priests and religious with guerrilla movements or with young persons who were guerrilla members. They showed films and slides, and hinted that if the church was not cooperative they would publish the information and would start a campaign to blame the bishops for not cracking down on subversives.

The military dictatorship found the bishops in a state of mind conducive to such arguments. The Copernican shifts introduced by Vatican II (1962–1965) and the documents approved by the General Conference of the Latin American Bishops at Medellín (1968) provoked a sharp internal crisis within the Argentine church. These events surprised and outstripped the bishops, who were not ready to take charge and provide leadership. The political developments of the 1970s, which were partly due to this upheaval, alarmed them. Their only concern was to get rid of troublemakers and return to the familiar order of things. The military took on part of the responsibility for the task of cleaning the dirty courtyard of the church, with the acquiescence of the bishops.

This sinister complicity explains something that Catholic observers from other countries have a hard time understanding: the amazing passivity of a body of bishops who stand by watching unmoved as bishops, priests, religious, and ordinary Christians are murdered, abducted, tortured, jailed, exiled, and slandered. The bishops' few complaints, only in episodes given major publicity, are formal in nature, and they even hasten to suggest excuses. The bishops had no problem accepting the false explanations given by authorities in the cases of Bishop Angelelli and of the Pallottine priests and seminarians, despite the fact that there was abundant proof that the government was responsible, evidence of which the bishops and the nuncio were quite aware. The murder of the bishop of La Rioja is not mentioned in any episcopal statement.

In some instances, the bishops themselves gave the green light. On May 23,

1976, the marines seized Jesuit Father Orlando Iorio in the Bajo Flores neighborhood of Buenos Aires. They held him in secret ("disappeared") for five months. A week before his arrest, Archbishop Aramburu had withdrawn his ministerial faculties without giving any reason or explanation. Various things Iorio heard in prison indicate that the armed forces interpreted this decision, and possibly also some criticisms from the Jesuit provincial superior, Jorge Bergoglio, as approval of their move against him. The military had undoubtedly alerted both the archbishop and his superior to the dangers he allegedly posed.

The extent and ferocity of this persecution are astonishing, as is detailed in chapter 8, below. The Argentine church has hundreds of genuine martyrs, who suffered and died out of fidelity to gospel principles—accompanied by the indifference or complicity of their bishops. What will history say of these pastors who instead of defending or rescuing their sheep, handed them over to the enemy!

There were bishops who went to see political prisoners, especially priests, within their dioceses: Marengo (Azul), Devoto (Goya), Witte (La Rioja), de Nevares (Neuquén), Kemerer (Posadas), Ponce de León (San Nicolás de los Arroyos), Zaspe (Santa Fe), Hesayne (Viedma), and Novak (Quilmes). But they were a minority. In no instance was there collegial action to confront the problem head on, including the situation of the arrested-and-disappeared.

From a pastoral viewpoint, there is something even more serious: the bishops' refusal to offer protection to the victims of illegal repression and their families, and to provide them with material and spiritual support. Bishop de Nevares formally proposed to the bishop's assembly that a special vicariate similar to the one in Chile be formed, but his initiative was rejected by a majority vote of the bishops.

It is common knowledge that the two cardinals and most of the bishops held a dim view of the human rights organizations and those made up of victims' relatives. I have previously quoted some of their public expressions along these lines. Privately they said that such organizations were "communist." If that were really the case, the bishops themselves would be at fault for not having done what their gospel mission and their responsibility in history demanded they should do. If the church had played a leading role in protecting the persecuted, not only would it have saved thousands of lives and mitigated a great deal of suffering, but its own pastoral work would have made unimaginable advances, and today it would not have to bear the wave of criticism rising from all sectors, and it would have prevented many thousands of Catholics from abandoning their faith.

I recall one of my last conversations with Archbishop Vicente Zaspe of Santa Fe, who was then the first vice-president of the executive committee of the bishops' conference. It took place on the grounds of the María Auxiliadora Retreat House in San Miguel, where the bishops were meeting in assembly. If memory serves me, it was 1977. At one particular moment he stopped, lowered his head thoughtfully, and said, "Look, Mignone, some years down the road, the church is going to be pilloried for this.'' At another time he said, ''This is so overwhelming that there's not enough time in the day to take care of the families of the disappeared who come from all over the country.'' He was clearly aware of the omissions for which the body of bishops, of which he was a member, was responsible, but he was not himself decisive enough to break free of the tangle of self-interest, preconceived ideas, and cowardice in which he was trapped.

The ones who did make the break were Bishop Jaime de Nevares of Neuquén, who was immediately willing to be honorary president of the Permanent Assembly for Human Rights (APDH), Bishop Miguel Hesayne of Viedma, who was also a member of that group and who was responsible for the most vigorous statements about state terrorism, and Bishop Jorge Novak, who was ordained for the diocese of Quilmes on September 19, 1976, and whose diocese, together with several Protestant churches, took part in the Ecumenical Movement for Human Rights (MEDH). It is important to point out that in these three bishops there lives, I believe, the most authentic Christianity of the Argentine church, together with community participation, theological openness, gospel poverty, and deep faith. In them the families of the arrested-and-disappeared, the murdered, and the tortured, found the consolation and support denied them elsewhere.

The hostility of most bishops toward the human rights organizations made it difficult for priests and religious to belong to them. There were three paradigmatic cases, those of Fathers Enzo Giustozzi, Mario Leonfanti, and Antonio Puigjané.

Giustozzi belongs to the Little Work of Divine Providence, a congregation begun by Don Orione. He is also a respected scripture scholar, and former editor of the *Revista Bíblica*. As an APDH member, he had a position in its secretariat, informally representing the Catholic Church. He was living in the diocese of Avellaneda, and Auxiliary Bishop Rubén H. Di Monte, who is now the ordinary, threatened Giustozzi with the withdrawal of his priestly faculties if he did not resign from the APDH. Archbishop Quarracino was involved in this decision. The solution was to transfer Giustozzi to Mar del Plata, where the distance would restrict his APDH activity.

The same sort of thing occurred with Father Mario Leonfanti, a Salesian, who was doing an admirable job of helping families of the ''disappeared'' and those who were in prison, through the MEDH. He had to withdraw because of the pressure put on his superiors by Archbishop Aramburu, who told them that otherwise he would withdraw his priestly faculties. Leonfanti nevertheless continued to work with the relatives of victims more discreetly in an office set up in the parish of Nuestra Señora de Los Remedios in the Mataderos neighborhood of Buenos Aires, where he did great work. He was later moved to Zárate.

The Capuchin priest Antonio Puigjané had to endure even more painful experiences. ''From the moment I got to know their dramatic situation,'' he said to Mona Moncalvillo of *Humor* magazine, ''the mothers of the disappeared have been at the center of my life.'' He was always there in the Plaza de Mayo.

He has been jailed and has been threatened repeatedly. Once when Cardinal Aramburu called him in and said that what he was doing was "contrary to the gospel," he replied, in his patient and unaffected manner, "What a confusing mess, your Excellency, because what you say seems to me contrary to the gospel!" The fiery public letters expressed in harsh language that Father Antonio has sent to the bishops' conference and Cardinal Aramburu are well known. The result was that he was sent off to Córdoba, to the slum disrict of Quilmes Oeste. He now exercises his ministry there among the poor in Bishop Novak's diocese; he is prohibited from celebrating Mass in Buenos Aires, Lomas de Zamora, or Tucumán. And the persecution goes on. From the chancery office in Buenos Aires and the nunciature goes a flood of accusations to the Holy See, and an official of the Sacred Congregation for Religious has written to his Capuchin superiors demanding that they take measures against him.

In view of the prohibition in effect in the city of Buenos Aires, priests active in the APDH reside elsewhere. Father Luis Farinello works in the Quilmes diocese. The Passionist Federico Richards is president of the APDH in Vicente López in the diocese of San Isidro where Bishop Alcides Jorge Casaretto has a permissive attitude. In Córdoba Father Felipe Moyano Funes is very active in the human rights field, but Archbishop Primatesta disapproves and he has had to give up his parish.

"I see that in the church we are not spurred into action by the plight of human beings, we don't risk our all. I think we are going to have to get down on our knees and ask the Argentine people for forgiveness," says Puigjané in a *Humor* interview. In another interview done by the same reporter, Father Farinello says, "You feel guilty for all the young persons who lost their lives. . . . You sometimes feel ashamed of belonging to the church. Why didn't the church measure up? It could have saved so many lives!"

The attitude of the bishops made things difficult for the victims' families, and it will be hard to overcome the resulting pain and resentment. The doors of the cathedral in Buenos Aires are always closed when the Mothers of the Plaza de Mayo meet. More than once, when they managed to enter, there were threats to call the police. It was hard to find a priest willing to celebrate a public Mass for the disappeared.

Father Rafael Carli, a Vicentian, the vicar of the basilica in Luján, once ordered that all the scarves left as offerings by the mothers of the arrested-and-disappeared be removed, because he did not want to be "involved in politics." This attitude provoked a public letter from Father Rubén Capitanio, who now belongs to the diocese of Neuquén because he cannot exercise his ministry in La Plata:

> I would ask Father Carli at least to be consistent in this stance he has taken against a group of Christian women: that he also order that the large number of military emblems, uniforms, and other memorabilia on display there be removed as well, for it is these same armed forces who have

committed and continue to commit the greatest crime ever committed against our people.

Capitanio is one of the priests who has spoken out most clearly. After the final report of the armed forces in 1983, he forbade members of the military juntas, governors, cabinet ministers during the dictatorship, and members of the armed forces and the higher echelons of the police to receive the sacraments within his parish, San Lorenzo, in Neuquén, "until they take the steps the bishops have required for reconciliation—that is, acknowledge that they have sinned, ask forgiveness, submit themselves to justice, and promise not to do it again." In an interview he said:

> I am in the church because of Jesus Christ, not because of de Nevares or Plaza. I love this church and hence I must acknowledge that it is in very grave sin, starting with the pope, and coming down through the nuncio, bishops, priests, nuns, and Christian communities. The church is responsible for millions of lives lost, not for having killed them, but because it did not save them. When the bishops realized they might be accused of omissions, they brought out a book recounting all the efforts they made. But this book that tried to justify them is nothing but a proof of guilt, for it shows that they knew what was happening. . . . I wonder what would have happened if, in April 1977, when their first letter was sent to the military junta, there had been a threat to excommunicate the junta, and that the military vicariate was going to resign, that all the military chaplains would resign, and there would have been a complete break with the government.[8]

THE SHANTYTOWNS

On June 9, 1978, the Team of Shantytown Priests of the archdiocese of Buenos Aires—Fathers Héctor Botán, Jorge Goñi, José Meisegeier, Rodolfo Ricciardelli, Daniel de la Sierra, Miguel Angel Valle, and Jorge Vernazza— appealed to public opinion by releasing a document entitled "Report on the Situation in the Shantytowns."

They courageously denounced the policy followed since 1977 by the imposed (unelected) mayor, Brigadier General Osvaldo Cacciatore, actively aided by the head of the Municipal Housing Commission, Guillermo Del Cioppo, who later became mayor, and his main assistant, police commissioner Osvaldo Lotito. This policy was that of dislodging some forty thousand poor families through all kinds of pressure, unkept promises, and especially the use of violence:

> We have been working in the shantytowns for over ten years. On previous occasions we have spoken about the precarious and pitiful condi-

tions of shelter and survival in which these brothers and sisters of ours live. . . . It is a deplorable situation, which has been getting worse for some time. . . . Today they not only do not receive any help, but there is an official policy that no help should be given them. . . . The only thought is to get rid of them in order to build expressways, or get back the land they occupy, or because they disfigure the city. But there is no concern for their immense human problems, the anguishing situation being created for thousands of families. And in order to make it easier to get rid of them, an untrue and unjust image of the situation is spread around, taking advantage of anecdotal isolated cases. . . . Three times now we have presented this situation to our archbishop, Cardinal Aramburu, and asked him to step in. This time we are appealing to public opinion.

The meaning of this last paragraph is clear. Like most of the population, the archbishop was not moved by this most serious violation of fundamental human rights. The forty thousand families, with their scant belongings, were hauled away in trucks, scattered and abandoned on lands belonging to the province of Buenos Aires, where they regrouped, worse off than before. Some returned to where they had come from, and a small number received a tiny subsidy from the municipal government that the diocesan Caritas office had obtained at the insistence of the shantytown priests' team.

The Team of Shantytown Priests put out a second and very well documented work entitled "The Truth about the Elimination of Shantytowns around the Federal Capital," dated October 31, 1980. It is signed by the same members, except for Father Goñi, who had died and was replaced by Father Pedro Lephalille.

There is little awareness of this crime committed by the military dictatorship, which those priests witnessed. In response to the criticism they had leveled at Archbishop Aramburu, the priests were sent a strong warning by the vicars of the area, who explained that such statements could disturb the negotiations underway with the city government. Among the advantages obtained through these efforts was the subsidy to construct a residence for the archbishop, as already described above. Aramburu's residence was built over the suffering and tears of many thousands of his children who were thrown out into the fields as their rickety houses were being mercilessly destroyed. I suppose that on rainy and cold nights, if God grants him such a vision, Aramburu, sheltered and well-clothed, will think about the brothers and sisters he abandoned, with their malnourished children shivering underneath a sheet of tin or a piece of cardboard.

Cacciatore and Del Cioppo accomplished their end, expelling more than two hundred thousand shantytown inhabitants from the city. With the aid of good-willed Christians, the efforts of the priests' team led to an interesting movement of housing cooperatives, which has built a number of barrios on the outskirts of Buenos Aires through various kinds of self-help projects. I should mention that the archdiocesan Caritas office helped out, with the approval of Cardinal

Aramburu. Some of the shantytown dwellers forced out now live in these modest but comfortable houses, but only a small number.

My wife and I were very close to this problem. We had connections with the makeshift barrio in Bajo Flores and the Santa María Madre del Pueblo parish, where our daughter Mónica was active. We are helping the Madre del Pueblo housing cooperative, which has built three barrios, with Fathers Ricciardelli and Vernazza providing effective guidance. When we were just beginning, there arose the possibility that a congregation of sisters might sell us for a very low price a piece of land close to where the highway that circles the city goes through the area of La Matanza. There was one obstacle, however. The nuns knew that the bishop of San Justo, Carlos Carreras, had had his eye on this lot for a seminary, and they did not want to make him angry. A commission headed by Carlos A. García, an engineer, went to see him. The meeting went well; the bishop had found another piece of property. When commission members told him what they had in mind, Carreras tried to discourage them, saying, ''I understand that cooperatives were invented by communists. Besides, why are you planning to bring poor shantytown people to a piece of land next to a convent of contemplative nuns surrounded by houses of the well-to-do?''

The barrio was built with the people's own sacrifice and today it is something wonderful come true, and its residents are no longer shantytown dwellers. Bishop Carreras retired and later died.

I am left with a question: How is it possible that a man with such criteria and prejudices should head a diocese with a large working-class population and have both voice and vote in episcopal meetings that dealt with the problems that resulted from state terrorism?

CATHOLIC SCHOOLS

The changes brought about by Vatican II and the Medellín conference led to a considerable renewal in Catholic schools, both those in parishes and those run by religious congregations. The military dictatorship was suspicious of them, regarding them as seedbeds of subversion.

In order to clean them out, the military made an arrangement with the Catholic hierarchy. This can be deduced from point 5, Appendix 5 (''Religious Sphere'') of the CJE directive no 504/77 (''Continuation of the Offensive against Subversion during the 1977–78 Period''), which can be found in a number of judicial proceedings. It reads:

Importance should be paid to various kinds of measures related to surveillance and control over religious schools, *a task that the religious authorities have decided to actively take on*. To that end, provision will be made to coordinate efforts, in order to avoid friction or premature unilateral actions [italics added].

The armed forces did not always live up to this agreement and there were incidents that left a great impact. An earlier incident was the November 29, 1976, search operation by a large military contingent at the San Miguel School run by the Missionaries of the Immaculate Conception of Lourdes, which was part of the Santísimo Redentor parish in the capital. The operation was led by the officer in charge of a subdivision of operations of the I Army Corps, Colonel Roberto Roualdés, and led to the arrest of Fathers Andrés Bacqué, Daniel Haldkin, Ignacio Racedo Aragón, and Bernardo Canal Feijóo. The last-named was forced to leave the country. The search, whose only result was the confiscation of a mimeograph machine, stemmed from accusations made by a few parents. A similar episode took place in Sagrado Corazón school in Pringles in the province of Buenos Aires.

Intense pressure on the schools created a climate of real terror. The intelligence services also used the media, and especially magazines published by Atlántida Press, to make accusations about alleged subversive activities in private Catholic schools. Protests from the schools led the permanent commission of the Bishops' Conference of Argentina to put out a communiqué on December 3, 1976, expressing two concerns: (1) repeated "publications in magazines and newspapers and the opinions of groups attacking the teaching given in some Catholic schools," and (2) "withdrawal of teaching credentials from sisters, catechists, or teachers without any reason given."

The fact is that the bishops had not made any protest when law 21,381, dated August 13, 1976, was passed, granting the state power to withdraw the credentials of teachers in private schools, and making it obligatory for them to be fired without severance pay and prohibiting them from teaching anywhere. Article 1 states:

Until December 31, 1976, the Minister of Culture and Education and the Military Delegate in this area are empowered to declare unauthorized to work in institutions of private schooling, including universities, teaching and nonteaching staff members who have been fired by the application of law 21,260 or *who are found to be connected with subversive or disruptive activities, or any of those who openly or secretly advocate or encourage such activities* [italics added].

Clause number 2 states that such a declaration of unauthorization is a legitimate reason for firing staff members and deprives them of severance pay. If such institutions do not fire such persons, they lose recognition by the state and any benefit derived therefrom.

This ruling was extended by means of laws 21,490 (December 30, 1976) and 21,744 (February 8, 1978), which kept it in effect until the end of 1978. However, the ruling was applied even after its expiration. In bulletin number 146 of the National Superintendence Office for Private Schooling (November 1979) there is information on eleven rulings of the ministry taking effect during 1979 and applied to eleven teachers.

Inasmuch as the law was applied to teachers of secular subjects *and* to teachers of religion, the bishops tacitly accepted the military government's right to supervise the teaching of Catholic doctrine. As I have written elsewhere:

> To my knowledge, this is the first time in the modern age that the church has handed over to the state the power to judge the orthodoxy of its members. (Recall that during the Inquisition it was the clergy who made this judgment. The "secular arm" only stepped in to punish those who were found guilty.)[9]

One of these cases was that of Sister Lidia Argentina Cazzulino, a teacher at the Institute of the Child Jesus, in Paso de los Libres, Corrientes. The delegate of the military junta in the Ministry of Culture and Education had her declared unfit to teach by a resolution on September 23, 1976, exercising the power given by law number 21,381, and he forced the school to let her go. The accused took legal action. The magistrates who took part (judge and federal court) declared the measure null, a sentence that became permanent in April 1981. In these procedures the ministry held that there were "security reasons" that needed no proof. But the court concluded that the measure was due to an accusation of "postconciliar" orientation in the sister's catechesis. The military delegate, Colonel Agustín Valladares, concurred with this judgment. He was thus playing the role proper to Archbishop Jorge Manuel López.

The very general way the first article of law number 21,381 was worded made it easy to declare teachers unfit. Any progressive or democratic expression could be interpreted as a covert way of fomenting subversion. Any interpretation of the teaching of the church outside the pattern of integralism or national Catholicism could be understood in this way.

Because it falls outside the scope of this work, I am not going to go further into what the military dictatorship did in the realm of education. However, I do not want to leave unmentioned two documents that bring out the truth of what has been said here.

The first is resolution number 44, dated October 11, 1977, handed down by the secretary of state for education. It has an appendix entitled "Directive on Subversive Infiltration in Teaching," which is a manual for school principals on spying, informants, and ideological control. Among other examples of how teaching can lead to subversion, it mentions "the tendency to modify the scale of traditional values," "the misinterpretation of the concept of private property," "a distorted interpretation of historical events, giving them a class-based meaning or one that sees them as representing popular interests against the excesses of capitalism," and "biased utilization of the social doctrine of the church to foment class struggle" (II-3-a,c,d, and e). Once again, it is for the military in the Ministry of Culture and Education to decide on the correctness of Catholic social doctrine.

In 1977, the Ministry of Culture and Education, under the aegis of Juan José

Catalán, distributed a 74-page booklet entitled "Subversion in the Realm of Education—Let Us Get to Know Our Enemy!" Like all material produced by the intelligence services, it is anonymous, although the introduction states that "the authorship and origins of this work guarantee the information it contains." The basic idea of the document, like everything else that came from this source, is simplistic and unhistorical. Subversion is defined as:

> The work of a commando force that, in the light of a clear ideology, has worked out all the details of its strategy and has at its disposal all the necessary means; it then carries out what is technically known as "international Marxist aggression."

CONFUSION OF ROLES

In such a context, roles are easily reversed. Bishops and priests like Bonamín and Zaffaroni become ardent warriors. Generals and admirals take on the task of interpreting the scriptures and lecture on theology, as bishops stand by in full acquiescence.

In Corrientes, on June 12, 1976, General Cristino Nicolaides said that an individual committed to a subversive organization is "irrecoverable," thus negating the basic Christian tenet that every human being is redeemable.[10] Archbishop López did not correct him.

On June 12, 1976, Lieutenant Colonel Hugo I. Pascarelli, in a ceremony to commemorate the sesquicentennial anniversary of Artillery Group I in Ciudadela, and in the presence of General Videla and the chaplains for that unit, advanced even further in theological innovation. He held that the struggle in which he was participating "knows no moral or natural limits; it takes place beyond good and evil, it goes beyond the human level, although it is human beings that bring it about. Not seeing or not wanting to see is not simply blindness, but the greatest offense against God and Fatherland."[11] This demigod of torture and murder sets aside the Ten Commandments. Offending God means not acknowledging the colonel's right to act outside the bounds of morality.

Meanwhile General Juan Sasiaín, head of the federal police, and Colonel Alejandro Arias Duval, superintendent of federal cooperation, held that Christianity is the only thing that can save the world. This idea guides their acts as military men and superiors in the areas under their command.[12] One could not detect this principle in the way they acted in those positions and others they held.

On April 29, 1976, Jorge Eduardo Gorleri, later made a general, ordered a huge book-burning in Córdoba, with these words:

> The command of the III Army Corps informs the public that on this date it is proceeding to burn pernicious material that affects the mind and *our Christian way of life*. In order that nothing of these books, pamphlets, and magazines be left, this resolution is being taken so that this material

will no longer deceive our young about the true goodness represented in our national symbols, our family, *our Church, and our most venerable traditional legacy, which is summarized in God, Fatherland, Home* [italics added].

General Gorleri, by then commander of the II Army Corps based in Rosario, was forced into retirement on September 1, 1986, after a meeting of the army high command, led by the minister of defense, José Horacio Jaunarena. In that meeting Gorleri opposed obliging those under him to appear in civil court to answer for crimes committed during the military dictatorship. This amounts to rebellion against the constitution. It is worth noting that human rights organizations had opposed his promotion to general, as proposed by President Alfonsín and granted by the Senate.

A fortnight previously, on August 15, 1986, General Gorleri presided over a ceremony in the Manuel Belgrano Catholic school run by the Marist Brothers in the capital. He gave a speech. It is significant that three years into a democratic government a book-burner and commander of an army unit is invited to preside over a ceremony and lecture in a Catholic educational institution. Rear Admiral José María Arriola, the commander of the naval base in Puerto Belgrano, was with him.

Ideological contamination also worried General Albano Harguindeguy during his brief period at the Ministry of Culture and Education. He marked his term by proscribing Paulo Freire's books *(Pedagogía del oprimido—La educación como práctica de la libertad; Acción cultural para la libertad; Concientización—Teoría y práctica de la libertad,* and *Las iglesias y la educación y el proceso de liberación humana en la historia.)* He said that Freire's idea of pedagogy "runs against the basic values of our Western Christian society."[13]

This theological progress reached its highest level of refinement in the marines. The gospel according to Massera was presented to Father Orlando Iorio during the time when he had "disappeared," with his hands tied, and a hood over his head in the Navy Technical School in mid-1976. "You aren't a guerrilla," his interrogating officer told him, "you're not involved in violence, but you don't realize that when you to go live there [a shantytown] you are bringing people together, you are uniting the poor, and uniting the poor is subversion." Later on another jailer explained to him:

You are mistaken and your error is interpreting Christ's teaching too materially. Christ talks about the poor, but that means the poor in spirit, whereas you have gone to live with the poor. In Argentina the poor in spirit are the rich, and from now on you must give more help to the rich who are the ones who are deserving, spiritually.[14]

The integralism and national Catholicism of some bishops continues to be well represented in the armed forces. On July 5, 1986, in Córdoba, during the monthly Mass for FAMUS and in the presence of the commander of the III

Army Corps, Leopoldo Héctor Flores, the Dominican priest, Daniel María Rossi exhumed the paleolithic teachings of Félix Salva and Julio Meinvielle, which Vatican II had buried. He rejected "the pseudo heroes who embody the French revolution in our country, for they are tearing apart the Spanish-American tradition." He went on to say that "the French triad of liberty, equality, and fraternity is utterly subversive." [15]

This worthy confrere of Torquemada agrees with another "distinguished thinker" in the army, General Justo Jacobo Rojas Alcorta. When he was a lieutenant colonel in charge of an infantry regiment in the province of Buenos Aires, he used to give illustrative and threatening talks to teachers in the areas under his jurisdiction. Standing beside a huge wooden crucifix, he used to explain that "the Jews passed on their secret practices and their symbols to the Masons, who try to destroy the Christian religious conception of things. In this respect, they do the same thing as communism." After attacking the French revolution and the ideas of Third World groups, he defended the "good violence" of the military, and said that religious freedom was only good for "hiding atheists." He ended by calling liberal democracy "false, because it supports popular sovereignty when, according to Christian doctrine, it is God who confers power." [16] He also held that the revolution of May 25, 1810 [independence from Spain], was a military coup, an idea that Gustavo Martínez Zuviría expressed some years ago in his book *El Año X*.

This madman has been promoted by the constitutional government, over the opposition of human rights organizations, who recall his terrorist role in the western part of Buenos Aires province. In July 1986, the Radical Party deputy from Tucumán, Juan Robles, accused Rojas Alcorta, who was then in charge of the fifth infantry brigade of Tucumán, of inciting political and labor groups for a coup that would take place in September, the classic month for such events. The source of the talkative general's outrageous ideas is no doubt his ideology, for he is fearful of the pluralism and freedom of our incipient democracy, just like some bishops.

Another officer promoted by the democratic government is Colonel Mohamed Ali Seineldin, who is also wont to indulge in theologico-fascist elucubrations, when, as military attaché in Panama, he engages in conspiracy against the government that inexplicably has promoted him. His tendency to mix the military and the religious led him to propose that the invasion of the Malvinas/Falkland Islands be called "Operation Rosary."

Isidoro J. Ruiz Moreno is a professor at the Superior War College and the author of a book on what our army commanders did during the Falklands conflict. He says of Seineldin:

> This soldier, who has a very exalted patriotic and religious mystique, knew how to impress on all the members of his subdivision of commandos (Special Team Falcon 8) an awareness that it was their absolute duty to carry out orders, that they should sacrifice themselves to the limit, and that they would find their reward in absolute obedience to the orders they

received. Despite his parents' religion, from the age of nine Mohamed was educated in the Catholic faith, and he became an open and militant supporter of it. ''God and Fatherland or Death!,'' the slogan of the Argentine commanders, became something real and not just something for speeches.[17]

Those attending the July 5, 1986, ceremony organized by Cardinal Aramburu in defense of the family were given a flyer with a profile of Colonel Seineldin and this procoup statement:

Brothers, there is hope. Here is a man, a soldier, who, when God so determines, will take up the best spiritual and moral weapons to defend the flag. He is the one who spared no efforts to defeat Marxist guerrila forces; he is the one who said, ''let the exploits of April 2 be named after the rosary to honor the Most Holy Virgin.''

The author of the book mentioned above is not embarrassed to explain that it was Seineldin who brought instructions on how to torture prisoners into military commands. As mentioned before, torture has been unconditionally condemned by both the papal and episcopal teaching of the Catholic Church, to which Seineldin says he belongs. Ruiz Moreno comments on the training of army commanders:

They even undergo what prisoners experience, because their camps do not meet the norms set down by the Geneva conventions, but have been adopted from the experience of Vietnam. The candidate is picked up by surprise, hooded, and beaten, in accordance with an established method. Instructors are not sparing in their use of the kinds of rubber hoses also used by the police, although a doctor and a psychiatrist are always on hand. Naked and put into a narrow hole in which they have to remain standing, or rather buried, the unfortunate individuals have a tin roof over them; it is roasting by day and freezing by night. They get only one meal a day, a hot corn mush that they must eat with their hands. There they must stay for three days, losing all sense of time. They are brought out only for questioning. In order to get the information they have, candidates are hit when necessary, and also when not necessary. Buried there, they are forced to listen to Central American folk music and subversive and Marxist slogans, played over a loudspeaker unendingly. They have time to think and pray, which is all they can do, and to decide whether to persevere to the end, even when the loudspeakers are broadcasting the screams of their comrades as they undergo interrogation.[18]

If this is what happens with comrades who are quite sure they will get through this ordeal alive and will receive medical attention, one can only imagine what happened to prisoners from whom information was wanted, such as the arrested-and-disappeared during the dictatorship. The commanders intended to use these methods of interrogation during the Falklands conflict, thus compromising commitments to which their country had solemnly agreed.

Among those commandos was Lieutenant Colonel Aldo Rico, a leader of the rebellion against the constitutional government in Holy Week 1987 in Campo de Mayo, near Buenos Aires. Rico is as fundamentalistic as Seineldin.

In July 1986 the federal judge in Neuquén, Rodolfo Rivarola, issued indictments against Second Lieutenant Dino Codermatz for using electrical charges with field telephones to torture conscripts. This means that torture is still being used with the approval of military authorities. The commander of the V Army Corps, General Enrique Bonifacino, defended this procedure and the military court released torturers.

From any point of view, this is very serious. It is urgent that the president of the country, as commander-in-chief of the armed forces, act without delay and that the Congress become involved in this matter. It is unacceptable that Argentine senior and junior officers should be trained to administer torture, or that they or ordinary soldiers be subjected to degrading practices. It is one thing to give physical and psychological training, as intense as it might be, and training for survival in hostile environments, but it is quite something else to cause suffering to and unleash brutality against the defenseless. Training should produce honorable officers, not beasts. That our armed forces still hold this doctrine was proven by presentations by the three heads of the high command before the defense committee of the Senate.

What Ruiz Moreno says, and what he regards as legitimate, has prompted the reaction it deserves, except for an article written by Horacio Verbitsky. And in the literary section of *La Nación,* Martín Alberto Noel praised the book without mentioning the facts I have mentioned and without showing any alarm. Bishop José Miguel Medina of the military vicariate has said nothing despite the fact that those responsible are under his jurisdiction.

This issue raises a final thought, related to the overall theme of this book. It seems that it is the officers who espouse Catholic integralism, championed by chaplains and bishops, who have been the most active in their enthusiasm for murder and their opposition to democratic principles. Ultimately, this is a result of the attitude and teaching of most of our pastors.

CHRISTIAN VON WERNICH

Since 1984, Christian von Wernich, a priest of the Nueve de Julio diocese in the province of Buenos Aires, has become notorious due to accusations that he was an accomplice in state terrorism. His name is mentioned in the CONADEP report and he is involved in two legal cases being pursued by CELS lawyers, as I will describe below. Both cases are pending in the supreme council of the armed forces.

Above and beyond these cases, however, it is von Wernich's personality, statements, and behavior that have made him notorious and turned him into something of a paradigm of a fascist priest, one who is identified with the armed forces and who cooperated with repression.

Several testimonies implicating von Wernich are listed and transcribed in part in the CONADEP report *Nunca más*. These testimonies are found in the following files: 683, testimony of Julio Alberto Emmed; 2218, accusation of the disappearance of Cecilia Luján Idiart; 2820, accusation of the disappearance of Domingo Héctor Moncalvillo; 2821, accusation of the disappearance of María del Carmen Morettini; 2852, accusation of the disappearance of María Magdalena Mainer and Pablo Joaquín Mainer; 6982, testimony of Luis Larralde; 6949, testimony of Luis Velasco.[19]

I will here reproduce only a part of the Larralde and Velasco testimonies, because the others are connected with the judicial cases I will treat below. On August 3, 1984, in the Argentine embassy in Madrid, Luis Larralde and Luis Velasco gave testimony in the presence of the congressional deputy, Hugo Diógenes Piucill, a member of CONADEP, Graciela Fernández Meijide, secretary of the commission, and embassy staff members, Carlos Rospide and Gustavo Asis. Among other things, Larralde said, "I was arrested, along with my wife María Josefina Roncero, at my house (*calle* Billinghurst 2143, 5-H, Buenos Aires), July 5, 1977, at 11:15 P.M. They took us to a clandestine center where we were tortured. I was listening when they tortured the former minister of the economy of the province of Buenos Aires, Señor Miralles. Father Christian von Wernich came to the investigation brigade every day, and spoke with those who were imprisoned there."

Velasco's testimony is given in the third-person singular:

On July 6, 1977, at midnight a large group of heavily armed men not in uniform forced open the door of the apartment where he lived with his mother in La Plata. They said they belonged to the Argentine army. They put him in a car, threw him on the floor, and blindfolded him. On July 8 they took him to "the little house." On that occasion and after the first session, a priest came up to him. Later on, he learned that it was Christian von Wernick. He saw him several times, and on one of these occasions the priest told him to take off the blindfold. When he refused to do so, he [von Wernich] took it off himself. This priest said his parish was in Nueve de Julio, Buenos Aires province. On one occasion he heard Christian von Wernich tell a prisoner who was begging not to be killed: "the life of human beings depends on God and your cooperation," and he spoke to the man, touching the hair on his chest and grinning as he remarked, "They burned off all your hair." On another occasion, he heard him defend and justify torture and acknowledge that he had been present during torture sessions. When Father von Wernich talked with prisoners about such matters, he used the plural, such as "When we carried out such-and-such an operation."

In a court case in criminal and correctional court number 3 in the city of La Plata, under Doctor Vicente Luis Bretal, office number 8, Domingo Moncalvillo, the father of one of the victims, accompanied by CELS lawyers, made accusations against the former chief of police of the province of Buenos Aires, Juan Ramón Camps, commissioner Miguel Osvaldo Etchecolatz, and Father Christian Federico von Wernich, who was regarded as an official with the rank of subinspector. They were accused of illegal constraint and unjust privation of freedom.

Von Wernich was given this rank by Camps in 1976, so that he could act as chaplain. (Later he would say to a reporter, "I was ordained in 1976 and because I am from Concordia, General Camps has known me since I was little, for he is from Paraná. Thus, with Archbishop Plaza's consent, I got to the point where I was entrusted with many matters during the antisubversive struggle.")

The court case stemmed from the arrests of Domingo Héctor Moncalvillo, Guillermo García Cano, Liliana Amalia Galarza, Cecilia Luján Idiart, María Magdalena Mainer, Pablo Joaquín Mainer, María del Carmen Morettini, and Susana Salomone.

These young persons were illegally imprisoned during most of 1977 in the general headquarters of the investigative police in the province of Buenos Aires, in La Plata. They were permitted to have contact with their families, and finally they were given the choice of jail for five years or leaving the country. Naturally, they preferred the latter.

During this period, chaplain von Wernich visited them frequently. Their families sought him out as an intermediary, and gave him money, so that he could start a fund to support them outside the country. On November 30, 1977, when the parents of these prisoners went there as was their custom, they were told that they had left that very day. Since then they have never heard anything more about them.

In his statement to the federal criminal and correctional appeals court in the capital, and in the trial of the former high commanders, von Wernich has explained that he took part in a departure ceremony and that at their request he went with them, in three groups, to the commuter airport and the port of Buenos Aires, from which they journeyed to Montevideo.[20] Despite this statement there is no doubt that they were murdered, like thousands of others of the arrested-and-disappeared, for there has never been any sign of life from them and it is inconceivable that they would be alive outside the country without contacting their families. Investigations carried out in Uruguay have not produced any results, although records indicate that Moncalvillo entered that country. The police officials insist on their position, suggesting that the former prisoners might be underground. Von Wernich was never able to provide a coherent explanation, nor has he shown any further interest in the matter.

Julio Alberto Emmed, a former police agent in the province of Buenos Aires, who worked as a driver and took part in various operations, gave CONADEP a very detailed account. He says the members of the group were driven in different vehicles. They were told they were being taken out of the country but they were brutally murdered on the way. According to Emmed, Father von

Wernich was present during all this, just as Emmed himself was. On the way back, commissioner Etchecolatz congratulated those who had taken part and, says Emmed, "Father von Wernich talked to me in particular because of the impact these events had had on me. The priest told me that what we were doing was necessary for the good of our country, that it was a patriotic act, and that God knew that what was being done was for the good of the country."[21] With regard to documents showing entrance into Uruguay, Emmed explains that they prepared documents with the prisoners' names on them but the photos were of police staff members. It must have been they who traveled to Uruguay.

It is true that Emmed, no doubt under threat, later denied these details in his statement to the federal court in the trial of the former commanders, and he said he would straighten out the statement he had made to the federal criminal court number 4 in the capital, presided over by Doctor Amelia Berraz de Vidal.[22] However, all indications are that he was telling the truth the first time, for it is reasonable to conclude that persons who disappear without a trace were murdered; this was not the first time.

In his long statement to the federal court, von Wernich acknowledges that he had something to do with this group of arrested-and-disappeared and confirms that he went to them to say good-bye, but denies knowing what happened to them. He also says that in a police station in Don Bosco he spoke with Jacobo Timerman and with the former minister Oscar Maralles, whom he found very depressed. He said he was not aware that they had been tortured.[23]

Another case involving von Wernich is that in which Arturo Andrés Lorusso has filed charges of unjust deprivation of freedom. It was initiated in the criminal and correctional tribunal number 4 of the capital, presided over by Doctor Amelia Berraz de Vidal, secretariat number 12, until this judge declared herself incompetent, and the case went to the supreme council of the armed forces. In this case, I am a plaintiff along with the fathers of other victims, with the support of CELS lawyers.

The origin of this case was the early morning arrest of Beatriz Carbonnel de Pérez Weiss, César Amadeo Lugones, María Esther Lorusso Lammle, Horacio Pérez Weiss, Mónica María Candelaria Mignone (my daughter), Mónica Quinteiro, and María Marta Vásquez Ocampo de Lugones, on May 14, 1976, by agents of the armed forces. None of them ever turned up again. Because of various pieces of evidence, which it would take a long time to explain, there is no doubt that they were taken to the Navy Technical School, where they were tortured and murdered. These young persons knew one another in the selfless project of human, social, political, and religious development that they were carrying out in the Bajo Flores shantytown and in isolated areas of Patagonia. That was also why they were done away with.

A brother of César Lugones, Eugenio, was a close friend of Father von Wernich. When Eugenio heard about the arrest, he went right to his friend looking for help. Eugenio was aware of von Wernich's ideology, how he stood with the armed forces, the fact that he was chaplain to the police in the province of Buenos Aires, and that he was friendly with Camps. He knew that he was a brother-in-law of Colonel Morelli, who was the head of the department of security in the federal police. Thus, he expected von Wernich to shed some light on the matter.

Von Wernich set out to check and a few days later he let Eugenio Lugones know that his brother César was alive. Eugenio told us the news right away. At that point, I wrote to Bishop Alejo Gilligan of Nueve de Julio, whom I knew from Mercedes, and I asked him to ask von Wernich, who was then pastor of the cathedral in that city, what he knew about my daughter Mónica. On August 4, 1976, Bishop Gilligan wrote back saying "the only information Father Christian has is that César Lugones is fine; he does not know anything about the others, where they are or who was responsible."

In 1984, when I began my suit in Judge Berraz Vidal's court, I brought in the letter and proposed that Bishop Gilligan and Father von Wernich be called as witnesses, the former to acknowledge his signature and the contents of the letter, and the latter to tell who had given him the information. Thus we would be able to move toward identifying who had committed the crime. The news came out in the papers, and caused a stir in Nueve de Julio. At this point, Mona Moncalvillo, the well-known journalist on the staff of *Humor* magazine and sister of Domingo, made statements about the case of the La Plata group. The bishop, who no doubt had forgotten about the correspondence, was very annoyed and wanted to make a statement denying it. Via the pastor in Trenque Lauquen, Guillermo Noé, I sent him a photocopy to remind him, so he would not make a big blunder. He then asked to make use of the right to be questioned in writing and in private. (This is a privilege that article 290 of the code of procedures in penal matters for the federal court gives to persons in the three branches of government, the members of military courts, clerical dignitaries, diplomatic ministers, consuls general, and all the military with the rank of colonel and above. This is one of the many inequities that violate article 16 of the constitution, and they are still in force in our laws and customs. It should be abolished.)

Gilligan acknowledged the letter and von Wernich was called by the judge. How did he get out of it? By lying. He said that the news that César Lugones was fine had come from Eugenio Lugones himself, who of course became unimaginably indignant. He asked for a face-to-face confrontation, which the judge granted. It was a very tense scene. Extremely nervous, von Wernich held his ground. To counter his statement we had only the word of Eugenio, and thus we were left without proof.

In legal terms, the way von Wernich escaped was brilliant. But it was at the cost of telling a lie, after a solemn oath before God and in front of a crucifix to tell the truth. I recall the words of the Lord in the biblical theophany where Moses receives the tablets with the Ten Commandments: "You shall not bear false witness against your neighbor" (Exodus 20:16), and I was saddened that a minister of God should have ignored those words.

The allegations against von Wernich drew the attention of the press. *Siete*

Días magazine sent Alberto Perrone, a reporter, and Mario Paganetti, a photographer, to the city of Norberto de la Riestra in the diocese of Nueve de Julio, to which von Wernich had been transferred as pastor. Swept away by vanity and his yen for publicity, von Wernich said a great deal, and when it was published in the July 30, 1984, issue, it created a sensation. The issue sold out and the story had to be reprinted in the next edition (August 1).

The interview with von Wernich, entitled "Priest Who Interrogated Disappeared Speaks," is well worth reading. There he lays bare his personality and his ideas. He says, "I never had any doubt about what I did." He is expansive about his relationship with the group of young persons who were imprisoned in the general headquarters for investigation in La Plata. "It was my responsibility," he explains, "to speak with them, in order to get information on how their Montonero organization was put together." With regard to the testimony given on the television presentation of *Nunca Más,* he says:

> I would like to find out whether those things are true. I doubt it. I suspect that all of it is false. On the contrary, it seems to me that the public was given the circus the present government needs to distract attention from the lack of bread. That's the way the left works in this country. . . . I was never in any police or military agency where any prisoner told me about being tortured. And, after all, I was in direct contact with Jacobo Timerman, with Minister Miralles, Papaleo, and many others. . . . Camps treated [Timerman] like a king. . . . If they told me that Camps tortured some poor devil that no one knows, well okay! But how could anyone imagine they would torture a journalist who was always at the center of worldwide attention!

The reporters describe the scene:

> We go into the large living room with a number of leather armchairs and with handmade brocades hanging on the walls. Christian von Wernich emphasizes that he had had this ranch-style house put up just a couple years before, where previously there had been a broken-down hovel. We then follow him into the room devoted to his ham radio activities. Certificates adorn the walls of this carpeted room. On a small bookshelf, alongside several religious books, are books by General Ramón Camps. Each one of them has a lengthy hand-written dedication, reminding his "priest and friend" that they have both given their all. Susana, the priest's sister and the wife of Morelli, one of Camps's military colleagues, is also there.

The account ends quoting von Wernich:

> I know very well what I did, why I did it, and who I did it with. At the proper moment justice will prevail. I have gone through a war, from an

ideological viewpoint, and that viewpoint is one of a centrist conservative. . . . As I said before, I am waiting for justice, especially divine justice.

"Christian von Wernich's statements have created a stir in the town," reported *Siete Días* in a second story, and there were numerous photos to prove it. At that point the priest realized that he had better not speak any more and he refused any further interviews. Bishop Gilligan defended him publicly, and also suggested that he keep quiet. Because of what he said, CELS started criminal proceedings, charging him with defending crimes. In federal court in Azul, von Wernich accused me of having made the threatening phone calls he received in Norberto de la Riestra, basing the accusation on a similar expression I had written in my letter to the pastor in Trenque Lauquen, Guillermo Noé. Of course, the judge ruled out such an absurd allegation. Court proceedings against von Wernich were then frozen. Meanwhile the government of the province of Buenos Aires has suspended him from his police post.

On Friday, April 25, 1986, the human rights commission of Nueve de Julio invited me to explain the case. Four hundred persons packed the auditorium in the municipal building, and there followed an interesting and enlightening dialogue. I wanted to invite the bishop but I could not contact him. Later I learned that he had approached the mayor, asking him to withdraw permission to use the auditorium. Such an attitude goes right along with the episcopal ideology I have described: seeking the protection of the state, and fearing the freedom of debate and pluralism.

Another instance of von Wernich's questionable activities is what he did in New York in late 1978. He has said that he moved there with a temporary contract with the archdiocese to provide pastoral care for the Spanish-speaking community, and for that purpose he moved into the parish of St. John Chrysostom in the Bronx. However, in the Lorusso case, María Eva Ruppert, who then lived in New York, gave testimony. She turned over a letter from von Wernich, dated September 27, 1978, in which he expressed interest in making contact with Argentine exiles connected with *Denuncia* magazine, which was engaged in a vigorous campaign against the Argentine military dictatorship.

According to Miss Ruppert's very detailed report, von Wernich met with her repeatedly and offered to work on tasks related to defending human rights in Argentina. He said he wanted to "type up a card file with data on 'contacts' in the organization with which she worked both in Argentina and in other countries."[24] He said he could get a short wave radio transmitter and a photocopy machine for this purpose. Because his attitude seemed suspicious, the Argentinians decided not to accept his offer.

In the Lorusso case, von Wernich was brought face to face with Miss Ruppert, but he denied knowing her and said he had never offered any help to human rights organizations, for that would have been outside the scope of his pastoral work. The lawyers present had no doubt that Ruppert was telling the truth.

Christian von Wernich was born in San Isidro, in the province of Buenos Aires, in 1938, but he belongs to a wealthy family in the city of Concordia, where he first went to school.

The ultranationalistic, rightist, Catholic integralism of Concordia has produced, besides von Wernich, Mohamed Ali Seineldin, mentioned above, and Father Raúl Sánchez Abelenda, who is now involved with the suspect Catholicism of French Bishop Marcel Lefevbre. Sánchez Abelenda, a disciple of Julio Meinvielle,[25] was once dean of the faculty of philosophy and letters of the University of Buenos Aires. According to rumors, he certified that von Wernich had passed courses in philosophy required for ordination to the priesthood—courses von Wernich never took.

A few years ago one of his brothers was involved in the bankruptcy of the Alvear Palace Hotel, which prompted various shadowy rumors. At one stage von Wernich moved to California, where he stayed for some time, learning English in the process. It seems that he was thinking of studying business administration.

All reports agree on his taste for a lavish and frivolous lifestyle, even during the period when he claims to have been in the seminary, studying to be a priest. Eugenio Lugones, who came to know him at the pool of the Ateneo de la Juventud gym in the early 1970s, says that some of his friends called him "the Priest" and others "the Count" or "the Duke":

> He obviously had a lot of money. . . . We went to Rio de Janeiro together, and spent about two weeks there during Carnival time. . . . In his car he had a siren, at least during the 1976–1978 period. I asked him why he had it, and now I realize that it wasn't to clear the way, or so he wouldn't be bothered on his way, as he said. Besides that, he had an identification card with his own photo but someone else's name. I know this personally because I saw it myself. I think the last name there was Salvo. I've had the identification card in my own hands. It was issued by the police commissioner of the province of Buenos Aires.[26]

Von Wernich's priestly ordination in 1976 at the age of thirty-eight was a surprise; he had attended more than one seminary and more than one bishop had refused to ordain him, including Archbishop Tortolo of Paraná. The bishop who decided to ordain him was Julio Alejo Gilligan of Nueve de Julio, who has a reputation for naivety. Thus, von Wernich ended up in Nueve de Julio, although he was not from there originally.

In the three cities where he has exercised his ministry—Venticinco de Mayo, Nueve de Julio, and Norberto de la Riestra—von Wernich gravitates toward a certain sector of the population because of his reactionary ideology, his free-and-easy style—he seldom wears a cassock and has a taste for high-powered cars—and his worldly tastes. As mentioned, he built his own house in Norberto de la Riestra. He spends a lot of money, presumably from his family or intelligence services, and frequently travels outside the country. During the period of military dictatorship, others were afraid of him because of his government contacts, although some say he saved a few young persons from that area. He fulfills his clerical duties (Mass, preaching, administering the sacraments), but his attitudes are secular. Hence, it is not surprising that he found no incompatibility between the priesthood and the activities of which he is accused.

Von Wernich tells his friends that he chose to be a priest because it is a profession in which—contrary to others—you work on Sunday and take it easy the rest of the week.

CHAPTER SEVEN

Institutions and Publications

CATHOLIC INSTITUTIONS

Authoritarianism is a characteristic feature of Argentine Catholicism. The institutions that make up, or depend on, the official church have no autonomy, and they are sanctioned if they dare to express any opinion not in accord with the line taken by the bishops. As a *Criterio* editorial puts it:

In Argentina the church desperately needs public opinion. There is a good deal of opinion, but what is missing is a climate sufficiently respectful of freedom so that such opinion can be expressed without fear of reprisal. The apparent calm could make many think that there is a greater degree of consensus than really exists. . . . We are quite afraid that in our church ideas are increasingly being repressed: the sooner controls are lifted, the less damaging will be the process of arriving at sincerity.[1]

The reprisals mentioned above mean sanctions applied by the bishops. Any attempt to say something to society that is not simply a commentary on their own ideas they call the work of a "parallel magisterium," not only with regard to theology but in issues of any kind. I have already noted two such situations. In chapter 1, I quoted passages from a document of the permanent commission of the Bishops' Conference of Argentina, in which the bishops scold the Argentine Conference of Religious (CAR) for suggesting that human rights violations should be confronted more vigorously. (The Latin American Conference of Religious [CLAR] is involved in a similar conflictive situation with CELAM, whose president is Archbishop Antonio Quarracino of La Plata. Quarracino has noted the split between the Brazilian bishops and CLAR, on the one hand, and CELAM, on the other, in an interview in *Nexo* magazine: "The fact that CLAR does not have an open dialogue and a spirit of solidarity with CELAM is simply a scandal that must be overcome.")[2] The Conference of Religious is forbidden to take public positions.

In chapter 6, I showed how the way priests in shantytowns were sanctioned when they denounced how thousands of their people were pushed off the land and the bishop remained indifferent.

Lay institutions in the Catholic Church usually keep quiet, except when they are given orders or they feel obligated to support a decision made by the bishops. They have no opinions, or if they have opinions, they keep them to themselves. That is what happened in the difficult question of human rights violations. Some of the organizations that spoke up did so only to heap praise on the military government.

Such is the case of the Corporation of Catholic Lawyers (CAC), a very small, nonrepresentative group, with a reactionary stance expressed in frequent public statements, where one can note the hand of Doctor Lorenzo J. Butler. When the Inter-American Commission for Human Rights came to Argentina, the CAC published a statement, signed by Ambrosio Romero Carranza and Virgilio Gregorini, with this astonishing paragraph:

> The Corporation believes that *we Argentinians enjoy a reasonable measure of freedom and that human rights are sufficiently protected by the law and Argentine authorities.* Individual cases of persons who have been imprisoned or who have disappeared are under investigation and will be cleared up. Most violations of human rights in our country have been committed by the very ones who, defeated by the armed forces and not courageous enough to take on the consequences of their actions, fled the country, and from there continue to injure Argentina with their hypocritical outcries on behalf of those very human rights that they did not respect when they themselves were in power [italics added].[3]

In 1982 the Federation of Parents' Unions of the Archdiocese of Buenos Aires, under the leadership of Ernesto Gómez Mendizábal, and with the vicar general of the archdiocese, Bishop Arnaldo Canale, as its advisor, began to publish a newsletter. The only thing in the first issue is the text of an instruction published in issue #6 of *Manual de Informaciones,* a magazine published by the chief army command, second headquarters. What is striking is that the teaching of a Catholic institution takes its inspiration from the armed forces.

The appropriate church body for defending human dignity is the National Justice and Peace Commission, which is dependent on the bishops. Pope Paul VI created this institution (which operates on different levels—worldwide, national, diocesan) in order to expedite implementation of the principles of his great encyclicals. That is what has happened, for example, in Spain and Brazil, where such commissions are widely known and highly esteemed. In our case the bishops' conference fulfilled the papal norm in a purely formal manner, as has been the case with so many other things. During the fiercest years of the dictatorship, the commission's president was Carlos Alberto Floria, who, for that reason, took part in the Puebla meeting, as I have explained. When, in the presence of the human rights activist Eduardo Pimentel, I asked Floria the reason for this passivity, he told me that the commission was explicitly forbidden to express opinions publicly. It was only occasionally called on to advise the bishops privately.

The Holy See became disturbed at the way the commission was being nullified in practice and sent the president of the Pontifical Justice and Peace Commission, the African Cardinal Bernardin Gantin, to try to change the situation. Some members were added and the officers were changed, but everything has gone on as before. Only once has the National Justice and Peace Commission become involved in the issue of human rights and expressed a stance different from that of the bishops' conference. It took place after the issuance of the so-called final document of the military junta. At that point, with the signatures of its president, Franklin Obarrio, and its secretary, Ignacio Palacios Videla, the commission declared:

> In the official document on the struggle against subversion we would have liked to have seen a rejection not only of the horror unleashed by guerrilla struggle, but also of the illegal repression that it prompted. The lack of objective truth and the absence of an explicit will on the part of the armed forces to rethink the issue of national defense, by abandoning the doctrine of national security, place the Argentine community at the mercy of the fluctuations of the internal politics of other powers.[4]

I never learned how the leaders of the bishops' conference reacted to this unique statement.

PUBLICATIONS

A scholarly analysis of the role of periodicals regarded as "Catholic" during the military dictatorship would demand research that for the present goes beyond my scant capabilities. Hence, I am going to limit myself to just a few indications. Catholic newspapers and magazines generally kept on safe ground, as did other areas of journalism. That was to be expected, given the reality of state terrorism and the fact that the bishops offered no protection. The usual practice was silence.

Esquiú-color, the clerical (rather than Catholic) weekly, was clearly on the side of the military dictatorship, and competed with the publications of Atlántida Press in defaming the victims of illegal repression and those organizations that defended human rights. The same line can be seen in *Universitas,* published by the Catholic University of Argentina, under the direction of Bishop Octavio Nicolás Derisi.

Criterio, the Catholic magazine for a more general public, which is more independent and serious, remained cautious during the hardest years, undoubtedly because of the circumstances. It frequently lauded the military dictatorship, especially its economic policies. At any rate, with its own approach and style, it makes a significant effort to assess and judge situations objectively. As the reader will have noticed, I cite it repeatedly throughout these pages. When it published an article on law 22,068, which set up conditions for declaring the presumed death of the arrested-and-disappeared—an article that contained significant errors and even praised the law—Augusto Conte and I went to see the editor, Father Rafael Braun. He listened respectfully and in issue number 1827–28, dated January 24, 1980, he published this letter of mine:

Buenos Aires
December 18, 1979

Father Rafael Braun
CRITERIO

Dear Friend:

I am sending you these lines about the commentary that appeared in issue number 1823, entitled "Scope of a Controversial Law," with a request that they be published.

The article is about law 22,068, by which special provisions are set up so that persons who "disappeared" between November 6, 1974, and the date of promulgation of the law—that is, September 12, 1979—can be declared presumably dead. I think the commentary fails to mention certain aspects that are essential to the ordinance and must be taken into account if readers are to have an informed opinion on the problem.

The core of law 22,068—and its purpose—is to be found in two phrases contained in articles 2 and 3, which the *Criterio* writer did not quote. The first phrase authorizes the state to request the declaration of presumed death *without any restrictions and without any juridical intervention*. The only requirement is a purely formal one, whose intrinsic truth a judge does not have to investigate: the declaration of a "disappearance," even one that has occurred only a few weeks previously. The second phrase is the repeated and emphatic statement that such a right can be exercised (by the state) "despite the opposition of other parties" (for example, the parents or spouse of a "disappeared") and brought to a final decision "that in no instance will be subject to further contention" (from art. 2 and 3 of law 22,068).

In other words, any day now the state, without any possible opposition, can seek to have the courts declare dead the thousands of citizens listed as "disappeared" in the files of the Ministry of the Interior, the Federal Police, or the Ministry of Justice. Thus, if it so desires, the state will quickly get such a judgment, without further ado, even if the immediate family of the "disappeared" is unwilling. For their part, judges are obligated by this law to declare this presumption of death without any investigation or other legal procedures—automatically. "Any answer, as long as it's yes," as the saying goes. Do we not have before us, I ask, an unjustified and dangerous—I would say, totalitarian—extension of the powers of the state, at the cost of the rights of the family, and a diminishing of the rights of the judiciary? Is this ruling compatible with Christian teaching in this area? By handing to the courts the power to certify presumed death, are we not witnessing the risk of a massive extension of that power in order to provide a "solution," as General Harguindeguy has said (*La Nación* August 22, 1979), for the problem of the "disappeared"? I let the reader decide. . . .

Some might point out that several officials, including the ministers of the interior and of justice, have said that the government will use this right only in cases of extreme need. But in law, the important thing is not the intention of the legislators, real or presumed, and even less the intention of future governments, but the text itself. Besides, who can guarantee that the successors of the present authorities will not use a different criterion? If that is the case, why pass this law, if law 14,394 is already more than sufficient? . . .

It is quite comprehensible why law 22,068 has been sharply criticized both in our country and elsewhere, and that it deserves to be indignantly rejected by its intended beneficiaries, among whom I myself am included, as you know. At his last press conference, General Videla regretted this "lack of understanding." Nevertheless, I wonder whether, given what I have said, it is not reasonable to think that the intention is—in Videla's own words—"to cover up an alleged or real crime" (*La Nación*, December 14, 1979). . . .

If the government really wanted to soothe our anguish, as General Videla expressed it on that same occasion, it has a very simple means: the truth—*the truth,* which, according to the slogan John Paul II chose for 1980, *is the precondition for peace.* . . .

Finally, I would like to express how disturbed I am to see law 22,068 mentioned in the exhortation of the permanent commission of the Argentine bishops, published in the newspapers on December 15, 1979, apparently without any recognition of the reasons why this new ruling is not necessary for solving the legal and inheritance problems mentioned there. . . .

Cordially,
Emilio F. Mignone

Another magazine that carries interesting and valuable material, *Actualidad Pastoral,* edited by Father Vicente Oscar Vetrano, the vicar for culture in the diocese of Morón, remained silent during the dictatorship. Although one of its features is broad coverage of the pope's activities and speeches, it failed to print one of John Paul II's references in St. Peter's square to the situation of the arrested-and-disappeared in Argentina. I wrote to Vetrano pointing this out and canceling my subscription. In doing so I also offered other criticisms of the publication, some quite harsh. He sent a skimpy but cordial reply, and said he would keep sending the magazine even if I did not pay for it. I have the impression that my observations were taken into account. He shows that he is broadminded and open, despite our disagreements, and I want to emphasize that. (When Bishop Emilio Ogñenovich took charge of the diocese of Mercedes, one of his first moves was to remove Father Vetrano from the chancery office, where he lived, and where he edited and ran the magazine. Vetrano had to be incardinated in the diocese of Morón. Apparently, *Actualidad Pastoral* does not suit the ideology of this wild man who enjoys episcopal rank.)

The December 1976 issue (no. 259) of the newsletter of the Center for Social Research and Action (CIAS) of the Jesuits, published an article by Father Vicente Pellegrini, S. J., "Human Rights in the Present Socio-Political Context in Argentina," which was reprinted in *La Opinión* in its weekly supplement dated January 30–February 5, 1977. That prompted the military dictatorship to close down Timerman's paper for three days. It did not do the same with the newsletter, which had a small circulation, but Pellegrini left the country for some time. He was an advisor to the National Justice and Peace Commission.

When read today, in the light of all that is now known, said, and published, Pellegrini's article looks pale, but taking into account the terror imposed by the dictatorship, the article, for those who knew how to interpret it, was a harsh and brave criticism of methods the military was using. Especially remarkable were the passages on torture:

> We should prevent the degradation of the armed forces by torture. It should be unthinkable to military honor. To transform an honorable military man, whose ideal is to struggle for justice, into a vile torturer, would be the greatest victory terrorism could have.

Obviously, such words could not have fallen very well on the ears of the military junta, degraded in its foul orgy of savagely torturing defenseless prisoners.

At that time most Argentinians were unaware of and could not imagine the genocide the armed forces were committing. Pellegrini spoke of "another kind of torture, mentioned by the Argentine bishops: the torture of relatives caused by long periods of detention, when they cannot receive any news about a person who has disappeared."

The CIAS newsletter did not return to the subject for a long time. In addition, the dominating role played by Father Jorge Bergoglio and his faction within the Jesuits lessened the center's vitality. Much earlier, in issue number 100 of the CIAS newsletter, Antonio Donini, then a Jesuit, published a sociological and pastoral analysis of what was called the Great Mission of Buenos Aires (August–September 1960). The article angered Cardinal Antonio Caggiano, his auxiliary, Bishop Guillermo Bolatti (subsequently archbishop of Rosario), and Bishop Manuel Menéndez, of the diocese of San Martín.[5]

That was the first time that the image of the Virgin of Luján was brought to Buenos Aires from its sanctuary. The second time the idea came from Bishop

Rubén Di Monte, and was carried out by Bishop Emilio Ogñenovich, for the mass demonstration called for on July 5, 1986, to oppose the divorce law.

Donini believes that, despite the immense effort put into it, the Great Mission did not achieve its objectives [a spiritual revival] and was a failure. Impartial observers have the same assessment of the antidivorce demonstration. It seems that moving her venerable image from its home ground in Luján does not impress the Mother of God.

Returning to Argentina after a long time away, Donini published *Religión y Sociedad,* a short summary of the history of Argentine Catholicism.[6] Curiously, he does not mention the Great Mission of Buenos Aires and skips over the 1976–1983 period.

One courageous publication was the bilingual paper *La Cruz del Sur (The Southern Cross),* edited by Father Federico Richards for Argentinians of Irish descent.

THE NOBEL PEACE PRIZE

In 1980, Adolfo Pérez Esquivel, an Argentinian whom the dictatorship was persecuting, won the Nobel Peace Prize. It was a surprise to most Argentinians and a slap in the face for the military government, which had held him in jail without grounds for a year and a half.

Pérez Esquivel is the coordinator of the Servicio Paz y Justicia (SERPAJ), a movement present throughout Latin America. It takes its inspiration from Christian principles, and also from Gandhi and Martin Luther King, Jr. What it advocates is active nonviolence on behalf of the dispossessed. In all the countries where it is active, it stands on the front lines of the defense of human rights. Adolfo Pérez Esquivel and his son Leonardo are among the founders of the APDH in Argentina.

Personally, Adolfo Pérez Esquivel is a committed Christian, a Catholic, and an upright man. Nevertheless, the Argentine hierarchy, as annoyed as the government over the awarding of the prize, did not offer a single word expressing joy or congratulations. Only a few bishops expressed support, those who were involved in the cause of human rights. Bishop Justo Laguna, then auxiliary bishop of San Isidro, where Pérez Esquivel lives, stated that he was a member of the church.

The weekly bulletin of the press agency of the archdiocese of Buenos Aires (AICA) published a snide commentary, seeking to make a clear distinction between SERPAJ and the National Justice and Peace Commission. In doing so, it made insinuations about the activities of SERPAJ and Pérez Esquivel.

However, in a communiqué dated August 18, 1976, the permanent commission of the bishops' conference had expressed concern about the fact that a meeting of bishops, priests, religious, and lay persons in Ecuador had been broken up, and many of its participants arrested or expelled. Among them were Archbishop Zaspe of Santa Fe, and Adolfo and Leonardo Pérez Esquivel.

INTEGRALIST CATHOLICS IN PUBLIC POSITIONS

During the military dictatorship, right-wing Catholics held high-level public positions, and by either their action or their omission, they played a role in the assaults made against the dignity of the human person. None of them were unaware of the deliberate state terrorism. I have personal knowledge of this with regard to Abelardo Rossi and Pedro José Frias, who were on the Supreme Court. Alejandro Caride and Federico Videla Escalada were also on that court.

Others to be named include Ricardo P. Bruera, Juan R. Llerena Amadeo, and Cayetano Licciardo; they were in charge of the Ministry of Culture and Education. (Education minister Juan José Catalán was a picturesque mistake made by Jaime Perriaux, Videla's advisor.) Among others of the same sort can be mentioned Alberto Rodríguez Varela in the Ministry of Justice; Jaime Lucas Lenon, rector of the University of Buenos Aires; Enrique Folcini, on the board of the Central Bank; and Mario H. Pena, in the psychology department at the university and president of the Chamber of Criminal and Correctional Matters in the federal capital. In the latter position, Pena approved autopsies and secret burials of the bodies of the arrested-and-disappeared brought in by the armed forces.

The National Commission on Scientific and Technical Research, Education, and Technology (CONICET) would require a separate study. Simply reading the list of the directors and researchers in its ninety-five institutes, thirty-six programs, and three services during that period, reveals the dominant influence of individuals distinguished by their integralist Catholicism and right-wing nationalism.

THE GLEAM OF THE SWORDS

It is only a short step from integralism and national Catholicism to pro–military coup sentiments. Those who advocate such ideas cannot stand pluralism or the rule of law.

The truth is that they are not Christians. The good news of Jesus is a message of conversion, spread by preaching the Word, prayer, and the testimony of one's own life. There is nothing more anti-Christian than to seek to impose the gospel by means of power and weapons.

In May 1986 there was a deplorable incident in the auditorium of the medical school of the University of Buenos Aires. A crucifix was pulled off the wall, damaged and defaced. Both university authorities and student organizations publicly repudiated the event, which naturally led to outcries from those who believe democracy paves the way for displays of anti-Catholicism.

Those responsible were not discovered. It is not far-fetched to think that they might have belonged to military intelligence services, and acting as provocateurs, just like the nine officers of the air force academy who were caught in acts of violence when Argentina was celebrating its victory in the world soccer championship in 1986.

La Nación, on May 10, 1986, published a letter of protest over the medical school incident, signed by thirty-eight fifth-year secondary students at the Don Jaime school in Bella Vista. Many of the homes in this particular part of Buenos Aires, near the Campo de Mayo, are citadels of right-wing nationalism and Catholic integralism. The Don Jaime private school, which belongs to the Montiel family, provides an education in accord with that ideology. General Videla's children, among others, have gone there. The name of the school, which is that of a medieval Spanish knight, is a symbol of the anti-Christian idea that the gospel may be imposed by the sword.[7]

In the present context of Argentina, the eight-line doggerel at the end of the letter, written by adolescents fronting for their parents and teachers, calls on the military to stage a coup:

> Oh, dearest Virgin so nigh,
> You have before with your glances
> Witnessed the progress of lances
> Setting up crosses on high.
> Look now with love our land towards,
> And if the crosses are falling,
> Tragedies bygone recalling,
> Show us the gleam of the swords!

THE FUTURE

In this new situation, the Catholic Church in Argentina is facing a clear challenge. This challenge will demand changes in the episcopacy, and some of those changes will be made easier by the age of the bishops. It also demands a concept of evangelization along the lines of Vatican II and the documents of Medellín and Puebla. There are very few dioceses where this kind of renewal is underway, but the overall picture offers interesting perspectives.

This challenge necessarily requires a self-critical debate about the role of the church during the period of military dictatorship, and the historical and doctrinal factors involved. I hope that this book will be a contribution to that indispensable purification.

CHAPTER EIGHT

A Persecuted Church

USING THE CHURCH

The 1976–1983 policy of the armed forces vis-à-vis the church was quite elaborate due to the complexity of the objectives they had in mind.

Given its ideological framework, the dictatorship sought to destroy the postconciliar sectors of the church. To achieve this goal it spared no means, resorting to terror, torture, and criminality. At the same time, it had to avoid conflict with the bishops and sought to use ecclesiastical structures for its own purposes.

Thus, the Argentine Catholic Church underwent a true martyrdom, which was nevertheless denied by its highest authorities. A strange case: a church that denies its martyrs!

This strategy is evident not only from what happened but also from secret instructions given by the army and the air force, which the Ministry of Defense introduced in the Giorgi case, heard by a federal judge in San Martín, in Buenos Aires province, and which CELS lawyers made public.

"These guidelines," reads a document of the air force chief of staff, "have been analyzed and adopted as the most appropriate in the opinion of government ministries and *as a corollary of discussions with the highest authorities in the Catholic Church* [italics added]." [1]

What are these guidelines about? They are found in a very detailed form in Appendix 5 ("Religious Sphere") of instruction number 504/77 of the army high command, signed by General Roberto E. Viola, attached to the court record mentioned above:

The army will act selectively toward religious organizations . . . in coordination with state bodies . . . to prevent or neutralize conflictive situations that might be exploited by subversive organizations, to detect and eradicate elements that have infiltrated [military units], and to support authorities and organizations collaborating with the legal forces. . . . With the PRN [Process of National Reconstruction] underway, the church

128

is not participating actively, but *it has expressed itself by understanding and accepting the basic principles laid down, while also pointing out certain aspects and indicating particular errors that could go so far as to undermine support for that process* [italics added].[2]

The document also states:

> The fact that there exists a body of progressive priests, some of whose members form part of the adversary *(el oponente)*, whereas others have a renewal orientation, cannot be allowed to affect the noble ideal of the Argentine clergy or justify a distancing from the church, *which is so necessary for attaining our basic objectives. . . .* The characteristics that the LCS [Struggle against Subversion] had to take on led to consequences that our adversary, in the form of various accusations, had skillfully directed toward the church, *so as to put it in a situation where it was committed to carrying out its pastoral mission of defending all those principles that are the essence of Christian teaching,* challenging the government and the armed forces. . . . Circumstances worsened this situation when *some chance events affected members of the clergy, particularly as a result of certain operations, which were justified even if they were not exactly on the mark. . . .* In the international realm, these events had a negative impact, projecting a totally distorted image of the nation and producing a reaction in the Vatican that in no way favors the PRN and the armed forces [italics added].[3]

The instruction recommends "a rapprochement":

> By means of dialogue and constructive cooperation with the various dioceses of the Catholic Church at all ecclesiastical levels in order to reverse this situation and to gain *the understanding and support of the clergy . . . which will enable us to take advantage of the persuasive role that the Catholic Church can carry out. . . .* Such dialogue, an indispensable objective that must be attained in order to reach the necessary goal, should not be limited to the level of the commanders of zones or subzones, or those responsible for areas,[4] in connection with archbishops and bishops. Clearly it should also be extended to lower levels of the hierarchy. . . . At the same time, the close contact that will be attempted in all dioceses so as to gain *unrestricted support for the LCS, will make it possible to detect problems of a subversive nature in which members of the clergy are, or might be, involved. . . .* Such problems, as important as they might be, should not become irritants that might eventually have a major impact. On the contrary, *they are to be managed with a great deal of tact, and they are to be referred to higher levels as quickly as possible in order to come to adequate solutions. . . . In this activity, military*

chaplains will be very important as advisors and participants in rap-prochement.[5]

The strategy prepared by the air force to deal with problems that could result from statements issued by the church or by sectors in it is also worth noting. Another section of this same document, which bears the signature of Brigadier General Teodoro G. Waldner, warns:

> Such public stances on the part of ecclesiastics can cause fissures, friction, or an atmosphere that would be negative for the PRN. . . . In addition, differences have arisen over certain publications that grow out of certain sectors of the Catholic Church, and they may do harm to the climate of cordiality we need.[6]

Next comes a list of the "Capabilities of the Enemy," meaning the church:

> Given its confessional nature, the Catholic Church can scarcely carry out activities of outright opposition. Nevertheless it can still have capabilities . . . by way of documents and statements providing criticism that intermediate bodies can use in opposition to the government. . . . Support, especially on the part of progressive sectors, for campaigns carried out by solidarity organizations. . . . Facilitating action by interest groups so that religious ceremonies and meetings can have or take on political or social accents (feast of San Cayetano).[7]

These passages speak for themselves. They confirm the basic idea developed throughout this book on the collusion between a large portion of the hierarchy and the armed forces.

Included is also a recognition that crimes were committed—"as a result of certain operations, which were justified even if they were not exactly on the mark"—such as the case of the Pallottine Fathers and the Chamical case, in which the military authorities deny any involvement.

Finally, these passages indicate that the military dictatorship made use of the church to achieve its political, social, and economic ends. The bishops allowed themselves to be used, which means that there was a tactical agreement in which each ally puts itself at the service of the other.

The authors of the military document clearly noted that repressive methods placed the church "in a situation where it was committed to carrying out its pastoral mission of defending those principles that are the essence of Christian teaching." The instructions are intended to prevent this obligation from being fulfilled, by avoiding confrontation. At that they were quite successful.

A PERSECUTED CHURCH

Starting in the 1970s the armed forces kept their sights trained on the progressive sectors in the Catholic Church, seen by them as subversive. During this period there were frequent conflicts, especially with the dioceses of Neuquén, La Rioja, and Goya, whose bishops—Jaime de Nevares, Enrique Angelelli, and Alberto Devoto—were regarded with mistrust.

In chapter 1, above, I talked about the conflict between de Nevares and Lanusse, the imposed president, over the strike in El Chocón. When I get to Bishop Angelelli, I will describe a similar situation.

In 1973 there was a respite, but the next year there began a bloody religious repression, one unprecedented in the Argentine Church. Until March 24, 1976, the crimes committed bore the marks of mystery and were carried out by the "Triple A" (Argentine Anticommunist Alliance), believed to have been founded by José López Rega [longtime Perón confidant, then minister of the social welfare and the power behind the throne during the presidency of Isabel Perón].

Without denying the criminal activities this individual carried out, I am convinced that attacks on priests and other members of the church were planned and carried out by the intelligence services of the armed forces, which began to act secretly a long time before the military coup. The Triple A was nothing but a cover for the illegal repression unleashed by military commanders, with help from some civilians who were part of gangs organized by the military. The proof is that on March 24, 1976, the Triple A disappeared as though by magic. Murders were still being committed, most of them after disappearances, but there was no longer any need for a disguise.

Hence, this analysis will encompass the 1974–1983 period. The sum total of this persecution is astonishing—a dramatic chapter in the history of the church, one unfamiliar to the public due to the silence of the bishops, who have not provided a history of what happened, or given the names of their martyrs.[8]

In order to draw up the following summary I have compared different pieces of research, which do not always agree.[9] From this material it can be concluded with certainty that between 1974 and 1983 sixteen Catholic priests were murdered or disappeared. Some sources also include the name of José Colombo, which would bring the number to seventeen. I do not include him, however, for I do not have data to confirm it. Here is the list:

1. Carlos Francisco Mugica, murdered in Buenos Aires, May 11, 1974.
2. Carlos Dorniak, murdered in Bahía Blanca, March 21, 1975.
3. Nelio Rougier, arrested in Córdoba in September 1975. Disappeared.
4. Miguel Angel Urusa Nicolau, arrested in Rosario, January 1, 1976. Disappeared.
5. Francisco Soares, murdered in Tigre, along with an invalid brother who was under his care, February 13, 1976.
6. Pedro Fourcade, arrested March 8, 1976. Disappeared.
7. Pedro Duffau, murdered in Buenos Aires, July 4, 1976.
8. Alfredo Kelly, murdered in Buenos Aires, July 4, 1976.
9. Alfredo Leaden, murdered in Buenos Aires, July 4, 1976.
10. Gabriel Longueville, murdered in Chamical, La Rioja, July 18, 1976.

11. Carlos de Dios Murias, murdered in Chamical, La Rioja, November 18, 1976.
12. Héctor Federico Baccini, arrested in La Plata, November 25, 1976. Disappeared.
13. Pablo Gazzari, arrested in Buenos Aires, April 8, 1977. Disappeared.
14. Carlos Armando Bustos, arrested in Buenos Aires, April 8, 1977. Disappeared.
15. Mauricio Silva Iribarnegaray, arrested in Buenos Aires, June 14, 1977. Disappeared.
16. Jorge Adur, arrested January 7, 1980. Disappeared.

To this list should be added José Tedeschi, a Salesian priest, who had been laicized, and who was arrested on February 2, 1976, in a shantytown named Itati, in the area of Bernal. A few days later his body was found with signs that he had been tortured. Héctor Federico Baccini, who is listed as a music teacher on the APDH list, was in the process of being laicized.

The names of Bishops Enrique Angel Angelelli of La Rioja and Carlos Ponce de León of San Nicolás de los Arroyos should also be added. Both died in similar car accidents, which took place on August 4, 1976, and July 11, 1977, respectively. With regard to Angelelli, the judge stated that it was a case of undeniable homicide, as we will see below. In the case of Ponce de León, there are also strong indications of a murder.

Thus we have a total of nineteen ordained men who were physically eliminated.

On the occasion of Bishop Angelelli's murder, August 4, 1976, the minister of the interior, Albano Harguindeguy, stated that ten priests were in prison. According to the information I have been able to gather, their names were Francisco Gutiérrez, Hugo Mathot, Gianfranco Testa, Silvio Liuzzi, Elias Musse, Raúl Troncoso, Francisco Javier Martín, René Nievas, Joaquín Núñez, and Omar Dinelli. That same year Dinelli was released and went into exile in France. All the others spent long years in prison.

The following priests were arrested, tortured, freed, and expelled from the country, or chose to go into exile: Néstor García, Patrick Rice, José Czerepack, Orlando Iorio, Santiago Renevot, Rafael Iacuzzi, Julio Suan, Bernardo Canal Feijóo, Luis López Molina, James Weeks, and Francisco Jálics—eleven in all. Iacuzzi returned to Argentina but had to leave again due to a court proceeding against him in the capital. Rice is executive secretary of the Latin American Federation of Relatives of the Disappeared (FEDEFAM), headquartered in Caracas, Venezuela. Iorio is incardinated in the diocese of Viedma, and Jálics, who is of Hungarian origin, is now with the Jesuits in West Germany. Weeks, an American, is doing pastoral work in South America.

I have compiled a list of twenty-two priests who underwent a period of imprisonment, usually including torture: Marciano Alba, Aníbal Coerezza, Pace Dalteroch, Jorge Galli, Gervasio Mecca, Luis Quiroga, Angel Zaragoza, Raúl Acosta, Roberto Croce, Juan Dieuzeide, Esteban Innestal, Diego Orlandini,

Eduardo Ruiz, Joaquín Muñoz, Juan Testa, Pablo Becker, Roberto D'Amico, Juan Filipuzzi, Antonio Mateos, Agueda Pucheta, Victor Pugnata, and Jorge Torres.

The preceding lists include sixty-two priests directly affected, but it does not include those who, out of prudence, left the country for good, or who changed dioceses. Among such cases is that of the priest-sociologist Duilio Biancucci, now in West Germany, who was a professor at the National University at Luján. It would not be an exaggeration to put the total number at a hundred.

Seminarians were also hit hard. Among the murdered and disappeared may be mentioned Salvador Barbeito and Emilio Barletti, of the Pallottines, killed July 4, 1976; Marcos Cirio, a novice in the Brotherhood of the Gospel, arrested and disappeared November 17, 1976; Carlos A. Di Pietro and Raúl E. Rodríguez, Assumptionists, arrested and disappeared June 4, 1976; and Juan Ignacio Isla Casares of Nuestra Señora de Unidad in Olivos, Buenos Aires province, who was arrested and disappeared on June 3, 1976. The seminarians Alejandro Dauza, Alfredo Velarde, Daniel García, José Luis de Stéfano, and Humberto Pantoja were arrested and tortured in Córdoba on August 3, 1976, along with Father Weeks of the community of La Salette. They spent a long time in jail. Thus, a total of eleven seminarians.

Among religious, the best known case is that of the French Sisters of the Foreign Missions, Alice Domon and Léonie Duquet, arrested December 8 and 10, in Santa Cruz church and at home, respectively. There is no official information on them, but many reports indicate that they were being held in the Navy Technical School, where they were tortured and later murdered. We may also add Brother Julio San Cristóbal, of the Christian Brothers, arrested and disappeared on February 5, 1976, and Henri del Salan Betumale of the Brotherhood of the Gospel, who was in prison from 1976 to 1978 and was then deported to France. Thus, a total of four religious, apart from those mentioned in other categories.

COMMITTED CHRISTIANS

The number of Christians, both Catholic and Protestant, who were committed to apostolic activities and were victims of state terrorism is hard to calculate. It no doubt includes an important segment of the thousands of those who were murdered, arrested-and-disappeared, jailed, and exiled at the hands of the armed forces between 1974 and 1983. I would rather not hazard a guess at numbers, and will simply highlight a few significant cases.

On May 9, 1975, María del Carmen Maggi, dean of the humanities department of the Catholic University of Mar del Plata, was abducted by a group of heavily armed men. On March 23, 1976, the day before the coup, her body was found on the beach near the lagoon of Mar Chiquita. She had disappeared ten months earlier. Dean Maggi had connections with Archbishop Pironio of Mar del Plata, who is today a cardinal in the Roman curia. There were indications that the abduction was the work of members of the National University Convocation, who were very active in the Atlantic coast area and were connected with the navy and the army.

In November 1975, army troops under the commander of the VI Infantry Brigade of Montaña de Neuquén (subzone 52), Brigadier General Juan Antonio Buasso, made a search of the Mamá Margarita school and residence in Junín de los Andes. They arrested two teachers, a cleaning woman (whom they tried to torture sexually), and Father Antonio Mateos. The incident led to a harsh public interchange between Bishop Jaime de Nevares and General Buasso, who defended what had been done.

In December 1975, Daniel Bombara, active in JUC (University Catholic Action) in Bahía Blanca, and José Serapio Palacios, a leader in JOC (Young Catholic Workers), in El Palomar, Buenos Aires province, were abducted. Bombara's body showed up a little while later showing signs of torture. Palacios simply disappeared.

As mentioned earlier, in the early morning of May 14, 1976, Beatriz Carbonell de Pérez Weiss and her husband Horacio Pérez Weiss, María Marta Vásquez Ocampo de Lugones and her husband César Amadeo Lugones, Mónica María Candelaria Mignone and María Esther Lorusso Lamle, were all arrested at their homes. At one in the afternoon that same day, Mónica Quinteiro, a former Mercy sister, was also arrested. There is no further information about them. Through the interrogation endured by Father Orlando Iorio, who lived in the same barrio, and by other indications, it is known that they were transferred to the Navy Technical School, where they were no doubt tortured and murdered.

The group that gathered around the parish of Nuestra Señora de la Unidad in Olivos and worked with La Manuelita neighborhood was practically decimated. Some of them were affiliated with the Fraternity of the Gospel and others with JIC (Independent Christian Youth). Their members included, among others, María Fernanda Noguer, José Villar, Alejandro Sackman, Esteban Garat, Valeria Dixon de Garat, and Roberto van Gelderen. Most of them were arrested and disappeared in June 1976.

During the last few months of 1976 the following active Christians "disappeared": Ignacio Beltrán, of Buenos Aires; Alberto Rivera, Horacio Russin, Néstor Junquera, and María Eugenia González, of Bahía Blanca; Luis Oscar Gervan of Tucumán; and Luis Congett, a Caritas leader in San Justo, in Buenos Aires province.

During 1977 others met the same fate: Antero Darío Esquivel, a Paraguayan citizen and a member of JOC in Lomas de Zamora; Eduardo Luis Ricci, a JEC (Young Catholic Students) leader in La Plata; Leonor Rosario Landaburu de Catnich and her husband Juan Carlos Catnich, active Christians in the capital; Susana Carmen Moras, president of the youth branch of Catholic Action, and Susana Antonia Marco, a member of Christians for Liberation, both of whom belonged to Nuestra Señora del Carmen parish in Villa Urquiza, Buenos Aires; Roque Agustín Alvarez, who belonged to a Catholic group in Avellaneda; Armando Corsiglia, a JUC leader in Florencio Varela; Cecilia Juana Minervine, who belonged to Christians for Liberation in the capital; and the married couple Laura Adhelma Godoy and Oscar de Angeli, of the Catholic University of Mar del Plata.

This bloody persecution did not cease in 1978. In January of that year the repressive agents sadistically tortured the married couples Gertrudis Hlaszick and José Poblete, Mónica Brull and Juan Guillén, as well as Mr. and Mrs. Gilberto Rengel Ponce. Four of them were handicapped and were participating in Christian organizations that brought them together. All were savagely tortured. In addition, Adolfo Fontanella, a militant Christian, was abducted and has never been heard from to this day.

Protestant churches were also victims of state terrorism. The most notable case is that of Mauricio López, with whom I enjoyed a very warm friendship. A theologian and philosopher, for many years he worked in the World Council of Churches, headquartered in Geneva, Switzerland. A native of Mendoza, he returned to Argentina and in 1973 was appointed rector of the National University of San Luis, a post he held until March 24, 1976. On January 1, 1977, he was arrested in Mendoza and, despite the intensive efforts made on his behalf in Argentina and elsewhere, there was never any official notice about his fate. Confidential information indicates that he was murdered in March that year.

The daughters of two Protestant pastors were also victims of repression. Elizabeth Käsemann, a German, was arrested, tortured, and murdered in 1977. She was the daughter of Ernst Käsemann, the well-known New Testament scholar. Patricia Anna Erb, an American, was abducted on September 13, 1976.

On April 4, 1976, Victor Pablo Boinchenko and Lilian Jane Coleman de Boinchenko, active members of the Evangelical Church in Cosquín, Córdoba, were arrested. There is no doubt that they were taken to the clandestine camp of La Perla and executed. On May 4, Oscar Alajarín, a Methodist and member of the Ecumenical Movement for Human Rights, "disappeared" in Buenos Aires.

There are shocking testimonies about the humiliating treatment suffered by committed Christians in secret detention centers. Such episodes reveal how much their captors hated the gospel message, and how twisted were their ideas of religion. Here are some accounts:

> Something astonishing happened at Christmas in 1977. Around fifteen of us prisoners were taken to a Mass celebrated in the social club of officers of the Navy Technical School. We had our feet shackled, our hands cuffed behind our backs, and hoods over our heads. Meanwhile, we could hear the cries of those being tortured and the noise of dragging chains of those who were being led to the bathroom in the "hooded" section.[10]

> Around December 24, 1976, Admiral Massera, Rear Admiral Chamorro, Captain Acosta, and some members of Task Force Three showed up [at the Navy Technical School]. Showing their unlimited cynicism,

standing in front of about thirty prisoners with shackled feet, they wished us all a merry Christmas.[11]

Twice they pretended they were going to kill me, once by firing squad and the other time by poisoning. Before that they asked me if I wanted to pray and handed me what they called a rosary. By touch (I was blindfolded) I could make out that what they had given me was not a rosary but the cross that my daughter always wore around her neck (it was handmade and quite distinctive). I understood that this was their sadistic way of letting me know that my daughter was also there. I prayed and wept. Then they showered me with obscenities, threats, and shouts. They said, "Shut up. This is what you get for being involved with that bearded guy, that queer (meaning Jesus Christ). That's why this is happening to you."[12]

They took us to station number 36 of the federal police in Villa Soldati. When I cried out, they whistled and made noise to drown out my cries. Then they took me to a dark cell and after a while some others came to tell me that I was "going to see the military," that I was going to realize that in comparison to the Argentine military, the Romans who persecuted the early Christians didn't know anything.[13]

PERSECUTION AND REACTION

This account is of course incomplete and gives only a rough idea of the scope and nature of the attack on the progressive sector of the Argentine church. It is to be hoped that detailed research into what happened will be undertaken and that the memory of the martyrs will be kept alive.

In almost five centuries the church in our region had not suffered such a bloody repression. Prior conflicts with the state were of a different nature. The expulsion of the Jesuits by Charles III in 1767 meant only that members of the society were sent out of the country and their property expropriated. Rivadavia's religious reform in 1822 was limited to suppressing religious houses and confiscating property. The clashes with Rosas were not especially significant. The high point of the events of the 1880s, during the presidency of Roca, was the forced departure of the nuncio, Luis Matera, and the breaking of relations with the Holy See.

We may consider at greater length the enmity between Perón and the church in 1954–1955. Besides the legislative and administrative measures, the most outstanding events were the expulsion of the auxiliary bishop of Buenos Aires, Manuel Tato, and of Canon Manuel Novoa, and the burning and other damage done to the chancery office and the churches of San Francisco, Santo Domingo, San Ignacio de Loyola, La Piedad, San Miguel Arcángel, El Socorro, San Nicolás de Bari, Las Victorias, and San Juan Bautista on the night of June 16, 1955. The death of the Redemptorist, Father Jacobo Wagner, was due to the injuries he incurred when he tried to escape over the roof of his rectory, and was the only incident of this nature. There are no indications that he had been beaten, as Juan Carlos Zuretti claims.[14]

I do not mean to justify these barbaric acts. I myself was watching from the hallway of the chancery office when the building was set on fire, and I can say that those who did it were small bands of arsonists, and that the police and army stood idly by. That is, it was not a spontaneous reaction by the people, who at noontime had suffered hundreds of deaths in a brutal bombing in the Plaza de Mayo carried out by navy airplanes.

These events prompted a harsh reaction on the part of the church. In late July the Argentine bishops published a joint pastoral letter, "Our Contribution to Peace in Our Country," denouncing the religious persecution. On June 16, 1955, the Vatican Secretariat of State published a decree excommunicating those responsible for deporting Bishop Tato.

In 1976 the assault was not limited to verbal attacks, confiscation of goods, expulsion of priests and church dignitaries, or the destruction of temples of stone or brick, which can be easily rebuilt. The victims were human beings, living temples of the Holy Spirit, created in the image and likeness of God. Two bishops, more than a hundred priests, religious, and seminarians, and thousands of committed Christians were the victims—but there was no joint letter from the bishops condemning the persecution or excommunicating those responsible.

What a strange spectacle, these bishops who exchanged favors with a regime that was terrorizing and slaughtering its priests and faithful!

Some might say that the persecution touched only one part of the church. That is true, but it does not excuse the pastors whose obligation it is to defend all the sheep in their flock.

One could argue that the government accused the victims of being involved in subversive activity, but that does not excuse the methods used. The bishops should have demanded a fair trial, and never allowed murder, disappearance, torture, or jailing without trial. As I state elsewhere in this book, one sometimes has the impression that some bishops were pleased to see such bothersome elements eliminated and even gave their approval for it to take place. In a letter to Angelelli attached to court proceedings, Archbishop Zaspe explains that in a meeting between the executive commission of the bishops' conference and the military junta in May 1976, Archbishop Tortolo asked that the bishop be advised when a priest was to be arrested. As is obvious, there was no demand for a trial, and they accepted imprisonment without due process. Yet not even this minimal demand was met.

The use of state power for persecution and criminal actions is common throughout the history of humankind. Hitler and Stalin eliminated millions, but neither of them claimed to be Christian or to be defending the church or Christian civilization. I recall how Auxiliary Bishop Daniel Pezeril of Paris told my wife and me how serious he thought this was. "What astonishes me is that the Argentine military junta should kill in the name of God and the bishops do not point out what a scandal this is." Pezeril had recently published a harsh criticism of the military regime in *Le Monde,* prompting a public exchange of letters with ambassador Tomás de Anchorena.

BISHOP ANGELELLI AND THE CHURCH IN LA RIOJA

In this context it is particularly important to examine the persecution of the church in La Rioja, which culminated in the murder of Wenceslao Pedernera, a Christian leader, Fathers Murias and Longueville, and Bishop Angelelli in July and August 1976.

After the arrival of Bishop Enrique Angel Angelelli, the church in that diocese began to stand out from other dioceses in Argentina. Angelelli had been born in Córdoba on July 17, 1923, had studied in the Colegio Pío Latinamericano in Rome, and was ordained in 1949. In Córdoba he served as JOC and JUC advisor, and in 1960 he was made auxiliary bishop. On July 11, 1968, Pope Paul VI appointed him bishop of La Rioja.

Starting with his first message, he gave a clear indication of what his pastoral line would be, saying "With one ear I listen to the gospel and with the other I listen to the people." He identified himself with the traditions of La Rioja, and with the lowly and dispossessed. He brought in a clear postconciliar thrust and quickly became a charismatic figure who revitalized the diocese. Around him there took shape a vigorous movement of priests (some of whom came from elsewhere), religious, and lay persons. He traveled around the province, moving from one community to another, and also speaking on the radio.

Angelelli did not stop at denouncing the difficult living conditions of residents of La Rioja and the exploitation they endured, especially the rural workers; he moved into action. He promoted the organization of farming cooperatives, and the division of large rural properties such as the Azzalini latifundium.

Because his activity affected vested interests, there began a campaign to get him out of La Rioja. To the powerful, he was dangerous. Incidents were created during the celebration of the patron saints' days in Anillaco; pseudo-religious organizations like the Crusade for the Faith published statements against him; denunciations poured into the bishops' conference, the Holy See, and the military government (presidents Onganía, Levingston, and Lanusse). In 1973, Paul VI sent Archbishop Vicente Zaspe as his personal representative to back up Angelelli's pastoral directioning. The newspaper *El Sol,* owned by Tomás Alvarez Saavedra, calumniated him every day, but another paper, *El Independiente,* supported him. He was called a communist, Third Worlder, and guerrilla.

The church of La Rioja, community-style, active, and prophetic, came under the scrutiny of the armed forces, the natural allies of the landholders. In 1976 the situation became asphyxiating. The commands of the engineering and construction batallion of La Rioja (area 314) and of CELPA, the air force base of Chamical, each with their own intelligence services, went into action, without waiting for the March 24 coup.

On January 1, 1976, at the conclusion of diocesan ceremonies, Angelelli spoke to the people about the situation. "I place the diocese in a state of prayer." At the air base Bishop Bonamín was preaching that "the people of Argentina had committed sins that could be redeemed only with blood." This statement led to a conflict with Angelelli, who, in a private letter to Archbishop Zaspe, said, "what Bonamín did in Chamical was preposterously wrong." On February 12, under army orders, the vicar general of the diocese of La Rioja, Esteban Inestal, and two young men of the diocesan rural movement, Carlos Di Marco and Rafael Sifré, were arrested in Mendoza. Their interrogation centered on the activities of the diocese. The officers asking the questions said, "John XXIII and Paul VI have ruined the church. They destroyed the church of Pius XII. The Medellín documents are communist and were not approved by the pope. The church of La Rioja is separated from the Argentine church." [15]

On February 20, Angelelli called the clergy together for priestly and pastoral reflection, and said, "The political situation in Argentina obliges us to discern our future mission in a gospel fashion." On February 25, he wrote to the Bishops' Conference of Argentina these decisive and prophetic words:

> In my understanding, this matter goes beyond La Rioja and affects us all. I appeal to my brother bishops, because it is urgent that we make a deeper assessment. We urgently need to clarify our mission to the dioceses and to the military vicariate. It is time to open our eyes and not let the army generals usurp our mission to watch over the Catholic faith. The fact that they want to oppose the church of Pius XII to the church of John and Paul is no coincidence. Today the victim was a vicar general; tomorrow (very soon) it will be a bishop. The thought that crosses my mind is that the Lord needs a bishop in jail or killed in order to make us wake up to our episcopal collegiality, and live it more deeply. For a diocese these tests are a grace from God; they are very helpful for uniting and deepening the priests and the rest of the diocesan community. This self-questioning poses for me once more the possibility that for the good of the church, I should consider the option that is well known to you: that I resign.

In March, on the day that school classes began, the commander of the air force base of Chamical, Vice-Commodore Lázaro Aguirre, interrupted Bishop Angelelli's homily during the Mass in the base chapel. He said the bishop, when he pointed to the social responsibility of Christians, was engaging in politics. As a result, on March 19, Angelelli decided to "suspend the celebration of religious services in the chapel within the jurisdiction of that air base."

The situation continued to become more critical. On March 20, Francisco Gutiérrez García, a Spanish priest, was transferred, under arrest, to La Rioja, under accusation that he was connected with the bishop of La Rioja. On March 24, the day of the coup, forces from the Chamical air force base, who had taken over the police station in Malanzán, arrested Aguado Pucheta, the pastor of the parish. In Olta, the pastor, Eduardo Ruiz, was jailed along with his brother Pedro. His imprisonment was to last six months. Sister Marisa, a member of the community of sisters working in the parish, was held by Second Lieutenant Peseta in Chamical, who questioned her about her relationship with Angelelli.

On March 28, the commander of the Chamical base, Vice-Commodore Lázaro Aguirre, told Father Gabriel Longueville to stay home quietly, and he called Fathers Francisco Canobel and Carlos de Dios Murias in to "have a conversation." The interrogation lasted five hours in the presence of Vice-Commodore Luis Estrella, the assistant director of CELPA and minister of finance of the province, and Second Lieutenant Peseta. Father Pucheta was arrested once more. On April 2, the army searched and closed the parish house in Olta; Father Ruiz, the pastor, remained in jail.

On April 18, the military authorities had the newspapers print a letter from Father Ruiz to Bishop Angelelli, in which he said, "You are mistaken; don't continue." When he was released, Ruiz said his intention was that the opposite be understood.

The priests of the diocese made a retreat in Sañogasta. At the end of the retreat they issued an Easter message, stating:

> We thought it important to recall once more what we have been teaching for so many years: the work of evangelization cannot ignore the serious issues of justice, liberation, development, and world peace as well as everything the church teaches about the dignity of the human person and the deep respect that that dignity demands of us as image of God.

On April 26, the priests of La Rioja wrote to Archbishop Zaspe:

> Our situation is becoming more suffocating and harder every day; our ministry is under surveillance and its meaning twisted; our pastoral activity is called Marxist and subversive. It is not the people of La Rioja who are acting this way, but the same group as always, those who previously started a campaign of calumny and now, with the change of government, are drawing up lists. There are house searches and arrests. They present La Rioja as a place that welcomes guerrillas and Angelelli as their main leader. This is one of the main topics in their interrogations. There is a conspiracy to achieve their purpose: to separate the faithful from their church.

Angelelli personally added this note:

> Certainly I cannot fail to take on the anguish of my priests, religious, and lay persons. I'll tell you something else: here in La Rioja the alarming unemployment among the people is creating a very painful situation. To top it off, there is still no clarification over the fact that there are two parallel governments: one, the army, which took over on March 24, and

the other, the air force, appointed by the central government. Witch-hunting is in full swing. This time no one can say that we did not give warning [to the bishops' conference]. Of course we are not the only ones, but it is time for the church of Christ in Argentina to discern our mission on a national level and not to remain silent in the face of these serious events that are taking place one after another. Once more I offer to resign so La Rioja won't continue to be a headache for the Holy See or the nuncio or my brother bishops. Either we get serious about backing one another up or another pastor for this diocese should be found.

Here are my suggestions for the document the bishops' conference is preparing: pose the question of the present situation in Argentina. . . . Don't sign a blank check for anyone—only for the gospel. Don't give up a constructive criticism from the viewpoint of the gospel. Issue a call to deepen ecclesial unity and don't allow ourselves to be divided for any reason whatsoever; clarify the mission of the military vicariate and its relationships to the dioceses. Deepen episcopal collegiality and sacramental unity among ourselves. We must provide this witness; all our diocesan communities need it.

At the bishop's suggestion, six priests left La Rioja. On June 17, six Sisters of Charity were arrested as they were entering the city. The police made them get out of their jeep, examined the vehicle and baggage, and even opened letters. The next day they were called to the police station where a file on them was started. The police chief explained:

This procedure is followed only with persons who seem suspicious. The situation in La Rioja is very serious because of Marxist ideologies, especially that of the bishop; the pope does not know the real situation of the church in La Rioja; he is misinformed. . . . I'm warning you that if you keep working in La Rioja, you may be stopped again.

During these difficult moments, Angelelli continued to put out messages. In one of them he said that the radio broadcast of the Mass from the cathedral had been stopped "by higher orders." It was replaced by Mass celebrated by military chaplains in the army battalion.

The situation reached its climax. Given the resistance of the church in La Rioja, the army and air force decided to use criminal activity to silence it and thus teach a lesson. On July 18, 1976, a group of men in civilian clothes who said they belonged to the federal police, asked to speak with the priests in Chamical, Gabriel Longueville and Juan Carlos de Dios Murias. The priests were having dinner in the parish house with some sisters. After speaking with the men apart, they explained to the sisters that they had to go with them to La Rioja to make a legal deposition. They said good-bye and left in the company of the group that had come to see them. The next morning their bodies were found in El Chañar, a few kilometers from Chamical, showing obvious signs of torture.

Gabriel Longueville was a 45-year-old French priest, who had been sent by the Bishops Committee for Latin America. He came to Argentina in 1972 and worked as the pastor in Chamical, where he was widely respected. The fact that he followed Bishop Angelelli's pastoral line and that he favored the poor had earned him the mistrust of the air force base. Carlos de Dios Murias was a 30-year-old Franciscan. He worked with the pastor and had plans to set up a house of his order in La Rioja. Before he was ordained, I got to know him on a trip to Patagonia, where my daughters were doing missionary work. He was a good priest, enthusiastic, dedicated to his gospel mission, and clearly post-conciliar in his mentality.

The murder stirred things up in La Rioja. Bishop Angelelli came to stay in Chamical and on July 22 he presided at the burial, giving an emotional homily. Meanwhile, in the provincial capital, the battalion communications chief, Colonel Osvaldo Pérez Battaglia, prohibited the news from the papers, even as a funeral notice.

On July 25 there was another killing. At night an armed group knocked on the door of the house of Wenceslao Pedernera in Sañogasta. When he came to answer, they murdered him point-blank in the presence of his wife and three children. Pedernera was a Christian who was active in farming cooperatives and in the parish of Sañogasta, and was involved in activities promoted by the bishop.

Angelelli understood that his hour had arrived. He wrote to the nuncio. He indicated it to his co-workers on a number of occasions. He said that they would try to disguise his death, perhaps as an accident. "Several persons have to die, and I am one of them," he said. He told his niece, María Elena Coesano, that in June he had been with the members of the military junta and said afterward, "Things look ugly. At any moment they are going to do away with me. But I can't hide the message under the bed." After the murder of Longueville and Murias, he went to Córdoba, visited that same niece, and explained that he had met with the commander of the III Army Corps, General Luciano Benjamín Menéndez, and Cardinal Raúl Primatesta. In that meeting, Menéndez told him to be very careful. He left that meeting certain that his fate was sealed. He felt isolated. No other bishop had attended the funeral of Longueville and Murias. To Zaspe, in whom he always confided, he wrote, "Among my brother bishops in Argentina I stand alone."

On August 4, he decided to return from Chamical to La Rioja. In his briefcase he was carrying important documents that he had gathered, documents that proved who was responsible for the murder of Longueville and Murias. In the parish house the night before they had the impression that men were prowling around outside. After lunch he left with Father Arturo Pinto, taking the old road. When they got to Punta de los Llanos, as Pinto later explained, a white

Peugeot came up from behind and swerved over, forcing him to turn sharply. The car turned over and Pinto was knocked out. Six hours later, Angelelli's body was found, twenty-five yards away, with his arms crossed and his skull smashed. Expert testimony in the court trial shows that he could not have gone through the windshield or through the door. All indications are that he was killed with a blow to the back of the neck and dragged away.

The report labeled his death a traffic accident and was quickly filed. The armed forces and security forces kept civilians and reporters away from the site. That same night army personnel tried to search Bishop Angelelli's living quarters. The vicar general, Esteban Inestal, refused and threatened to notify the nuncio, and so they gave up. The nuncio, Pio Laghi, and ten bishops attended Angelelli's funeral. Archbishop Zaspe spoke about his longtime friend, as did other speakers.

No one was deceived. Everyone knew he had been murdered. In Rome, Cardinal Eduardo Pironio told the Methodist theologian José Míguez Bonino that the Holy See had no doubts and would speak as soon as word came from the bishops' conference. But that word did not come. On the contrary, Cardinal Aramburu, speaking in Tucumán, said, "In order to call something a crime you must prove it, and I have no indication of that sort. None of the investigations left any possibility that it might be the kind of thing rumored about."[16] Cardinal Primatesta said something similar, even though he had direct knowledge of the facts. The evidence piled up in the nunciature, but nothing was said there either.

Years went by. On January 26, 1983, a former police officer, Rodolfo Peregrino Fernández, made a formal statement explaining that he had seen Angelelli's briefcase with documentation on the killings of Longueville and Murias on the desk of Interior Minister Albano Harguindeguy. On July 31 that same year Bishop Jaime de Nevares of Neuquén said openly that Angelelli's death was deliberate and he provided details. At a press conference organized by CELS in the Permanent Assembly for Human Rights, Arturo Pinto, who had been with Angelelli, provided decisively important elements.

The court case was reopened in La Rioja. When constitutional government was restored and Doctor Aldo Fermín Morales was appointed judge, the investigation moved ahead. Angelelli's successor, Bishop Bernardo Witte, provided very important elements of proof for the case. The provincial government, headed by Carlos Saúl Menem, and the under secretary of government and human rights, Graciela Petray, offered their help. On July 19, 1986, the appointed judge pronounced an interlocutory judgment, *"Declaring that the death of Bishop Enrique Angel Angelelli was not due to a traffic accident, but rather to a coldly premeditated homicide, which the victim was expecting"* (italics added). In the supporting documentation, it is said that the proofs are conclusive. The label on the file was changed from "accident" to "undeniable murder." This change prevents the case from being closed.

A few weeks later, lawyers from CELS came forward in a case representing the bishop's niece, María Elena Coesano, and she was recognized as a litigant. The task ahead is to identify those who were responsible, directly or indirectly, for the bishop's death.

These events took place at a time when the whole country was involved in a movement to keep alive Bishop Angelelli's memory, his activity, and his teaching, on the tenth anniversary of his death. These events climaxed with the ceremonies that took place in La Rioja on August 4, 1986, with pilgrims from different places, especially the dioceses of Neuquén, Viedma, and Quilmes.

On the eve of this liturgical celebration, the board of ATC Channel 7 prohibited a part of a program with the CELS lawyer, Jorge Baños, from being broadcast at 11 P.M. Sunday night on the program called "A Fondo," hosted by Mona Moncalvillo. It was said that Baños was going to announce the names of fifteen persons involved in the crime. This shows the veto power still held by the armed forces.

With regard to the bishops' conference, Cardinals Aramburu and Primatesta have not changed their 1976 statements, despite the judicial decision contradicting them. The ceremonies in memory of Angelelli were not supported by the bishops who side with them, although his successor, Bernardo Witte, and some of the bishops who follow the same pastoral line, did support them.

Similarly, there has been no explanation from the officers in charge at La Rioja when the murder took place. In particular, I am referring to the commander of the battalion 141 of engineers and construction (area 314), Colonel Osvaldo Pérez Battaglia; the second-in-command, Lieutenant Colonel (now General) Jorge Malagamba; and the commander and assistant commander of the CELPA air base in Chamical, Commodore Lázaro Antonio Aguirre and Vice-Commodore Luis Estrella.

On August 2, 1986, Bishop Bernardo Witte stated that the time had come to look into the life, works, virtues, and "fame of sanctity or of martyrdom" of his predecessor, Enrique Angelelli. For that purpose he has set up a diocesan commission made up of theologians, jurists, pastoral experts, priests, and lay persons. "There is no doubt that he was a true pastor and prophet in the storm; he was a sign of contradiction in the gospel tradition," he said.

These are the first steps in the process by which the church declares a person a saint.

In the same document the bishop of La Rioja says that "in deep silence, for nine years we have patiently investigated the life, documents, deeds, attitudes, and works that will provide us with the light and truth about Bishop Angelelli." He ends by stating that the judge involved in the case has produced the first proof that what took place was murder.

On August 5, 1986, after the tenth anniversary of the murder of Angelelli, the secretary general of the Bishops' Conference of Argentina, Bishop Carlos Galán, made a statement reported by the Catholic News Agency. This statement is utterly disgraceful, for it maintains that his death was an accident and, using incorrect statements, tries to diminish the value of the court declarations. The statement says in part:

They [Primatesta, Laghi, Aramburu] carried out all the investigation that it was in their power to do. Those in charge of the church never have the resources available to the civil power for making such investigations, and certainly at that time even Bishop Angelelli's best friends thought it had been an accident. Now, with the passage of time, a judge is telling us something else. In fact, as we know, he is a recording judge. Later on there will be a fuller process in order to come to a more decisive conclusion.

These statements are misleading. First, Angelelli's friends and the people of La Rioja always held that it was murder. The judge is a penal magistrate who is empowered to pronounce a sentence. The judicial decree changing the classification of the file has been given within the legal process.

BISHOP PONCE DE LEÓN

From *Nunca Más* I take this important information:

On July 11, 1977, Bishop Carlos Ponce de León of San Nicolás de los Arroyos died in a suspicious highway accident. The bishop was on his way to the capital with Víctor Martínez, who worked with him, in order to bring to the nunciature documentation about the illegal repression (abduction and torture) being carried out in the diocese of San Nicolás, and also in Villa Constitutión, in the province of Santa Fe. This documentation implicated General Carlos Suárez Mason, commander of the I Army Corps, Colonel Camblor, commander of the regiment at Junin, and more directly Lieutenant Colonel Saint Amant, commander of the regiment in San Nicolás.

The documentation the bishop had with him disappeared, and the chancellor of the diocese, Monsignor Robert Mancuso, who was also the chaplain of the prison in the city, made no effort to claim it.

Víctor Martínez recalls that after attending the funeral of Bishop Angelelli of La Rioja, Ponce de León had said at a meeting: "Now it's my turn."

Following the automobile accident, the bishop was taken to the San Nicolás clinic, along with Víctor Martínez, and he died there a few hours later as a result of his injuries. It has been established that the bishop's personal physician was not allowed to enter the intensive care unit. A few days after the accident, Víctor Martínez, who was doing military service in the prefecture of Saint Nicolás, was arrested by order of Lieutenant Colonel Saint Amant, and had to undergo all kinds of physical and mental torture during his imprisonment. "There they beat me until I fainted. Then they began to ask me about what the bishop did, who visited him, how many extremists he had hidden" (file 734).

Bishop Ponce de León had been receiving threats for a long time. "In addition," says Víctor Martínez, "there were personal threats from Lieutenant Colonel Saint Amant: 'Be careful; you're considered a red bishop.' That officer had prohibited him from celebrating the field Mass in the regiment, because 'We don't let communist priests in here.' "[17]

THE PALLOTTINE FATHERS

Very early on the morning of July 4, 1976, Fathers Alfredo Leaden, Pedro Duffau, and Alfredo Kelly, and the seminarians Salvador Barbeito and Emilio Barletti, all members of the Pallottine community in the parish of San Patricio in the Belgrano district of the capital, were murdered.

Father Leaden, 57, was a representative of the congregation called the Society of the Catholic Apostolate, founded by St. Vincent Pallotti; Father Duffau, 65, was a teacher; Father Alfredo Kelly, 40, was the director of catechesis in Belgrano and a teacher in the high school of the Servants of the Most Blessed Sacrament; Salvador Barbeito, 29, was a seminarian, a teacher of philosophy and psychology, and also principal of San Marón school; Emilio Barletti was a seminarian and teacher.

On the night of the crime, neighborhood residents saw a black Peugeot 504 with four men inside parked for a long time in front of the parish house. They also saw a patrol car stop in front of them and then move on.

The first persons who came to the parish in the morning found writing on the walls and on a carpet: "This is how we take revenge for our colleagues in the federal headquarters" (where a bomb had been placed in the dining room a few days before) and "This is what happens when you poison the minds of the young." Papers and other objects had been taken from the parish.

On July 7, 1976, the executive commission of the bishops' conference sent a letter to the military junta "about the unspeakable murder of a religious community," but also including the exculpatory language I have referred to before. But the commission did not demand an investigation, nor did it provide the elements of proof that were to be found in the Buenos Aires chancery office and in the nunciature. On the contrary, the bishops imposed silence, just as they had in the cases of Angelelli and Ponce de León. Cardinal Aramburu delayed the ordination of the surviving seminarian, Roberto Killmeate, until 1978, and he forbade him to give sermons until 1982.

Nevertheless, as I have said before, officials in the chancery office in Buenos Aires and in the nunciature were aware of evidence incriminating the authorities. Yet, the military and the bishops were present at the funeral side by side.

On August 20, 1986, the federal prosecutor, Aníbal Ibarra, requested that Judge Néstor Blondi try Patrolman Romano, who was then an aide in division 37 of the federal police, and the former police chief there, Rafael Fensore. The patrolcar driver who questioned the men who had the Pallottine fathers under surveillance belonged to that section. The agents in the car recognized his credentials and allowed him to remain there. The prosecutor contends that the ones who committed the crime were those inside the Peugeot, which was in the vicinity at 2 A.M. The suspicious position of the two cars, which communicated back and forth with their lights, made Julio Martínez, the son of General Martínez, then the governor of Neuquén, alert police station 37, for he was afraid of a terrorist attack on his father who lived in the same neighborhood. The police station sent out a patrol car to look into the matter, with the result already mentioned.

On September 2, 1986, the judge decided to put these persons on trial. An investigation into these elements of proof, of which church authorities were already aware, makes it clear that this investigation could have been carried out in 1976.

I recall that even in 1976 the nunciature gave me the name of Martínez, the witness.

The former police chief is currently the head of Rosil, S.A., one of the largest insurance companies in the country, with 958 branches. He holds 80 percent of the stock.

THE BROTHERHOOD OF THE GOSPEL

The Little Brothers of the Gospel—also called the Brotherhood of the Gospel—were founded in France by Father René Voillaume in 1933, as a branch of the Charles de Foucauld spiritual family. The group follows the guidelines of spirituality of this well-known French mystic who was killed in Africa in 1914.

The characteristic feature of the priests of the brotherhood is that, in addition to an intense prayer life, they support themselves by working in humble kinds of labor and they live in marginal communities sharing in the hardships of the poor around them.

As I have explained before, the military saw these characteristics as subversive, and the members of the brotherhood, who had been in Argentina since 1960, were eliminated, some through murder and others by being expelled. In 1973 they had fifteen religious living in six fraternities. None of them survived.

As I have already indicated, Brother Henri del Solan Betumale was arrested and deported to France in 1978. Father Pablo Gazzari was arrested and disappeared in 1977. An Uruguayan, Father Mauricio Silva Iribarnegaray, who worked as a municipal street sweeper and lived in a crowded slum, shared the same fate in 1977. Nelio Rougier had been kidnaped and murdered in 1975.

The one who could tell of their ordeal was Patrick Rice, who was saved from death by the forceful intervention of the embassy of Ireland, his homeland. As he relates in an interview, in 1976 he was working in Villa Fátima in Soldati. He witnessed how persons there were persecuted and he shared in their struggles. He was arrested and taken to the police station in Soldati, along with some others. The fact that his arrest had been witnessed and the solidarity of his colleagues helped to have his case recognized. And the news came out in the papers. As he later testified:

After being tortured for three days, I was taken out and interviewed by a hooded army officer. Another day I was taken to the central police headquarters and after a few days my ambassador was able to visit me. I was in prison for two months and in December 1976 I was expelled and came back to Europe. . . . I had been subjected to sessions of dunking in water; I had my hands and feet tied for twenty-four hours; on the second day I was tortured with electrical shock before being interrogated.[18]

From outside the country, Rice carried out an intense campaign to make known what the Argentine dictatorship was doing. He now lives in Caracas, Venezuela, where he serves as executive secretary of the Federation of Families of the Arrested-and-Disappeared in Latin America (FEDEFAM).

OTHER CASES

I have referred to Father Santiago Renevot in passing. This French priest, pastor in El Colorado, in the province of Formosa, was arrested on November 17, 1975, by the armed forces. Bishop Raúl Scozzina and the clergy of the diocese protested by suspending religious services, and seventeen of them went on a hunger strike. Father Renevot remained imprisoned and was expelled from the country on May 27, 1976.

I have also mentioned the American priest James Weeks and the seminarians who lived in his house. Weeks was subjected to all kinds of torture for about two weeks, starting August 3, 1976, until his country's embassy got him released. When he was in Washington, he visited the first ambassador of the Argentine dictatorship, Arnaldo Musich. That prompted a reprimand from Admiral César Augusto Guzzetti, who was then the foreign minister, and Musich had to resign.

I am very familiar with the arrest, disappearance, and release of the Jesuit priests, Orlando Iorio and Francisco Jálics. Both lived in the shantytown of Bajo Flores and were arrested at noon on Sunday, May 23, 1976, in an operation that involved more than fifty marines, as Father Gabriel Bossini was saying Mass. They showed up in a swamp in Cañuelas five months later, on October 23. Neighbors said they had been left there at night by helicopter. The priests said that they had been held in the Navy Technical School, which they recognized, for three days, tied up and hooded. Then they were transferred to a country house in Don Torcuato, thirty miles from Buenos Aires, where for the rest of the time they were hooded, handcuffed, and had their feet tied, but they were not tortured. In legal statements and before CONADEP, Father Iorio, who is now in the diocese of Viedma, was questioned about Mónica Quinteiro, María Marta Vásquez de Lugones, and my daughter Mónica.

On July 1, Admiral Oscar Montes, who was then chief of naval operations and subsequently foreign minister, met with me and with José María Vásquez, the father of María Marta. He said he knew nothing about our daughters, but admitted that Fathers Iorio and Jálics had been arrested by the marines. Meanwhile, Admiral Massera denied that his branch of the service was involved. In September of that year, I passed this information from Montes on to Colonel Ricardo Flouret, who assured me that he would pass the new data on to General Videla, on whose orders he was preparing a briefing.

I have already commented on the questionable intervention of Cardinal Aramburu and the Jesuit provincial, Jorge Bergoglio, in the arrest of these priests.

CARLOS MUGICA

I end this chapter and this book with a brief reference to the first priestly victim of persecution, Carlos Mugica, who was gunned down in front of the parish of San Francisco Solano, in Buenos Aires, on May 11, 1974.

I do so with a quote from the biographical sketch with which his colleague, Jorge Vernazza, begins the introduction to his writings:

> In *El Padre Mugica cuenta su historia* ["Father Mugica tells his story"] he himself points out the main factors that led a young student from a well-off family, who was thus conditioned by the mind-set of that class, to become a priest marked by the "preferential option for the poor" long before that catch-phrase was launched by the Latin American bishops at Puebla in February 1979.
>
> He was born on October 8, 1930. At 21 he left law school to enter the seminary in Villa Devoto. Shortly after ordination in 1959, he went to spend about a year with Bishop Iriarte of Reconquista in the northern part of the province of Santa Fe. Upon returning to Buenos Aires, he was an assistant pastor in the parish of Nuestra Señora del Socorro, and at the same time private secretary to Cardinal Caggiano. He was also an advisor to university students, and taught theology in the University of El Salvador. But none of that prevented him (perhaps just the opposite) from seeking out in the Retiro area the persons to whom he wanted to dedicate his best time and priestly energies. He spent a good deal of 1968 in France doing further study.
>
> When he returned to Buenos Aires at the end of that year he joined the pastoral team for shantytowns, which was approved by Cardinal Aramburu of Buenos Aires. He also began to participate in the activities of the Movement of Priests for the Third World. On May 11, 1974, he had a discussion with couples who were preparing for marriage and he celebrated his usual Saturday evening Mass in the parish of San Francisco Solano. As he was leaving the church, he was shot down by someone who had gotten out of a car, and who got back in and sped away.
>
> In a little more than thirteen years of priestly labor, he had become widely known in our country. Argentinians were very deeply moved by his murder. Thousands filed by his coffin, first in the parish of San Francisco Solano and then in the chapel of Cristo Obrero in Retiro. A huge crowd, with persons from all social classes, but especially from among

the poor, marched more than fifty blocks to the Recoleta cemetery, in an outpouring of faith whose depth of religious and popular sentiment was unprecedented in our city.

In such a short sketch of events and dates, how can we explain the far-reaching impact of his life and the sorrow caused by his death? Perhaps it can be summed up in this answer: it was his *authentic religion, totally committed to the service of his brothers and sisters,* and especially the poorest, with intense human and spiritual vitality.[19]

I have brief but intense memories of Carlos Mugica. I recall his speaking in public events, and also in Rome on November 16, 1972, when we were together on a flight to accompany Perón on his return to Argentina. I recall him at a meeting of young persons in our house, organized by my daughter, Mónica.

His death was a foretaste of what was to come. He was a symbolic and charismatic figure whom the oligarchy, who considered him a traitor to his class, and the armed forces could not allow to live as they went on preparing their gigantic slaughter.

Notes

CHAPTER ONE

1. See *El Diario del Juicio* (Buenos Aires), año 1, número 18 (Sept. 24, 1985), pp. 389–94.

2. Horacio Verbitsky, *La última batalla de la tercera guerra mundial* (Buenos Aires: Editorial Legasa, 1984), p. 15.

3. *Clarín* (Buenos Aires), April 2, 1986.

4. Alain Rouquié, *Pouvoir militaire et société politique en République argentine* (Paris: Presses de la Fondation Nationale des Sciences Politiques, 1978), p. 472.

5. Comisión Nacional sobre la Desaparición de Personas, *Nunca Más: Informe de la Comisión Nacional sobre la Desaparición de Personas* (Buenos Aires: EUDEBA, 1984), pp. 261–62.

6. S. E. R. José Miguel Medina, Vicario Castrense, *Introducción a la Pastoral Castrense* (Buenos Aires, Sept. 1982), Boletín no. 70, 6 pp.

7. *Nunca Más,* pp. 262–63.

8. Ibid., p. 262.

9. Marcial Castro Castillo, *Fuerzas armadas—Etica y represión* (Buenos Aires: Editorial Nuevo Orden, 1979), p. 13.

10. Ibid., p. 150.

11. See Antonio López Crespo, *Projecto de Investigación, Estructura de la represión en la Argentina y su acción sobre la Iglesia y la educación.* Commissioned by the Ecumenical Movement for Human Rights. Part 2, ''Acción sobre las Iglesias.'' Edición para uso interno. Argentina, April 1986, p. 19.

CHAPTER TWO

1. Henri-Irénée Marrou, *Desde el Concilio de Nicea hasta la muerte de san Gregorio Magno,* translated from the French (Madrid: Ediciones Cristiandad, 1984), Nueva Historia de la Iglesia, vol. 1, p. 390.

2. ''La Iglesia y los derechos humanos—Extractos de algunos Documentos y Memoria de algunas intervenciones de la Conferencia Espicopal Argentina acerca de la violencia y sobre diversos derechos humanos—1970–1982.'' Buenos Aires: Conferencia Episcopal Argentina, 1984, 65 pp.

3. Ibid., p. 4.

4. *La Nación* (Buenos Aires), May 6, 1983.

5. *Caras y Caretas* (Buenos Aires), Aug. 1984.

6. *Documentos del Episcopado Argentino 1965–1981—Colección completa del magisterio postconciliar de la Conferencia Episcopal Argentina* (Buenos Aires: Editorial Claretiana, 1982), 490 pp.

7. Hans Küng, *On Being a Christian* (Garden City, N.Y.: Doubleday, 1976), pp. 341–42.

CHAPTER THREE

1. *El Diario del Juicio* (Buenos Aires), número 2, June 4, 1985, p. 26.
2. *La Nación* (Buenos Aires), June 27, 1976.
3. Jorge Rouillón, "Argentina's 'Dirty War' on Trial," *National Catholic Register* (Los Angeles), Aug. 11, 1985.
4. Ibid.
5. *Acta Apostolicae Sedis*, 17 (1884–1885) 561.
6. Roger Aubert, *La Iglesia católica desde la crisis de 1848 hasta la primera guerra mundial* (Madrid: Ediciones Cristiandad, 1977), Nueva Historia de la Iglesia, vol. 5, p. 76.
7. *Clarín* (Buenos Aires), Jan. 6, 1986.
8. *Caras y Caretas* (Buenos Aires), Aug. 1984.
9. *Tiempo Argentino,* Jan. 16, 1983.
10. See *Humor* (Buenos Aires), April 12, 1984, p. 124.
11. *Clarín,* June 14, 1982.
12. *Clarín,* Sept. 3, 1979.

CHAPTER FOUR

1. *La Nación* (Buenos Aires), Nov. 20, 1978, and *Clarín* (Buenos Aires), Nov. 21, 1978.
2. *Clarín,* Nov. 24, 1978.
3. *La Prensa* and *La Razón* (Buenos Aires), Nov. 20, 1978.
4. See *Clarín* and *La Prensa,* Dec. 31, 1983.
5. *La Razón,* May 25, 1985.
6. *La Razón,* Dec. 8, 1984.
7. Orestes Plana, "El escándalo de la secta Moon—El Vaticano absuelve a monseñor Plaza," *El Periodista* (Buenos Aires), Nov. 24, 1984, p. 11.
8. Alfredo Silleta, *La secta Moon. Como destruir la democracia* (Buenos Aires: El Cid Editor, 1985), p. 37.
9. *El Diario del Juicio* (Buenos Aires), número 25, Nov. 12, 1985, p. 470.
10. Silleta, *La secta Moon,* p. 41.
11. "La Iglesia ante un desafío," *Criterio* (Buenos Aires), número 1947, July 11, 1985, pp. 327–28.
12. *La Razón,* May 13, 1977.
13. *Buenos Aires Herald,* Aug. 2, 1978.
14. *La Opinión,* June 8, 1978.
15. *La Razón,* Jan. 23, 1983; *La Voz* (Buenos Aires), Jan. 24, 1984.
16. *La Razón,* Sept. 12, 1979.
17. Ibid.
18. *Somos* (Buenos Aires), Sept. 7, 1979.
19. *Clarín,* Aug. 8, 1979.
20. Newspapers of San Juan, May 15, 1977.
21. *La Prensa,* Jan. 31, 1978.
22. *Convicción* (Buenos Aires), Sept. 13, 1979.

23. *Crónica* (Buenos Aires), Sept. 13, 1979.

24. *El informe prohibido. Informe de la O.E.A. sobre la situación de los derechos humanos en la Argentina* (Buenos Aires: CELS, 1984) p. 14.

25. *La Nación,* May 27, 1978.

26. See *Convicción,* April 3, 1983; *Tiempo Argentino,* April 3, 1983; *Esquiú,* April 18, 1983.

27. *Convicción,* April 3, 1983.

28. *Clarín,* April 6, 1985.

29. Interview given to *Familia Cristiana* magazine, reprinted in *Clarín,* March 13, 1977.

CHAPTER FIVE

1. Opening address by John Paul II at the Third General Conference of Latin American Bishops, Jan. 28, 1979, in John Eagleson and Philip Scharper (eds.), *Puebla and Beyond* (Maryknoll, N.Y.: Orbis, 1979), p. 58.

2. Ibid., p. 65.

3. Ibid., p. 66.

4. Discourse to members of the *Consilium de Laicis,* Oct. 2, 1974, *Acta Apostolicae Sedis,* 77 (1974) 568; later quoted in *Evangelii Nuntiandi,* #41.

5. Quoted by Juan Carlos Zuretti, *Nueva Historia Eclesiástica Argentina—Desde el Concilio de Trento al Vaticano II* (Buenos Aires: Itinerarium, 1972), p. 40.

6. Emilio Ravignani, *Asambleas Constituyentes Argentinas* (Buenos Aires: Instituto de Investigaciones Históricas de la Facultad de Filosofía y Letras de la Universidad de Buenos Aires, 1937), vol. 4 (1827–1862), p. 532.

7. Enrique Udaondo (*Antecedentes del Presupuesto de Culto en la República Argentina* [Buenos Aires, 1948], p. 144), estimated their value at 2.046 billion pesos in the Argentine currency of 1948.

8. Juan Isérn, *La Formación del Clero secular de Buenos Aires y la Compañia de Jesús (Reseña historica)* (Buenos Aires: Editorial San Miguel, 1936), p. 204.

9. Emilio Fermín Mignone, *La educación cívica en la escuela media argentina* (Buenos Aires: Comisión Permanente en Defensa de la Educación [COPEDE], 1984), p. 2. See idem, *"La vuelta a la escuela normal,"* Criterio, número 1,641 (Buenos Aires), April 13, 1972, pp.170–72.

10. Vatican Council II, "Pastoral Constitution on the Church in the Modern World," in Walter M. Abbott, S. J. (ed), *The Documents of Vatican II* (New York: Guild-American-Association, 1966), No. 76, p. 288.

11. Ibid.

12. *On Evangelization in the Modern World [Evangelii Nuntiandi]* (Washington, D.C.: U.S. Catholic Conference, 1976), #41, p. 32.

13. Faustino J. Legón, *Doctrina y ejercicio del Patronato Nacional* (Buenos Aires: J. Lajouane Editores, 1920), pp. 601–3.

14. Ibid., p. 584.

15. Héctor Félix Bravo, *El Estado y la enseñanza privada* (Buenos Aires: Editorial Belgrano, 1984) p. 52.

16. Ibid.

17. *Fidel Castro y la religión. Conversaciones con Frei Betto* (Buenos Aires: Ediciones Legasa, 1986), p. 187.

18. Leonardo Boff, *Iglesia: carisma y poder—Ensayo de eclesiología militante* (Santander: Editorial Sal Terrae, 1984), p. 17.

19. Ibid., p. 25.

20. As Carlo Caretto has written: "Oh, how I wish that the church born of the council will be a church concerned less about the length of girls' skirts, and more about problems having to do with love in the world; a church that, out of love for others, can renounce its own rights and privileges; a church that ignores self-defense and goes on the way of its exile, small and poor, as did Jesus' family on its flight to Egypt" (cf. *Love is for Living* [Maryknoll, N.Y.: Orbis, 1976], pp. 145–46).

21. *Criterio,* número 1,641, April 13, 1972.

CHAPTER SIX

1. See José María Rovira Belloso, "Sociedad perfecta y Sacramentum Salutis; dos conceptos eclesiológicos, dos imágenes de Iglesia," in *Iglesia y sociedad en España, 1939–1975* (Madrid: Editorial Popular, 1977), pp. 317–52; Leonardo Boff, *Iglesia* (chap. 5, n. 18, above), pp. 20–28.

2. Juan María Laboa, *El Integrismo, un talante limitado y excluyente* (Madrid: Narcea S. A. de Ediciones, 1985).

3. *Criterio* (Buenos Aires), número 1,959, Jan. 23, 1986, p. 3.

4. The integralist "bible" is the work by the Catalan priest Félix Salva y Salvany, *El liberalismo es pecado: Cuestiones Candentes,* published in Barcelona in 1884, which was reprinted in countless editions. In Argentina the main exponent of integralism was Father Julio Meinvielle, who was a prolific writer. He was influential among various groups until his death in 1973. Among his books we may cite the following: *Concepción católica de la política* (Buenos Aires: Cursos de Cultura Católica, 1932); *El judío* (Buenos Aires: Editorial Antídoto, 1936); *Los tres pueblos bíblicos en su lucha por la dominación del mundo* (Buenos Aires: Adsum, 1937); *El Comunismo en la revolución anticristiana* (Buenos Aires: Ediciones Theoría, 1961); *La Iglesia y el Mundo Moderno* (Buenos Aires: Ediciones Theoría); *De la Cabala al progresismo* (Salta: Editora Calchaqui, 1970).

5. See Charles Maurras, *Encuesta sobre la monarquía* (translation and notes by Fernando Bertrán) (Madrid: Sociedad General Española de Librerías); Enrique Zuleta Alvarez, "Charles Maurras," in *El Nacionalismo Argentino* (Buenos Aires: Ediciones La Bastilla, 1975), vol. I, pp. 27–32; idem, *Introducción a Maurras* (Buenos Aires: Nuevo Orden, 1965).

6. *Clarín* (Buenos Aires), Aug. 3, 1986.

7. *La Razón,* (Buenos Aires), May 13, 1977.

8. *El Periodista de Buenos Aires,* July 7–13, 1985, p. 13.

9. Ibid., March 24, 1986.

10. *La Opinión* (Buenos Aires) June 12, 1976.

11. *La Razón,* June 12, 1976.

12. *La Prensa* (Buenos Aires), Sept. 12, 1979.

13. *Clarín,* Oct. 20, 1978.

14. *Nunca Más,* (chap. 1, n. 5, above), file 6328, p. 349.

15. *El Periodista de Buenos Aires,* número 96, July 11–17, 1986.

16. Ibid., número 95, July 4–10, 1986.

17. Isidoro J. Ruiz Moreno, *Comandos en Acción—El Ejército en las Malvinas* (Buenos Aires: Emecé, 1986), p. 36.

18. Ibid., pp. 41–42.

19. *Nunca Más,* pp. 259–61.

20. *El Diario del Juicio* (Buenos Aires), número 3, June 11, 1985, pp. 56–59.

21. *Nunca Más,* p. 60.

22. *El Diario del Juicio,* número 3, June 11, 1985, p. 60.

23. Ibid., pp. 56–59.

24. María Eva Ruppert, holographic report, pp. 478–80.

25. See n. 4, above.

26. *Siete Días* (Buenos Aires), Aug. 1–7, 1984, pp. 6–7.

CHAPTER SEVEN

1. Buenos Aires, número 1,947, July 11, 1985, p. 328.

2. Buenos Aires, número 8, second trimester of 1986, p. 13.

3. *La Prensa* (Buenos Aires), Sept. 15, 1979.

4. *Clarín* (Buenos Aires), May 5, 1983.

5. Antonio Donini, "Aspectos sociológico-pastorales de la Gran Misión de Buenos Aires", CIAS monthly newsletter (Buenos Aires), número 100, Jan.–Feb. 1961.

6. Buenos Aires: Editorial Docencia, 1985.

7. José Enrique Miguens, in his book *Honor militar, conciencia moral y violencia terrorista* (Buenos Aires: Sudamericana-Planeta, 1986), argues tellingly that the concepts of knightly and military honor, as championed by integralist Argentinians, are anti-Christian and immoral.

CHAPTER EIGHT

1. Comando de Agrupaciones M.I.—Buenos Aires, Anexo "Lima" (Relación entre autoridades militares y eclesiásticas), Plan de capacidades 1982. "For internal use." (hereafter, Anexo "Lima")

2. Secreto. (Cdo. J.E. [EMGE]—Jef. III Op.) Buenos Aires, 2D 1200 abril 1977. CRA—127. Anexo 5 (Ambito religioso) a la Directiva del CJE [Comando en Jefe del Ejército] Nr. 504/77 (Continuación de la ofensiva contra la subversión durante el periodo 1977/78). 1. Situación a). (hereafter, Anexo 5)

3. Anexo 5, 1. Situación, c, d, e, and f.

4. For the purposes of repression, the country was divided into five zones, corresponding to command numbers 1, 2, 3, and 5, and the army's military institutes. Excluded were the regions corresponding to the navy and the air force. In general, "subzones" correspond to brigades, and "areas" correspond to regiments, schools, institutes, or other units. Details on the repressive structure can be found in the book put out by the Centro de Estudios Legales y Sociales, *692 responsables del terrorismo de estado* (Buenos Aires, 1986).

5. Anexo 5, Ejecución, 1, 2, 3, and 7.

6. Anexo "Lima," 1. Situación 2, 3, and 4.

7. Anexo "Lima", III Capacidades del Enemigo, Factor religioso, 145, 1, 2, and 3.

8. See *La sangre por el pueblo: Nuevos mártires de América Latina* (Managua: Instituto Histórico Centroamericano, and Panama City: Centro de Capacitación, 1983). See also Martin Lange and Reinhold Iblacker (eds.), *Witnesses of Hope: The Persecution of Christians in Latin America* (Maryknoll, N.Y.: Orbis, 1981).

9. The following sources have been consulted: Comunitá Ecuménica Italo-Argentina, "La Chiesa In Argentina sotto la dittadura militare" (Rome, n.d.), 13 pp.; "La persecución a la Iglesia Argentina" (Buenos Aires, May 1978), 16 pp.; "La situation de l'Eglese Catholique en Argentine" (n.d.) (a note says, "document presented to UNESCO"); Bishop Antônio Fragoso, "Prière et solidarité avec l'Eglise des humbles persecutée en Argentine" (1976), 14 pp.; Marcela Bosch de Paulucci, "Lista de víctimas de la represión ligadas con la Iglesia" (Buenos Aires, n.d.), 2 pp.; Dr. Antonio López Crespo, *Estructura de la represión en la Argentina,* part 2, *Acción sobre las Iglesias* (Buenos Aires: MEDH, 1986), 25 pp.; *Nunca Más* (Buenos Aires: EUDEBA, 1984), 350 pp.; CONADEP, *Anexos,* Anexo I, (Buenos Aires: EUDEBA, 1984); Asamblea Permanente por los Derechos Humanos, *Lista de los detenidos-desaparecidos registrados en la Asamblea Permanente por los Derechos Humanos* (Buenos Aires, n.d.), 115 pp.

10. *Nunca Más,* testimony of Lisandro Raúl Cubas, file 6874, p. 348.

11. *Nunca Más,* testimony of Graciela Daleo and Andrés Castillo, file 4816, p. 348.

12. *Nunca Más,* testimony of Leonor Isabel Alonso, file 5263, p. 348.

13. *Nunca Más,* testimony of Father Patrick Rice, file 6976, p. 348.

14. See Juan Carlos Zuretti, *Nueva Historia Eclesiástica Argentina* (Buenos Aires, 1972), p. 423; José Oscar Frigerio, "Perón y la Iglesia" in *Todo es Historia,* no. 210, Buenos Aires, Oct. 1984, pp. 1–64.

15. These references and those following are taken from documents in the files of the chancery office in La Rioja. Some of them have been added to the documentation of case number 23,350, "Angelelli, Angel Enriques/Homicidio calificado y tentativa de homicidio calificado," which is in process in criminal court number 1 in La Rioja, under the responsibility of Doctor Aldo Fermín Morales; Mabel Lucía Fallabrino, secretary. Other documents have been taken directly from the files. These last I owe to the kindness of my friend Rubén Dri.

16. *El Periodista* (Buenos Aires), no. 97, July 18–24, 1986.

17. *Nunca Más,* pp. 259–60.

18. *Humor,* no. 137, Oct. 1984.

19. *Padre Mugica: una vida para el pueblo,* Prologue by Justo Oscar Laguna, bishop of Morón; Introduction by Jorge Vernazza (Buenos Aires: Pequén Ediciones, 1984).

Index

157